SOUL SURVIVOR

SOUL SURVIVOR

The Autobiography

P.P. ARNOLD

NEB 005

First published in the UK in 2022 by Nine Eight Books
An imprint of Bonnier Books UK
4th Floor, Victoria House, Bloomsbury Square, London, WC1B 4DA
Owned by Bonnier Books, Sveavägen 56, Stockholm, Sweden

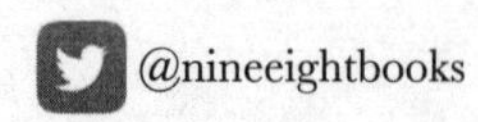
@nineeightbooks

@nineeightbooks

Hardback ISBN: 978-1-7887-0578-3
Trade paperback ISBN: 978-1-7887-0601-8
eBook ISBN: 978-1-7887-0579-0
Audio ISBN: 978-1-7887-0529-5

A CIP catalogue record for this book is available from the British Library.

Publishing director: Pete Selby
Senior editor: Melissa Bond

Cover design by Luke Bird
All cover images © Gered Mankowitz
Typeset by IDSUK (Data Connection) Ltd
Printed and bound in Great Britain by Clays Ltd, Elcograf S.p.A

1 3 5 7 9 10 8 6 4 2

Nine Eight Books is an imprint of Bonnier Books UK
www.bonnierbooks.co.uk

For the constant love, support and guidance they gave me that formed the foundation of my life, this book is dedicated to:

My sons, Kevin Arnold and Calvin Kodzo.

The memory of my beloved daughter, Debra Elaine Arnold; my parents, Theora and Mary Cole; my brother Ronald Edward Cole; my grandparents Theodra and Estella Cole; and my grandmother Mattie Benjamin Gray.

My sister, Elaine, my brothers Larry, Kenny and Theo, and all of my nieces, nephews, cousins and dear friends.

And in remembrance of Vernon and Rashied James. I had to cut a lot of our growing-up and the many experiences we shared – that's another book. Soon come!

CONTENTS

PART 1

Present Out of Past

'When dat ar ole chariot comes,
I'm gwine to lebe you.'
– 'I'm Bound for the Promised Land'

1

1965 (LA)

Mysterious Ways

'When you make your bed hard you have to lie in it.' Daddy's favourite quote rang in my head. I was living proof. Here I was in an abusive teen marriage. My husband David was abusive, physically and mentally. I was seventeen and working two jobs to support two young children. But my husband was never going to love me or treat me right. He couldn't stand the sight of me.

Once, a Sunday morning for me had meant getting up early for Sunday school and, after that, putting on my choir robes for the eleven o'clock service. And then I'd sing. I loved to sing. Now I was cooking, cleaning and washing clothes, trapped in a hell I'd created for myself. I knew what a hard bed was alright!

I had prayed for a way out for a long time. This particular morning, I wanted to know that God still loved me in spite of everything. 'Lord forgive me for my sins,' I prayed. 'I know I've brought this all on myself, but I'm afraid and I don't know what to do.'

The phone rang. It was Maxine.

Maxine Smith was my brother Ronnie's ex-girlfriend. She had a look of Diana Ross and a funny little lisp when she talked. She was really into the Supremes and we used to sing with each other around the house. She was now dating a singer named Jimmy Green, who had a little studio at the back of his house. I had already done one session there with her, for an artist Jimmy was writing for called Bobby Day, well known then for his big hit 'Rockin' Robin'.

The other singer on this session was Gloria Scott, who was the lead singer of Ike and Tina Turner's backing singers the Ikettes. Actually, there were two sets of Ikettes: one, the real Ikettes (Robbie Montgomery, Venetta Fields and Jessie Smith), toured with the Ike & Tina Turner Revue; while the other ones toured with *The Dick Clark Show*. Gloria sang with this 'B' group.

Dick Clark was a superstar DJ, famous for hosting *American Bandstand*, the long-running TV show which gave many rock 'n' roll artists their first national exposure, including Ike and Tina, Smokey Robinson and the Miracles and Stevie Wonder. It was one of the first shows where black and white performed on the same stage to unsegregated live studio audiences. Its live show toured throughout America and Ike, a shrewd businessman, had one set of Ikettes performing with Clark while the other toured with him.

Gloria could sing her ass off. She had a Texas sound like mine and our voices sounded really good together. She was very confident and polished. She'd toured on the same bill as the Supremes and many other Motown acts.

She had called Maxine to tell her that the Revue's Ikettes were quitting and that Ike and Tina needed girls to go on the road with the Revue. Maxine had suggested me.

'You've got to come to this audition with me.' I said I'd love to, but no way is David gonna let me. 'Just say you're going to collect the money from the session we were never paid for. Be ready. We'll pick you up in thirty minutes!' She hung up before I could say no.

I scrambled a lie together and David agreed to babysit. My hair was a mess, so I put on my black feather hair-net cap. Now I just looked tacky. It was the latest fashion, a kind of feather Afro, but a quick fix better suited to going shopping than for an audition.

Maxine rang the doorbell and I kissed the kids goodbye. At the end of the lawn, a big black and green Cadillac was idling. I freaked out.

'Quick,' I told the driver. 'Drive off before my husband sees this car.' I knew if David saw me sneaking away and climbing into the Cadillac, that would be it. I looked very young. I was still jailbait and the driver cracked up, seeing me sneaking away like that. 'Drive,' I pleaded. 'If he sees me, he will kill me.' He checked his mirrors, still laughing as he pulled away from the kerb. The driver was Jimmy Thomas, who sang with the Revue and moonlighted as a chauffeur and valet. He was real cute. He had this gold tooth, which was very country by LA standards. I liked him right away.

We arrived at a sprawling ranch-style house located in the hills above Crenshaw Boulevard, in a very exclusive area called View Park. This was still a 'white' Hollywood neighbourhood, but several black sports celebrities and actors now lived there, as well as entertainers like Ray Charles and Nancy Wilson. I had never been to Hollywood before.

An absolutely stunning black woman with beautiful cheekbones and a warm smile asked us in: 'I'm Ann. Ike and Tina are waiting.' The audition would take place in a very modern living room, with cheap-looking furniture, like you'd see in one of those stores on Crenshaw Boulevard. My father was an upholsterer, so I could tell that this design was not in good taste. There was a coffee table shaped like a guitar and gaudy velvet portraits of Ike and Tina on the walls.

And there stood Ike and Tina themselves.

Tina was even more glamorous and beautiful in person than on television. She was enchanting. She was dressed comfortably and casually, in a simple Sunday-afternoon blouse and trousers, her sepia-brown skin, high cheekbones, full mouth and long black wig giving her an air of elegant glamour. The sparkle in her eyes and her infectious enthusiasm just slapped you in the face. I liked her instantly. She welcomed us warmly as she looked us over. 'Hi, girls, glad you could make it!' She spoke quickly and precisely, in a friendly but professional tone. Maxine and Gloria were both very fashionable. I wasn't. But Tina didn't make me feel uncomfortable.

Ike had processed hair and was dressed immaculately. Slacks, a V-necked sweater and sharp shoes. He reminded me of Sammy

Davis Jr and also of my Uncle Book. He was dark-skinned and medium height, but also somehow gangly, with a long head that was too big for his body, sharp, angular features and large eyes. He was a little bow-legged, which some find sexy in a man. He was also funny, with a southern sense of humour, but I wasn't sure how I felt about him. He wasn't ugly, but then he wasn't particularly handsome either – and he told too many dirty jokes, which made me feel awkward and embarrassed. He asked my name with this weird little laugh and seemed fascinated with the size of my ass. 'Like Miss Porter,' he said to Tina and they ended up nicknaming me Porter. Apparently Miss Porter was a generously backsided neighbour of Ike's back in Mississippi. I was not amused.

Gloria he knew, so he joked around with her and Maxine. There was a white woman there too, which I thought was strange. She was called Rhonda. She was very tall with a girlish face and sparkly eyes.

We were the last girls to audition that afternoon. I was scared shitless and following the others' lead. I felt completely out of my depth and concentrated on my harmony to 'Dancing in the Street'. Then we sang another song, improvising on the spot.

'Alright, girls, you sound great!' They seemed impressed. 'You've got the gig!' said Tina. It was that easy. I couldn't believe it. Maxine and Gloria were ecstatic. I was less so. 'There's no way I can go,' I said immediately. I explained I'd only come to help Maxine and Gloria. 'I'm married with two young children; the youngest is just fifteen months old. I told my husband a lie to get out of the house! I'm already two hours late. I'm gonna get my ass kicked when I get home.' 'Well,' said Tina. 'If you're going to get your ass beat for nothing, you might as well come to Fresno tonight and see the show. You might change your mind.' Everyone was trying to convince me. Ike chimed in and told me to call David and ask him to come over. 'If David found out I was here,' I told him, 'I won't be going to Fresno. I won't be going anywhere.'

Ike and Tina weren't taking no for an answer. This was a day full of surprises and I was definitely already under Tina's spell. She had planted a seed. 'Okay, I'll go,' I said, 'but I'm not calling David.'

I had nothing to lose. Better to be hung for a sheep as a lamb.

We went to Tina's bedroom. It was very modern and beautiful. In her dressing room were sequined gowns and fur coats, so much jewellery and shoes for days. She was very feminine, with an amazing strength about her. We all laughed and talked and giggled. Tina told us about Robbie, Jessie and Venetta, whom she loved very much. They were the current Ikettes who were leaving and the Revue was due on the road in five days. I had always loved their rich gospel sound. They had a hit single called 'I'm So Thankful' and wanted to pursue their own careers and not be tied to the Revue. Ike was cursing them and calling them ungrateful. The song was released on a label Ike had nothing to do with and it wasn't produced by him, so he wasn't happy about their success. Tina didn't comment. They had been friends for a long time and I could tell she was really going to miss them.

The drive to Fresno seemed endless. The Cadillac was a real smooth ride. A Fleetwood Brougham, with space to spare, like a limo. *I could easily get used to this*, I thought. Us in the back with the Turners, like royalty, and Rhonda sat up front with Jimmy. Everyone else was in their showbiz element, but mostly I remember being nervous as hell. David was gonna kill me when I got home.

If I felt underdressed before, I felt like a real country bumpkin in the club. Everyone on the dance floor was dressed to the nines, fired up and having the best time. I'd only been out of LA once before, to see Ray Charles at the Fillmore Auditorium in San Francisco with my sister Elaine and my cousin Cookie. It was my first concert and I was thirteen. This was the first time that I'd ever been to an actual nightclub. It was dark. The vibe was hip, intimate and raw. It had a real bluesy down-home atmosphere.

As the potential new Ikettes, we were asked to remain in the club and not to venture backstage, in case things got awkward at that last gig together between Ike, Tina and the old Ikettes. Maxine and Gloria had immaculate hairdos, hip attire and make-up, but I looked underage and green – I was underage and green! – and certainly not a future Ikette. They were also both used to ordering drinks in clubs. I had a Coca-Cola and sat quietly in a corner taking in the scene. And there was a lot to take in.

The MC introduced the Revue and Ike took to the stage, immaculate in his green mohair finery. With his band the Kings of Rhythm dressed in black suits, he opened the show with a twenty-minute set. They were incredible. Live and funky to the bone. Ike was a charismatic performer and played great lead guitar. The male singers, Jimmy Thomas and Bobby John, resplendent in blue and gold mohair, with picture-perfect conked hair, gold teeth and the most soulful voices and hottest dance moves, were a sight to behold.

The bandstand was smoking as the Ikettes were introduced for their own short set: 'I'm Blue', 'Peaches and Cream', 'Dancing in the Street' and 'I'm So Thankful'. They were so sexy and they sounded completely on point. Their harmonies were tight and their routines elegant and funky.

But when Tina hit the stage, all hell broke loose. She was beautiful and wild, her wig flying back and forth with a non-stop Pony groove. She broke into 'Shake' – and boy could she shake her money-maker. The Ikettes rattled maracas in a frenzy behind her as they joined in the choruses: 'Shake, loosen up your shoulders!' It was mesmerizing.

The three of us were totally blown away. Maxine and Gloria were thrilled because they'd be on stage as Ikettes in a few days. I hadn't yet allowed myself to even imagine such a thing. As the final set ended with a sexy, high-energy version of Ray Charles's 'Tell the Truth', Jimmy and Bobby joined Tina and the Ikettes on stage. The rhythm increased and everyone simultaneously launched into the Shag, a dance routine against a flickering, iridescent light. It was like a Charlie Chaplin silent movie. They seemed to dance even faster and shagged their way off stage, leaving the audience dumbstruck with glee. Tina was dynamite. She was the female James Brown. Everybody loved her.

As the band packed up afterwards, we still weren't introduced and there was definitely an atmosphere. This group had experienced so much together and had been close for a long time. All the girls had boyfriends in the band. It was a very tight unit.

We left for the long drive back to LA. And my inevitable ass-whipping.

All the way back, Ike and Tina tried to convince me that I should bring David to their house the next day and let them talk to him. I didn't dare think about being an Ikette; I was too afraid of what would be facing me when I got home. But they really wanted me and time was running out. Four days from now, there was a show in Columbus, Ohio and Ike needed a 'yes' from me by the following afternoon. Compared to the older, more sophisticated Ikettes, we were pretty green, but we were in tune with the latest trends. We were like a baby Supremes, only raunchier. Our youthful zest is what Ike and Tina liked. We could inject their show with that high-energy teen Go-Go vibe.

The tour itself would visit the south, the East Coast and parts of the north before returning via the Midwest to LA and the West Coast. It would last ninety days and the salary would be $250 a week. Ike failed to tell us we'd be paying for our own hotel and food costs out of that. Today you'd get per diems to cover travel, hotel and basic food expenses, but not back then. Still, $250 a week seemed a lot of money to me.

I figured it was a moot point anyway. I had a one-track mind, thinking only about what would happen to me when I got home.

We arrived in LA at about 5 a.m. and I was back at my house around 6 a.m. 'Let me come in with you and help explain,' Maxine offered. 'Thanks, but I know what's going to happen,' I told her. I knew David would unleash his Mad Dog personality. He was never very well restrained at the best of times.

I was right.

Bracing myself for the inevitable, I put my key in the door. As I opened it, he was there waiting. I was barely through the door when he was already punching me repeatedly in the head, asking me what the fuck I thought I was doing. Punches first, questions second. Even by his standards, this onslaught was quick out the blocks. He hit me so hard maybe he knocked some sense into me, because now I knew I was going on the road. I told him what had happened. 'I didn't call because I knew you wouldn't let me go!' I cried. 'You're crazy if you think that you're going anywhere,' he screamed. 'You have two kids and a husband!' As I took my beating, I knew I would be accepting Ike and Tina's offer. I believed God had answered my prayer and sent me a way to escape the hell that I was living in. He had shown me a way out and I was going to take it.

I took my whipping without talking back. I always did. Talking back would only result in harsher punishment. Kevin and Debbie were awake now and screaming. I fixed their breakfast and dressed them, changed my clothes and pretended to get ready for work as usual. My lip was a little swollen and I was sore. But I was also pissed off and I felt a renewed strength and determination. My ride to work every morning was with my good friend Frances. As far as David knew, I was dropping the kids off with my mother, but I had another plan, which I explained to Frances. She was shocked because she knew how obedient I was. She couldn't believe I was thinking about being an Ikette. Couldn't believe I even had the opportunity. The lumps in my head were killing me by the time I reached my mother's. I was exhausted.

I broke down the moment I walked through the door. My mother knew why I was crying. David had called looking for me, angry that I'd left him alone with the kids. 'Everybody was worried and thought that something bad had happened to you,' Mama said. They'd called Maxine's house and heard all about Fresno, so she knew David would beat me when I returned home. I told her about my miraculous day and begged for her help with the kids. This was my once-in-a-lifetime shot to try to make a success of singing professionally. Pregnant twice and forced into a loveless marriage, I'd also messed up my education. I knew the odds of going back to school were slim. I was working two jobs. Whatever money David made he spent on himself.

I explained how trapped I felt. God had given me a talent and shown me a way out of my hell. I was determined to see where it might lead me. I had to try. I knew that sooner or later David would hurt me bad or I would hurt him protecting myself. I had suffered in silence for far too long.

'Calm down and get some rest. Let's see what your daddy has to say,' was all she could reason. I explained about Columbus, Ohio and the pressing four-day window in which I had to learn everything. I told her Ike and Tina needed to know straight away. 'Well, that's as may be, but they'll just have to wait until your daddy gets home,' she said.

I called Tina and explained the situation. She spoke with Ike and said, 'We can give you until six o'clock.' They would find another girl if I couldn't go. Rehearsals were starting. I would have to be in View Park no later than seven o'clock, to work through the night. They wanted to meet David. Ike would talk to him. He thought he could make it right, one alpha male to another.

I was drained. Around three o'clock, I would call David and let him know my plans, so that he could come over by four o'clock, when Daddy got home. I ate a little and got some rest in my old bedroom. Aside from my lip, I had no facial scars, but the blows I'd taken to my head and my body had me aching all over. My mind was racing, but somehow I managed to get some sleep. It was the strangest, most painful answer to a prayer. I guess. *God really must work in mysterious ways*, I thought.

2

1847 (Tyler, Texas)

The Coles and the Hawkins

My parents were Mary Lewis Valoo Gray and Theora Cole. My two grandmothers were Estella Hawkins Cole (who was called Stella, Stel or Grandma by us kids) and Mattie Mae Benjamin Gray (who we always called Big Mama). At fifteen, Estella married seventeen-year-old Theodra Cole (who we called Pop or Poppa Thea).

Jack Cole, my great-great-grandfather, was born in 1847 (in Arkansas or the Indian Nation; the 1870 and 1880 censuses disagree). My great-great-great-grandmother Jane Wiley Denmon (1813–95) was born in Alabama and died in Arp, in Smith County, Texas. She was the slave wife of a Major Wiley, born in 1800 in Mississippi, a white plantation owner. He and Jane had two sons together and a daughter, Eliza Denmon Wiley, who married my great-great-grandfather Jack Cole. They had eight children. The fifth, Don Cole (1878–1938), was born and died in St Violet, Smith County. He was father to my grandfather Theodra.

Don's wife, Carrie Johnson Cole, was also from Arp. She died at an early age of ptomaine poisoning after eating canned corn, but not before she bore nine children – one of whom was Theodra.

My great-great-grandfather Mouser Hawkins was born in 1836 and hailed from Alabama. He married Catherine (born 1839, also from Alabama). In the census of 1870, Mouser and Catherine are listed as thirty-eight and thirty years old respectively, living in Smith County with four of Mouser's ten children by various mothers. I'm not sure when he or Catherine passed away, but their first-born son was my great-grandfather Webster Hawkins, born in 1863 in Tyler, Smith County.

Mouser and Catherine are both said to have been farm labourers, which likely at that date and place means hardworking sharecroppers picking cotton. Catherine evidently had four very young children – Webster, James, William and a baby girl, Evaleen. I can imagine her working in the fields with Evaleen tied on her back while her boys played in the fields close by.

Texas had been a province of Spain and Mexico until 1821 and its name comes from its first known inhabitants, the Caddo Indians, known to Spanish explorers as Tejas, meaning 'friends'. Smith County is named for James Smith, a general during the Texas Revolution of 1835–36 – and its first immigrants were Cherokee and Kickapoo retreating across the Mississippi River ahead of the westward movement of European settlement. In the decade before the Civil War, the county tripled in population, to more than 13,000 in 1860, nearly 5,000 of them negro slaves. When Tyler, the largest city in Smith County, was officially incorporated in 1848, it had a population of 1,024. In 1860, more than 350 of its population were slaves. Many of my relatives ended up in Tyler from small cities and counties close by or else from neighbouring states.

My African roots are most likely from Ghana. My Native American roots I believe to be Choctaw. Before I studied the 1870 census, I thought that all my people were from East Texas, so I was surprised to learn that Mouser was from Alabama. It means he was either a runaway slave or was one of the first free slaves to get the hell out of the deep south after the Civil War – meaning that he was lucky that he wasn't caught or lynched for no good reason. They were still hanging black men in Texas when my family migrated to California in the early 1940s. But possibly he was simply sold to someone who lived in Tyler. I hope his dream of freedom was realised, though. I hope when the Civil War ended in 1865 that Tyler gave him a better life, if indeed such a thing then existed for black men.

The Choctaw were one of the 'Five Civilised Tribes'. Those tribes adopted European ways – which meant owning slaves to work on plantations after some were taken as captive in war or purchased from settlers. When the Choctaw were forced to hand over territory and move west with other Native Americans, their slaves were made to migrate with them. When the Civil War erupted, most tribes fought with the north – but the Choctaw were promised their own state if the south won. They became allies and their slave laws mirrored those of the Confederacy.

Black life and Native American life were often deeply intertwined. Fugitives were often given sanctuary and there were benefits to intermarriage. Tribal slaves of various backgrounds often worked side by side sharing recipes, remedies, myths and legends. The colonists tried to restrict anything that drew Native and African Americans together, including marriage. Slaves who escaped into tribal territory were hunted and captured. Nevertheless, the 1860 census found several Choctaw households that were predominantly African American. When the south lost the Civil War and slavery was ended, slaves owned by the Choctaw were to become freedmen with full citizenship of the Choctaw Nation (incredibly, as of 2021, some were still legally battling for this status).

All of which ensures that the tale of my own personal roots are tangled. Certainly I don't know if or how some of my forebears migrated to Texas from the south-east. Were they indentured servants, freedmen or escaped slaves? Were they tribespeople on the Trail of Tears? The migration took many forms.

In 1887, Webster Hawkins married Sarah Jane Irvine (born 1869, Tyler). The youngest of their eleven children was my grandmother Estella, born in 1909 in Clayton, Panola County, Texas. Panola County was formed in 1846 from sections of Harrison County (north), Shelby County (south) and Rusk County (west). It was named after a Choctaw/Chickasaw word for cotton. The family were sharecroppers in Tyler, Texas, picking cotton and working in the fields to make their money. The unfairness of the sharecropping system meant they never made enough to climb any social ladder. This was a close community, everybody knowing everyone else and many related in one way or another. But I suspect my Grandma Stel knew little about Mouser and Catherine's generation. She told me that the only thing she remembered about her grandmother was that she was an American Indian woman with hair long enough to sit on. She never spoke of her parents, who died when she was quite young – though she had one very handsome photo of them. They both looked very regal, decked out in coats with fur collars. She herself was a cross between a beautiful American Indian squaw and an African Queen, with high cheekbones, broad nose and those dark-brown eyes that held so much wisdom.

At the turn of the twentieth century, Webster was thirty-six and Sarah thirty, with six of their eleven children: my great-aunts Frances and Catherine (who I remember very well), plus Pearl and Marie (who passed away before I was born) and two great-uncles I never knew or heard about. My Grandma Stel would come later, as would two younger brothers who I vividly recall – Uncle Goldie and Uncle Hubert. Uncle Goldie played blues guitar in the fashion of Blind Lemon Jefferson and T-Bone Walker. He was quite a character; tall, lanky and rugged-looking, a party animal that drank a lot of whiskey. Estella loved him. Uncle Hubert was more withdrawn and kind with that unique inherited nasal tone that marked him out as a Hawkins.

My grandparents Papa Thea and Grandma Stel met when they were living in Smith County. By the time Stel was twenty and Theodra twenty-two, they were already raising my father Theora and uncle Booker Timothy. Thea was registered as a farm labourer; Stel was 'without occupation'. Both left school after sixth grade but Grandma never let this keep her from success in life. She was a creative, spiritual woman, with a great, quick mind.

The majority of the Hawkins-Cole relatives were sharecroppers. Pop's side of the family were rich in Indian, African and Caucasian ancestry. Wild and good-looking. Most of the men were heavy drinkers and gamblers. Pop grew up in Tyler, picking cotton like everybody else. He was a very handsome man, with a strong resemblance to Fats Domino and a head full of thick, wavy hair with a distinctive widow's peak.

I loved to hear him sing. 'Don't worry about the mule being blind, just load the wagon and shake the line' was a favourite. As a young girl, these were just 'Pop's songs', but to Pop they were life – and had helped him make it through every back-breaking, cotton-picking day.

But Pop had a damaging weakness for women and an even greater one for whiskey. My father had to grow up fast.

3

1965 (LA)

Becoming an Ikette

I woke up just after 3 p.m. in my sister's bed. My aching head and body brought it all back. Daddy would be home soon and my fate was in his hands.

I didn't hate him or blame him for making me marry David. I'd brought it all on myself. My father was a strict disciplinarian and although we all loved him dearly, his own violent nature kept us from being closer to him. He and Mama had worked hard, sacrificed and experienced a lot of tragedy and pain. I had watched him control and abuse my mother for years and now I was in the same boat. But as with many victims of abuse, I had become used to blaming myself.

Still, I knew I couldn't keep kissing David's ass. One of us was going to get hurt. And who knows, maybe Daddy could convince David that I could make something better of my life? Daddy was the closest thing to a father figure that David ever had. Perhaps he could make him listen.

Every day when Daddy came home, he would wash up for the dinner my mother always had ready for him and sit in the den in his favourite chair in front of the television to eat it. This was his daily ritual. Today my mother told him I needed to talk afterwards. When he finished his meal, I presented my case to him, like his den was a courthouse and he was the judge. He listened intently, his left eyebrow raised. He knew I was fundamentally a good girl. That I'd become stupidly infatuated and that David manipulated me, abused me. He knew all of that, but he also knew that I could sing. I could sing, but he didn't think for a minute about me going into show business.

Silence descended on the room as it always did when we could see that Daddy was thinking. Calmy, he delivered his verdict: 'You know nothing of the dangers of show business,' he said. 'How can you expect to leave your husband and children and go out on the road with just a week's notice? This is the position you're in and it's your own fault.'

I knew I had messed up. I'd put on a happy face; I'd suffered in silence. And now I begged and pleaded. My life was going nowhere; I wasn't even sure I had a future with David. This was my way out. Singing was my heart. All I wanted was his love and support.

Daddy sat with his forehead knotted in frowns. I'd seen this many times before. This meant 'leave me alone'. I sat quietly sobbing in the kitchen. Nobody said a word. I needed some compassion from Mama, but she would never go against my father.

Daddy finally broke the silence. 'Tell David to come over here.'

When my husband arrived, I was greeted with nothing but rancour and disdain. If looks could kill! He explained that he was angry with me staying out all night with Ike and Tina. I apologised for lying and said I hadn't planned on going, but, if I'd have called to ask for permission, he'd have flatly said no.

And then Daddy spoke. It was time for some home truths, as he saw it. He told us how he felt partly responsible for forcing us to get married at such a young age, how this overwhelming sense of responsibility could be frustrating for a young man – especially one as hot-headed and nefarious as David. While I was admonished for my hush-hush flit to Fresno, he also chastised David for the violence, which, in his words, 'had got out of control' – as though there was a more reasonable, acceptable level of spousal abuse. We were young, we had been stupid and life had taken a sharp turn that nobody expected, he said. But he also pointed out to David the opportunity at hand. How my talent could turn things around and how it wouldn't hurt for him to meet Ike and Tina and get the measure himself.

Whether it was a respect for Daddy and his calculated speech or – more likely – the allure of someone else's hard-earned dollar signs flashing in front of his eyes, David considered the situation. 'Tell Ike and Tina that we're on our way.'

We drove in silence. The View Park area of LA was beautiful and the Crenshaw District had a great shopping centre. I was surprised how familiar David seemed with the area, but there was a lot that I didn't really know about him.

When we arrived, everyone was in the living room going through the Revue routines. I was convinced Ike and Tina would change their minds about me – especially when I arrived with two kids and a husband in tow – but when they took a break in rehearsals, they went straight into the hard sell. Ike apologised for the short notice and ushered David into the office to fill him in.

Tina introduced me to her kids, Craig, Ike Jr, Michael and Ronnie, the baby who looked so like Tina. 'Leaving your kids to go on the road is the hardest part for me,' she said, 'but my boys are fine. They're well-loved and looked after and that's the most important part.'

My parents would look after Kevin and Debbie. They would be happy about this; it was me that it would be hard for. We waited anxiously. Tina and the girls showed me the moves they'd been working on. I never found out exactly what Ike had said to David in that office, but he promised they would look after me. I imagine that my $250 a week helped smooth the deal.

I was ecstatic. I was an Ikette! While I was more wary of Ike, I was determined to pay Tina back for changing my life. But for now, it was work time. There wasn't a moment to waste. We rehearsed long and far into the night before Jimmy drove us home, exhausted.

When I got in, David was waiting to talk. We should try to save our marriage, he said. We had two children to think about. His mother Mae had already agreed to help. He would get a job and we could start saving money. I agreed to send the bulk of my earnings home and David would pass some to my mother. He made everything seem so logical but, this close to getting out of the frying pan, I wasn't too eager for the fire.

The next morning, we dropped the kids at Mama's and David drove me over to Olympiad Drive. My life as an Ikette started right away. It was drill-yard discipline and back-breaking work. Tina was very vocal but Ike was in charge. During a break, he told us the rules and regulations. He talked real fast and cursed frequently without once cracking a smile.

If you were late you'd be fined.

If you fucked up a routine you were fined.

If you sang out of tune you were fined.

If your uniforms and shoes weren't clean and perfect you were fined.

If you talked during rehearsals or on stage you were fined.

In short, you were fined for anything if he saw fit.

And if you missed the bus you would have to make your own way to the next gig on time. And be fined.

It was a page right out of the James Brown book of costly punitive measures.

Ike did not allow drugs or excessive drinking. You were paid on a weekly basis and you paid for your own food and hotels. They would provide costumes and wigs but if we lost or damaged them, we paid to replace them. We were to conduct ourselves as 'ladies' at all times and be mindful of our appearance on and off stage. If we were unhappy about anything we were to tell Tina, who would then discuss it with Ike. He took no shit from anybody. And if there were problems, you were fired and sent back home. He had a huge phone book with the names and numbers of every available singer and musician in the country and warned us we could be replaced as quickly as we'd been hired.

And just to remind us, we now had less than four days to learn the whole show.

I was a good dancer, but this was my first professional gig. I had never had to learn routines under such pressure. We were working day and night to get those dance moves down. Luckily the Cole family were all dancers. These routines incorporated a bit of everything. We rattled our maracas and shook our fit little asses.

We did the Shotgun, bending our knees and sinking down low, propelling ourselves around imitating a shotgun with our arms.

We did the Jerk, with its powerful, sexy shoulder action and that little skip in the middle.

We fused the Temptation Walk into our moves, rolling our hands with that cool little kick before forming a line with Tina to do the Twist or the Pony.

We'd stand side by side for that funky groove to 'Fool in Love', singing into one mic together, so close we could hear each other's heartbeats.

We did the Shag, we did the Funky Chicken and, if James Brown was king of the Mashed Potatoes, Tina was the queen. Boy, could she mash those potatoes!

I was in my element.

If we took a break from the routines, it was to get our harmonies super tight. Tina was always driving hard but I remember those rehearsals with fondness. We worked our butts off but there was laughter as we all became accustomed to one another's personalities and idiosyncrasies. Ike made rude and wicked remarks, teasing us about our most insecure body parts, my ass, the shape of Maxine's mouth, Gloria's big head. He was clearly a sex maniac and something of a predator, but yet you couldn't help liking him, with his funny long waist and bow legs. He certainly had charisma. He talked real fast, his laugh was contagious and you could always tell when he was lying because he stuttered. It was a good tell.

While Tina also had a great sense of humour, she would laugh affectionately at all of Ike's jokes. She was also really into astrology and kept explaining everyone's birth signs. She'd asked my star sign at the first meeting and I didn't understand at all. 'When's your birthday?' I said 3 October. 'That means that you're a Libran. I'm a Sagittarian.' Gloria was Pisces, Maxine Taurus, Ike was a triple Scorpian. I had no idea what all this meant, but apparently our star signs were harmonious and we should all get along well.

And they would always laugh at me. I was still so young. I didn't really know anything worldly. That was all about to change.

My brain was fried from memorising so much in such a short time. But most of the harmonies had a gospel feel that I connected to immediately. All my years singing in the choir were paying off. Ike's music was down-home funky and soulful to the bone, the show was high octane and the two of them were perfectionists. We would work late into the night until Jimmy once again dutifully took us home.

In the meantime, I would have to prepare for life on the road. We would be away for ninety days and I didn't even have a suitcase. I'd never been away from home before. I bought a big one and packed a little bit every night and morning, as well as everything the kids would need for my parents' house. I was going to miss them.

Besides the songs and routines, we were attending what I called the Tina Turner Finishing School: a crash course in lady-like behaviour, make-up, hair, beauty tips and etiquette. She had such easy class. A great sense of elegance and grace. It was fair to say that Tina was everything I wanted to be and she appeared to have everything a woman wanted: a beautiful home, beautiful clothes, fur coats, jewellery, enough shoes to open up her own store, wigs for weeks, her own Lincoln Continental, fame, fortune and four cute sons. (At the time I thought they were all her children by Ike, but Ronnie was their only child together.)

One break we were taken downtown to shop for our stage clothes. We went to wholesale stores where we bought some cheap little sheath dresses, but the outfit that I loved best was a Go-Go dress with a black-and-white plaid skirt and a white turtleneck top with suspenders to go with white Go-Go boots.

As for high heels, Maxine and Gloria always had their own and until we had time to go shopping, I would wear Tina's. Except her shoes were two sizes too big for my very small feet. It helped that they were also narrow, but I had to stuff the toes with toilet paper. There was nothing else I could do.

At the time the only cosmetic company that catered for black folks was Max Factor. We went to the Max Factor studio and bought pancake foundations. Maxine and Gloria showed me how to put on false eyelashes, but aside from the latest Day-Glo orange and pink lipsticks I had never worn make-up before.

Everybody laughed at how unsophisticated I was, but after my first session, I couldn't believe the transformation.

After Max Factor, we went to a wholesale wig store. Wigs were a key part of the Ikette look. Tina's would transform her into an Amazon beauty and were longer and more sophisticated high-quality versions. Ours were temporary because the best place for wigs was in East St Louis. Gloria, who had the confidence that came with being the better singer, wore a reddish-brown one like Venetta Fields had worn. Maxine was sexy and sassy and her wig was dark brown and swept to the side to clone Robbie Montgomery. Mine was jet black with bangs, which was supposed to make me look like Jessie Smith. Ike was shrewd. We were being cloned into an image of the former Ikettes – and if we didn't work out we could just as easily be cloned ourselves. When I looked in the mirror at my new wig and Go-Go boots, fake eyelashes and made-up face, the abused and downtrodden teen wife was nowhere to be seen. I felt very pretty.

By the third day, we had somehow learned the whole show. But in the room with all of this experience and these big personalities I'd started to fold in on myself. Tina went to work on this straight away. 'There's no room to be shy on my stage. You have to open up your mouth and sing out, like you do when you're talking with Maxine and Gloria.' She wanted to hear me loud and clear, to shake my ass and be confident. I began to work real hard on letting go of my inhibitions. And letting go of the old Patricia Arnold.

I had no idea how much my life was about to change.

4

1870 (Rusk County, Texas)
The Benjamins and the Grays

I know much less about my mother's family. Her mother Mattie was from Tatum, one of seven children born to my great-grandparents Aaron and Ella Minor Benjamin.

Aaron was born in 1870 in Rusk County, which borders on Smith and Panola. His father was from Georgia and his mother from Alabama and he was a farmer who owned his own house, but that's pretty much all I know. He had six children with my great-grandmother Ella (born 1874), who was the firstborn of Isham Zepher (born Mississippi, 1846) and Liddy (born Texas, 1853). Mississippi had been Choctaw country, but Zepher sounds European and so does Liddy's maiden name, Minor. Aaron and Ella's second child, Mattie, my grandmother, was born on 18 December 1901. Ella died in 1920 and Aaron re-married in 1930.

Mattie's siblings were very close; strong, stylish, good-looking light-skinned people known for their sense of humour. The women had come from a line of house servants and Mattie was always well versed in the indoor habits of white folks. We children were always on our best behaviour around her and it was hard to speak and be relaxed in her company. This fear and lack of communication is why I know so little about her, including her life before she married my grandfather, Percy Gray.

My great-great-grandparents on his side were the Wrights, Noah (1834–1912, born North Carolina) and Harriet (1836–1923, born Georgia). Noah fought as a private for the Confederacy in the Civil War, while Harriet lived right through the First World War. Their first-born of eleven children was my great-grandmother Victoria Wright, who married Peter Gray. They had twelve children; the youngest was my grandfather Percy, born in March 1900.

Percy met and married Mattie in Henderson in Rusk County, Texas and they had four children, including daughters Hattie Ruth and my mother, Mary Lewis, who was born on 26 January 1924 in Henderson. Hattie Ruth I knew as 'Aunt Baby Ruth', which I always thought was strange, as my mama was the baby. Maybe it was connected to the popular Baby Ruth chocolate bar.

We called Mattie 'Big Mama' and we always knew Percy as 'Little Daddy'. Whereas my Grandma Stel was a very beautiful dark-brown-skinned woman with long black beautiful hair, Mattie had very Caucasian features. She and Percy were committed churchgoers but they divorced in 1931, when my mother was just six years old. He became a Methodist minister and married a woman in Dallas whom I only knew as, of course, 'Little

Mama'. I only remember meeting them once when they visited us in LA.

After the divorce, to support her two daughters, Mattie worked as a live-in housekeeper and cook. 'We spent our childhood moving from pillar to post living with various relatives while your Big Mama worked,' Mama always said. As a result, she always felt badly treated, like an outsider. A similar fate befell my mama, who always lived in the shadow of her seemingly more popular older sister. It caused an envious rift between the sisters that would last a lifetime. When my mother spoke of her childhood, it was always with sadness. If she had friends, she never spoke of them. She swore that she would never let her kids grow up in a broken home, no matter how unhappy her life became. It was a promise she kept.

Eventually Mattie saved enough money to move to Tyler, about 35 miles from Henderson. Things start to move fast. In May 1942, my parents Theora and Mary met in a club called The Green Top. I've been told that it was love at first sight. According to Mama: 'Your daddy was the most handsome man in the club and by far the best dancer.' And Daddy would say, 'Your Mama was the most beautiful, most shapely and sweetest girl in the room.' They tied the knot in August of that same year after a short, whirlwind courtship.

In January of 1943, with my mother married and Hattie Ruth in college, Mattie was ready to spread her wings. She'd heard that there were better opportunities in California for 'Coloured people', as African Americans were then called (at least that is when we weren't called Niggers). She wanted to escape the Jim Crow racism of East Texas. She could no longer live with the poverty and limitations of the south. She moved to Los Angeles and found a job at the Post Office and then as an elevator operator in a hotel, before returning to her former profession of live-in cook and housekeeper.

Mattie was the pioneer of the family's migration, the first in my family to move west to California, but Grandma Stel was right behind her. By June 1943, Stel had grown tired of Papa Thea's womanising. She left Uncle Book with him and set off for Los Angeles herself.

5

1965 (On the Road)

Ike and Tina Turner

We covered nearly 2,000 miles on that tour, rehearsing relentlessly on the road. It's easy to tell if someone's out of tune in the close confines of a car and Ike was always on our ass if anything was wrong. We had so many vocals and harmonies to learn. Gloria took the lead on everything and that was fine with me.

Ike Turner was a serious, hard businessman. 'I've been in show business since I was a young boy,' he told us. 'I know everything about it.' His booking agency was called Sputnik, which Ann Cain ran. She was from Louisiana, very smart and intelligent with a lovely smile, high cheekbones and big dark eyes. When she was young she had sung in a girl group and had toured with James Brown and Little Willie John. Ike first met her at the record store she owned on La Brea Avenue in LA. Her first role was minding the kids while Ike and Tina were on the road, but it soon became apparent to Ike that she had other skills that he could exploit and he made her manager of Sputnik. She booked all the gigs.

Rhonda Graam was the road manager. Originally from Texas, she had grown up in the San Fernando Valley. Like Ann, she was first hired as housekeeper and nanny. She was tall with long sexy legs, a kind face and innocent blue eyes. She wasn't glamorous like Ann or Tina, but she was pretty. In those days, having a white woman travelling with a black revue was pretty revolutionary and at times a little dangerous. But Rhonda wasn't fazed and nor was Ike. Initially I was surprised that he only had women running his business. I would soon learn why.

Maxine and Gloria helped me to get made up. After my eyelashes and lipstick were applied I checked my reflection in the mirror. I was amazed at this person looking back at me. No way David could call me ugly now! Tina insisted we wore corsets, waist cinchers, garter belts and silk stockings, but when we put on our dresses and high-heel sneakers, the transformation into Tina's sexy background singers was complete. Three sexy bags of nerves ready to hit the stage. Tina glowed with pride when she saw how we looked: 'Don't worry about anything,' she said. 'Just concentrate on your lyrics and routines. You don't want to upset Ike.' It was meant as encouragement, but the threat lingered in the air as we heard our introduction, took our places on stage and hit our marks perfectly.

When Jimmy announced Tina, the place erupted. The band broke into 'Shake' as we shook our maracas and Ms Turner arrived on stage, moving like a hurricane in front of us. Wigs flying, butts shaking, we moved in and out, our harmonies perfect.

Ike and Tina nodded in our direction after that first song. It was the surge of confidence that I needed. Before long we were Shagging off the stage and our first gig was over. Everyone was elated. Except for my aching feet, I felt great. I was really looking forward to wearing my own shoes.

The band were all really friendly, but I was so shy, which they all found really funny. Ike was happy, but as we stopped to eat a late-night breakfast he reminded us we could still do better. He and Tina gave us notes on what they wanted improved for the Cleveland show the next night. It was a two-hour drive away. We would have time to shop for my shoes before leaving.

Alone in our hotel room, Maxine, Gloria and I talked excitedly about our first official gig. They'd already set their sights on the band members they liked. 'I think Rayfield [the baritone player] is real cute,' giggled Maxine. 'I got my eye on Sam [the bass player],' laughed Gloria. As for me? I was just tired and missing my babies. I put on my pyjamas and fell asleep.

The mood was upbeat as we drove out of town after shopping for high heels the next morning. Ike was on top form. Tina was laughing at his teasing. They seemed such a happy couple. We sat in the back and tightened up our harmonies, keeping the lyrics fresh in our minds.

The drive to Cleveland went real fast and that second gig was even more nerve-racking. 'You're still on trial,' Ike reminded us. Remembering all the moves and lyrics was still a challenge. But with their help I was making the transformation from an abused child bride into a cute and sexy Ikette. My first pair of high heels felt good. No more borrowed shoes with tissue paper filling out the toes.

As soon as they changed out of their uniforms – wet from that night's perspiration – Ike and the band would be back in the club doing their Mack Daddy thing. They all had different women swarming around them like bees to their sweet honey. Jimmy had introduced me to his wife in Columbus, so I was surprised when he introduced a second beautiful woman as his wife in Cleveland. I was still learning about the habits of musicians.

Ike brought an attractive young girl to the dressing room, to see Tina and to introduce the three new Ikettes. She sang acapella in front of us with no inhibitions. It was a not-so-subtle reminder that his telephone book was full of names and numbers. We could so easily be replaced. We had made it through a very hard week, but this was only the second show of a ninety-day tour. We would still have to be on our guard.

Gloria could act a little spoiled but I liked her a lot. Maxine was just plain cool, stylish and hip. We were all petite, but she was also super-confident and sexy. She sang all the top notes and had a funny way of talking that made us all laugh. And I was the shy one that just loved to sing. All this hard work and performing was slowly taking my mind off the last three years of pain.

The third show was the first time we really messed up. Ike was really pissed and he let us know it. 'You motherfuckers fucked up tonight!' he screamed. He could be a mean, merciless asshole. Of course, they had a reputation to uphold, but mistakes happen. Everything had just fallen apart.

Ike kicked us out of the car. And just like that, we were relegated to the bus with the rest of the band. The fairy tale was over. The real on-the-road world was about to unfold.

The bus was dark and dimly lit and the band members all had their seats. It was very territorial. Maxine and Gloria always knew we'd be travelling with them eventually and they found some seats and slipped effortlessly into the joking and laughter. More cautious, I found an empty place to sit. It was still overwhelming to me. These were some of the best musicians around, moving from band to band depending on pay and how they were treated. The horn players in particular were all seasoned jazz musicians. And I was cutting my teeth working with them. They became my road family.

The band line-up at that time was Thomas 'Nose' Norwood on drums, Sam Rhodes on bass guitar, Ernest Lang on piano, Baby Huey on guitar, Rayfield Porter on baritone sax, Herman Ralph on trombone, Clifford Solomon on tenor sax, Max Johnson on trumpet, Bobby and Jimmy as male vocalists and Clifford's wife Bess along for the ride. When they played together it was magical, a musical alchemy. But they were all interchangeable. Not everyone went the distance.

That first night on the bus was hard. I kept my eyes and ears open. It wasn't a Cadillac, but you did have a whole row of seats to yourself so you could stretch your legs across the aisle. Duke Thornton, a big, dark-skinned man with an untidy conked process and red, bloodshot eyes, was our bus driver. He was also the road manager and sound man, so he got less sleep than anybody.

As the night went on, I prayed to God to protect us from all hurt and harm as the band gossiped about Ike and Tina and life on the Chitlin' Circuit.

The Chitlin' Circuit was a string of venues throughout the eastern, southern and upper Midwest of the United States. Ballrooms, auditoriums, nightclubs and honky tonks. The shows were one-nighters filled to the brim, located in the heart of black communities. Club owners sold chitlins[1] and other soul food dishes in their kitchens. Black-owned and/or promoted, in the late '50s and early '60s the circuit was crucial for the likes of Ray Charles, B. B. King, Otis Redding, Aretha Franklin and most of the jazz and R&B artists of the time.

Our bus had seen better days. It was unattractive and raggedy and we spent the majority of our time on it, sometimes travelling up to 400 miles a day. We mostly stayed in Holiday or Ramada Inns as many chains wouldn't allow blacks back then. They were clean and cheap with restaurants and swimming pools. For a hotel novice like myself, this felt like luxury. Sometimes Maxine, Gloria and I still shared a room, but generally they slept with their men – Maxine had hooked up with Rayfield and Gloria with Sam – so I'd have the room to myself. Once everyone

---

[1] Chitterlings are pig intestines, a soul-food delicacy: when slave masters threw them away as kitchen scraps they became a staple part of the black menu. They had to be washed and cleaned well to get rid of the fat and bacteria, then cooked for many hours and spiced to taste. I would only eat my mother's.

understood that I planned to stay faithful to my husband, I was left alone. Nobody hit on me. And like the youngest member of the family that I was, I was protected. Clifford and Bess even jokingly called me 'daughter'.

I'd heard horrific family stories about life in the south, but I was still not accustomed to segregation first hand. In LA, we had our own communities and didn't mix much. In the south, black and white mixed more, but only because the former worked for the latter. They still knew their place! Lincoln's Emancipation Proclamation was back in 1863, more than a hundred years before, but if slavery at least had been abolished, in reality, black people in America were still oppressed second-class citizens.

One day as we travelled, I needed to go to the toilet real bad. I kept asking Duke to stop the bus at the next gas station, but he never would and I got angry. When he finally stopped, I ran off the bus. Nobody followed me. Naively I huffed off towards the ladies' room where an irate redneck shouted at me: 'You know you cain't go in there! Your toilet is always at the back of the garage.'

I was unnerved by the way he spoke to me but I went around the back. An unpainted door had a big sign on it: 'For Coloureds'. When I opened the door there was just a big dirty hole, with a filthy toilet seat on top of it, flies everywhere. I gagged at the smell and ran back to the bus. I didn't need to pee so badly now. Duke looked at me hard: 'Now you know why I didn't stop. This is redneck country. They don't care nothing about Negroes down here.'

Most of the others were born and bred in the south, including Maxine and Gloria. They had let me learn the ugly truth about racism the hard way. I was angry and humiliated. Duke stopped where he thought it was safe and everybody got off the bus and ran behind a bush or tree. Back on the bus, I was schooled on the dangers and realities of being black on the road in the south.

Another time we stopped at a Greyhound bus station to get a bite to eat. When we sat down to order, the waitress, a real redneck, rude as well as nasty, refused to serve us. She said something Tina didn't like and the next thing I knew Tina had jumped out of her seat and was kicking her butt. Ike pulled Tina off her and we got out of there real fast, before the police showed. Tina might've been submissive to Ike, but she wouldn't take no shit from anyone else.

There were so many characters on that bus. Sometimes the jokes could be cruel. For example, drummer Nose and Bobby John were both gay and everybody knew they were a couple. They got their fair share of ribbing. Bobby was an outrageous gossip and kept everybody in stitches – but he also had terrible piles, moaning and groaning like Papa Thea after he had drunk too much whiskey. And with women waiting every night at every gig ready to hang out and party, there were always eye-watering stories to share the next day.

But outside of the bus confines, Ike ruled all with an iron fist and Clifford had the scars to prove it. The diamonds on Ike's fingers were major bling but also serious weapons. Clifford was an amazing saxophonist, but they'd had a falling out and Ike punched him in the nose, splitting a nostril. It needed stitches and left a visible scar. Yet Clifford had forgiven him and would stay with the Revue for many years. Maybe this is why Bess was always allowed to travel with us.

This was all before the cocaine-fuelled '70s. Many of the musicians drank alcohol, which wasn't a problem as long as it didn't interfere with their playing. While I worked with the Revue, drugs were not tolerated, at least not on the bus. Ike knew some musicians smoked a bit of weed in their hotel rooms, but as long as they didn't get busted he was cool. I'm sure Ike had his own vices.

I wasn't really interested in drinking or smoking back then. I learned how to play blackjack and became quite good. It helped pass the time and I won often, which gave me some pocket money. I barely had enough to eat and unlike Maxine and Gloria I wasn't able to do much shopping. Sometimes a band member bought me lunch or dinner, but not often. They knew I wasn't giving up sex for a free meal, so why waste the money?

6
1943 (LA)
California Dream and Reality

Theora Cole was newly married and soon to be a family man. Tyler only offered farm work and he wasn't into shining shoes, that wasn't the life he wanted to lead. With just a high school education to his name, he headed out to California just two weeks after his mother. His first stop was LA. 'We had no idea how to get around,' our cousin Thomas Jackson later told me, 'but we caught the streetcar to 54th and Central Avenue, close by where your grandmother lived. Then we caught the bus and went further north to Vallejo, where we found work in a shipyard.'

Pregnant with her first child, Mama arrived in LA in late July and moved in with Big Mama. Hattie Ruth had stayed in Texas, where she studied to be a teacher and got married. This caused more upset between Mama and her sister and only served to widen the cracks in their already fractious relationship. It was something they never truly repaired.

To save money, Big Mama moved in with a family in Beverly Hills, as a live-in domestic. There was now more room, so Daddy returned from Vallejo and Papa Thea arrived with my Uncle Book. He and Grandma Stel were reunited and our family migration was complete. In January 1944 my brother Ronald Edward Cole was born. In June, Daddy was drafted into the army and in early 1945 shipped off to the Philippines.

I was conceived on a thirty-day leave and born Patricia Ann Cole on 3 October 1946. Thursday's Child with far to go. Straight away I suffered a black right eye thanks to pneumonia. Mama said it settled under my eye, whatever that meant. It was the first of the many battles ahead of me.

Daddy was proud to be a soldier for Uncle Sam and looked very handsome in his uniform. The Second World War was over, but with a wife and two kids to support, he decided to re-enlist. There were financial benefits and the more money he could save towards buying a home the better. My mother became pregnant a third time on another one of his potent thirty-day leaves and my sister Elaine was born the following August, just ten months younger than me. Elaine was six weeks old when Mama found out she was pregnant again. Daddy was certainly making sure she didn't stray while he was away.

LA is beautiful, full of Spanish architecture, palm-tree-lined streets and exotic tropical plants, with beaches from Hermosa to Zuma, mountains and (in those days) fresh air and sunshine. It must have seemed like a paradise for migrating black families. But they soon encountered new kinds of racism. The mansions in Hollywood and Beverly Hills needed domestic servants and there were poorly paid jobs as factory workers, janitors, cooks, waiters, waitresses and bellhops. Even the railroad was becoming more racially stratified, but with black workers confined to jobs like portering.

The NFL had instituted a lock-out for black football players in 1932 and George Preston Marshall, founder-owner of the Boston Braves (who became the Washington Redskins) had openly refused to have black athletes on his team, reportedly pressuring the rest of the league to follow suit. But in 1946, the Los Angeles Rams would sign Kenny Washington and Woody Strode, breaking the colour bar. And for those with the talent and the ambition, there was Hollywood. For sure, black actors mostly still only played butlers or domestics or dancers, but Hattie McDaniel, Dorothy Dandridge, Lena Horne, Cab Calloway, Louis Armstrong, Ethel Waters and Ruby Dee had all broken through and in 1956 Woody Strode, already a sports legend, would play a slave and a king in *The Ten Commandments*.

It was enough for my parents to feel some optimism. They could work hard, save their money and – God-willing – perhaps buy some property. It wasn't as easy as they'd hoped, nothing ever is, but it was still better than being in Texas.

After his discharge from the forces, Daddy got work at Restwell Upholsterers, where Papa Thea was also employed. They were the only blacks there alongside many Mexicans. None of them liked their white employers. They would rip them off all the time.

Everyone was now living with Grandma Stel and Papa Thea on Naomi Avenue in Watts, South Central LA and everybody worked, except for Mama, who was always pregnant. When she was hospitalised with Elaine, Papa Thea's younger sister Bertha Cole moved in to help with childcare. This was my mischievous Aunt Bert, who straight away set about teaching me her favourite curse words.

My first clear memory is one of our raucous family parties. I was just two years old. Everyone playing cards, drinking and having a good time Texas-style. There was even a jitterbug contest between Daddy, Uncle Book and Otis, Aunt Bert's son who had just arrived from Tyler. Everybody was laughing and shouting and egging the revellers on. I was caught up in the energy of it all and when I heard Otis shout out my favourite new word, I mimicked him. 'Motherfucker!' I repeated proudly.

Daddy stopped dancing, grabbed me hard and busted my little ass real good in front of everybody. I didn't understand what I had done wrong. I was just copying Otis and nobody said anything to him! Why Aunt Bert thought it was funny to teach me a curse word so foul I'll never understand. She certainly didn't say it was a bad word. How was I supposed to know? I was so hurt and embarrassed. I was sent off to the back bedroom where I cried and cried.

This event certainly taught me not to curse in front of grown-ups. Not out loud anyway. Don't get me wrong, I love my family and I understand now why things were like they were, but it was hard work being a part of it. I'm just not sure that my parents had enough time to deal with a little girl with a mind as active and inquisitive as mine. I was already developing my strength and awareness, as well as my rebellious independence and my insecurities. The negative sides of which I'm still working hard to eliminate!

The house in Naomi Avenue had two and a half bedrooms, but it seemed smaller with so many crammed into it. It was on the north-east corner of the street in a sort of cul-de-sac where the streetcar turned around on Slauson Avenue, with the main railroad track just across the street. There was a fair-sized yard, but it was not properly fenced in. Elaine and I were always supervised as we played there, but Ronnie was allowed to play outside, with his friend Boo Boo. He was constantly warned not to play near the tracks. But when you tell a child not to do something, nine times out of ten, curiosity will get the best of them.

He was just four years old and had no fear. For two-and-a-half years he had been the baby and he was spoiled. Nobody knows for sure what happened, but one day Ronnie and Boo Boo ventured across the street with their toy trucks and trains. I'm told that they heard a whistle blowing in the distance. My cousin Thomas and my Uncle Book were teenagers then, sixteen and eighteen years old. Thomas thinks Ronnie was somehow trying to copy them: 'His parents didn't know Ronnie had been watching us jump on and off the railroad cars as the train passed in front of the house.'

Ronnie dropped his toy tractor onto the track and was trying to get it when the train rolled over his foot. The driver was unable to stop in time or perhaps simply hadn't seen him as he was so small. Miraculously he was not killed. But his foot was so badly mangled they had to amputate right up to the knee. Terrified of a whipping, Ronnie lied and said Boo Boo had pushed him. The lie had haunted him until he confessed, years later, as a grown-up. None of us know what happened to Boo Boo and how this lie affected his life. Belts or switches from trees were supposed to be how children were kept in line and out of trouble. But the fear they instilled in us stifled our ability to communicate openly. 'Spare the rod and spoil the child'? I'm still not sure.

Theora and Mary would never be the same again. Five years earlier they'd been teenagers full of hope. I can only imagine the torment and the despair they went through. They had very little insurance on Ronnie and, with no proper legal representation, they got ripped off big time. The railroad company all but turned a blind eye and paid out very little. Ronnie would spend a large majority of his childhood in the hospital, undergoing many operations.

The tragedy was devastating for all of us. Grandma Stel and Aunt Bert helped my parents look after Elaine and me and – when he was born – my younger brother Larry. I was still just two years old, but there was no time for me to be a baby. Somehow in my infant consciousness I knew I had no choice but to grow up fast and help my mother as best as I could.

Two years later we moved to 232 East 117th Street and a fresh start, but as for Naomi Avenue itself, all my memories of that place are dark and tinged with sadness.

7
1965 (Still on the Road)
On Tour

I was missing my kids badly. I would gaze out the window at the changing scenery, amazed how my life had changed in such a short space of time. Moving from show to show, gas station to Holiday Inn, I didn't understand that I had travelled from one hell and on to the next.

I was calling home two or three times a week and sending the lion's share of my money to David – $175 a week; $50 of which was for Mama, leaving $75 for food and hotels. The idea was to save enough for a down payment on our own house. My Grandma Stel was an estate agent; she would find us a nice house to start off in. I was so naive.

David had our itinerary, but he never once called. One day, Mama said, 'David's not giving me regular money. You'd better speak to him.' I did, but he always found an excuse.

Ike was moody. He fined people to keep them in line, anything up to $100. He'd slap you so fast for $25 for what you thought was nothing, that you couldn't talk your way out of it. If he thought a drink had affected your performance, you could be fined on the spot, so we girls weren't allowed to drink at all. You'd be fired and on a Greyhound bus with your replacement ready at the next gig.

Ike also had a habit of chasing us around the dressing room with his dick out. Everybody else laughed, Tina most of all, but I thought this was just nasty. He and Tina were always talking about giving head. I would gag imagining her doing this, but they said it opened up your throat to sing better.

It was also obvious by now that Ann Cain and Rhonda were more than just employees. Ann was extremely jealous of Rhonda, which created friction, but all of them, including Tina, were afraid of Ike's temper, so they tolerated one another. Safety in numbers. He never let them forget that he was in control and he took his temper out at a second's notice. He had women in every city and he callously paraded them backstage in front of Tina. I stayed well out of all this unless we were summoned for a meeting. By now I disliked and feared him, although I trusted at least that Tina would look out for me. I wasn't prepared for what was about to happen.

Maxine and Gloria were out with Rayfield and Sam so I was on my own watching television and doing my laundry. There was a knock on the door. It was Ike. 'Porter,' he whispered, 'open the door.' I hated being called Porter and didn't want to let him in. I had never been alone with him. But he was the boss.

He made small talk, then rushed me, sticking his tongue down my throat and putting my hand on his crotch to feel his dick. I begged him to stop: 'Please, Ike, stop, don't do this, you know that I'm married.' I was terrified but he didn't care. He kept saying things like, 'You know you want this' and 'Let me help you out.'

Before I knew it I was pinned down on the bed wrestling with him in vain. I was in tears, but he didn't stop. He pulled my panties down and stuck his big, black, ugly dick inside me. 'Don't this feel good?' he kept saying. I was shocked and scared. And he was really hurting me. He pulled it out before he came.

When he was finished, I begged him to leave. He then tried to give me money. Money! Like I was some cheap hooker! I knew that if I accepted his money there would be no going back. He tucked his dollars back in his billfold like nothing had happened and left. I was terrified.

I took a bath and cried and cried. I didn't know what to do. If I told my family they would demand I come home. I couldn't tell Tina. I really didn't want her thinking I was after Ike. I was used to always defending myself with my father and David and whenever I tried explaining myself to Tina, I always sounded defensive. She always thought I was being argumentative. Most importantly, I didn't want to lose my job.

I never told Maxine and Gloria. I think Ike was surprised I didn't take his money. Did he think I would let him pimp me the way he pimped the others? I was naive but I wasn't stupid. I'd already married one violent, egotistical, chauvinist abuser. Did Ike think I was a fool twice over? I was starting to enjoy being on the road, but every time I began to feel good about myself, something happened to take another swing at my already fragile confidence. I certainly wasn't going to let Ike intimidate me. I was not one of his women. In fact, I was underage and I could really make trouble for him. But I felt so alone and afraid and ashamed.

Not long after, I was using a dressing-room toilet when Ike suddenly appeared. Putting his finger to his lips, he picked me up and put me on the basin. As he was preparing to do his dirty deed, Gloria entered, saving me from a second forced sexual encounter. I was so embarrassed, but Gloria was there for me. She knew not to say anything to anybody.

In my whole life, I've only told my sister, Elaine, and a couple of very close friends about any of this. All this time later, I'm surprised at how affected I still am. I don't understand how I've managed not to hate the men in my life. My grandfather, my father, my husband and now Ike Turner. So many people I put my trust in let me down. They either abused me emotionally, physically or sexually, yet I was able to carry on living among them without letting them completely take away my self-respect. I was wounded, but I was also strong and I buried these secrets without becoming hard or bitter. This ability to survive has served me well.

I now avoided being alone with Ike, but I behaved as if nothing had happened. All I wanted was to do my job, get paid and get back home. I'd developed a persona: I'd joke around like everybody else, stay focused on my work and keep away from the in-crowd. I loved the glamour but I wouldn't sell my soul for it. This was my chance to become independent and perhaps to leave David. I still wasn't free like the other girls.

I told no one and as far I know neither did Ike. Did Tina know? In her autobiography *I, Tina*, Maxine says something that suggests Tina wanted me out because she felt Ike had his eye on me – but if so I never knew about it. Of course, she was aware of all Ike's women. She accepted that she had to share him. She didn't like it, but there was nothing that she could do about it. She was the star of his empire but he controlled her on every level.

I loved Tina. I wasn't refined or glamorous in the way that she was, but she had inspired me to question my whole way of thinking. She laughed at me because I was so shy and inexperienced. She liked me, although I knew I wasn't one of her favourites.

But I still really felt for her. She had developed this thick skin to deal with all of his controlling abuse. She had been with him for many years, laughed at his jokes, shut up when told to and was so strong for all of us. Of course, unbeknown to us, she was also broken inside. Yet they seemed very close, this dynamic duo that had everything going for them.

Ike knew the industry inside out. Sputnik was his management and personal booking agency. He produced his own records and his distribution deals kept them financially independent. They had it all. And although nobody could match Tina's high-powered live performances, it was Ike the perfectionist who drove her hard. Because Ike knew that the empire, the riches, the cars, the beautiful home all depended on Tina and her amazing gift. He himself was as sharp as any player out there and his own talent was undeniable. Their act together was sexy and raw. But Tina was the star.

As we travelled the south, I was also learning what our country was. Mostly the people at our gigs were the hardworking poor letting their hair down in hot, funky, sweaty little clubs. Some were rowdy as hell and sometimes there'd be trouble. Fights would break out and we would run off stage and take cover as gunshots rang out. Wisely, Ike demanded his money before each show. Normally we played two shows and if he didn't get his money, half before the first set and half before the second, we didn't go on.

A highlight for me was the East Coast Theatre circuit. It possessed a sophisticated big-city energy that was very different from down south and LA. The Apollo in Harlem was legendary. The audiences were serious and if you didn't have your shit together, you would be booed and pelted with fruit and vegetables – and even shoes – while you tried to take cover and run for the wings. But they loved Ike and Tina; they always delivered. One afternoon James Brown came backstage. We were introduced briefly and then the Godfather of Soul was ushered into their dressing room. Ike didn't like us getting above our station and fraternising with their VIP guests.

In East St Louis, Illinois we bought new wigs. By now we really needed them. This was all before Afros, when you either got your hair processed or conked or you just got a press and curl – which would look great until you started sweating or got caught in the rain or had a bath.

So, unless you were lucky enough to have 'good hair', you needed a wig on stage, because we would sweat so much while performing. But this meant we had to maintain them as well as wear them. You had to wash them in very lukewarm water, because if it was too hot the synthetic hair would draw back into the cap of the wig – then you had to brush and pray that you wouldn't lose too much of it. Gloria found this out the hard way. Her wig was so thin we all died laughing at the state of it. And we also had to pin them on our own hair so that they wouldn't fly off during our routines. People were always asking if the wigs were our real hair – as if the majority of black women had long, straight hair! Of course they weren't, but Ike would gently pull on them while we were on stage, making people think that it was our real hair. If your wig wasn't pinned on tight with bobby pins, it would come off in Ike's hand and you can imagine how embarrassing that could be. We all dreamed of owning good-quality human hair wigs like Tina's, which were made by Hallam's in East St Louis. Once you had a Hallam wig, you never went back to synthetic!

8

1947 (LA)

232 East 117th Street

As a child, I remember wishing I knew what Tyler, Henderson, Dallas and Fort Worth, Texas were like. My parents, grandparents, all of my older relatives and so many kids I knew had been born in Texas – but I had to make do with stories. True, many of the stories angered and humiliated me – stories of slavery, cotton fields, black men lynched, black women raped, segregation and sharecropping. And, while I definitely didn't regret not picking cotton, there was a romance about life in the country close to nature, about old-time revivals, about picnics and parties. Everybody seemed to miss absent friends and family, all the colourful characters. Maybe Texas without the racism wouldn't have been a bad place. It hardly seemed to matter. The actual pain of being black in America eclipsed any such notions.

The area I grew up in was predominantly black Americans looking for a better deal. Families who had migrated west in search of their own piece of the American Dream. All the while, the black families were moving in, the white families were moving out towards the suburbs. The large Mexican and South Korean migration hadn't yet begun, so our neighbourhood was a mix of families from Texas, Mississippi, Alabama, Louisiana, Missouri and Oklahoma. LA was just one big country town.

My parents, Theora and Mary Cole, weren't bourgeois or middle-class. They were hardworking Baptist Christians with a young family. Daddy worked two jobs, sometimes three, including Saturdays and any overtime he could lay his hands on. When Mama wasn't pregnant, she worked, too. Hoping to save money for their own future home, my grandparents lived with us.

They only had high school diplomas, but their Texas education had been a good one. Daddy was very disciplined and hardworking, with dreams of one day being his own boss. Mama was a born mathematician and a natural comedian, her true calling. A sense of humour was really necessary being married to my father. My grandparents also both left school young, but Grandma Stel had a good business mind and Poppa Thea knew how to turn one dollar into two.

Despite the setbacks, the Coles remained optimistic. I don't remember leaving Naomi Avenue, but I do remember arriving at 232 East 117th Street. Elaine and I were running back and forth exploring our new environment as the grown-ups unloaded furniture. Ronnie had mastered getting around on his crutches. My mother worried he'd open the wounds from his most recent operation, which created painful infections for him, but he never seemed to care.

Everyone was so happy that day. Located on the outskirts of Watts and Compton, with its front yard and big porch, our new home was a palace compared to Naomi Avenue.

Stel and Pop had the front bedroom, Mama and Daddy the big one in the back. I had a new brother now too, Kenneth. He was so cute, with a little flat head that made everybody laugh. He slept in a crib with Mama and Daddy.

There was a big backyard, with peach, apricot, banana, fig and loquat trees. There were tropical plants all over, like a jungle and a grapevine along the back fence. It was a great house.

Ronnie was two years and nine months older than me, but he spent so many of his younger years in hospital. It was always a big event when he was allowed home. I loved him so much. He made me feel so proud. I would do anything for him. He had already had so much pain and tragedy in his young life but still he hardly complained. He was my hero. He hated to be separated from the rest of us and wouldn't always tell Mama when he was hurting.

He loved watching television. Western movies were his favourites. In pride of place on the family mantle was a photo of him on a pony in a cowboy outfit, complete with hat. We all watched cowboys on TV, plus *I Love Lucy*, *Ozzie and Harriet*, Gene Autry and Shirley Temple films and every Marx Brothers movie. And we loved *Amos 'n' Andy* and *The Little Rascals* with Alfalfa, Stymie and Buckwheat. These were black characters who were slower and more ignorant than all the white characters, always scared and buck-eyed. As kids, we weren't aware of the racist stereotypes their characters perpetuated. We just thought they were funny. Shocking as it is now, we were just glad to see black kids on TV.

When Ronnie wasn't home there was serious pressure on me. I felt frustrated. My parents had the idea that Elaine was the sweet little angel and that I was the opposite somehow. I couldn't decipher it. How had they come to this conclusion? I would watch the grown-ups real hard to know what kind of example I was supposed to be setting, but I also realised early that this could be misleading. I had to make a decision: should I play innocent or let them see how fast I was learning? I wanted them to be proud of me, but nobody took the time to understand me. I learned to take care of myself and, by the age of five, I was already fiercely independent. I don't remember being unhappy; I was quite happy with myself and I loved my sister and brothers, but there was so much stress around me and the grown-ups seemed always to be doing all the things they told us kids not to do.

You felt the tension as soon as Daddy came home. Automatically everyone was on their best behaviour, unnaturally quiet, tip-toeing around him. He was so intense and serious; we were all afraid to do or say the wrong thing. Often he and my mother would argue and it was always over the most petty things. Still, she would always try her best to please him. She used to cry a lot, I remember and I never liked how he treated her, even then. 'Your daddy is under a lot of strain,' she would often say, making excuses for him.

In terms of putting food on our table, my father was a great provider, but he could be mean. I think he regretted having so many kids so fast, but that wasn't our fault and it isn't an excuse. I wish he'd spent more time nurturing our natural talents and personalities rather than relying on violence and fear to chastise us.

He was old-fashioned about everything and very chauvinistic. He couldn't bear to be wrong and we all suffered from his pride and ego. But as he saw it, he was always right. Whatever he said was law. He paid the costs to be the boss, he would say. There was just no room for our opinions and if we reacted to anything he said we had the shit knocked out of us. We took it for granted that your parents had a right to beat you if they thought it necessary. We were not aware that we were being physically and mentally abused. It was a very different world.

He was an angry man. Angry that his own youth had been cut short, angry that he had so many mouths to feed, angry at the system that made it so hard for a black man, angry that Ronnie was disabled and angry at having to work so hard and make so many sacrifices to succeed in LA. He tried to be a serious, religious man, but his demons often got the best of him and he took his frustrations out on those closest to him.

Despite all this, I loved him and did my best to get his approval and maybe even a bit of affection when I was real lucky. I always wanted him to know how much I appreciated everything he did for us and that I really understood how hard it was for him and Mama.

Mama was wonderful. A dedicated wife and mother. But, like the rest of us, she was also afraid of my father. She did as she was told or she got beat, too. She was servant to everyone. She was loving and warm and worked her butt off day in and day out. I wondered if all women were totally subservient, until I realised it wasn't like this in everyone's home. Once, I asked my mother why she'd married so young and she replied simply, 'We were in love and we felt that we were ready.' After almost sixty-four years married to my father, she died miserable and unfulfilled.

9

1965 (California)

The Roots and Reality of Violence

When Ike was on a rampage, any member of his on-the-road harem might get beaten. It was a lottery. When I joined the Revue, I'd assumed Tina's life to be a bed of roses, but she bore the brunt of Ike's controlling behaviour. And the evidence of his abuse was written all over Tina's face; a bruise here, a black eye or a busted lip there. I guess it was ironic that it had been Tina who persuaded me to disobey David, but really it was pretty disturbing. I'd enjoyed three months of not being abused, but I couldn't understand why Tina put up with this. She hid her sadness behind her sense of humour, but her pain was common knowledge to everyone in her circle.

One time, so desperate to leave, Maxine, Gloria and I gave her money for a bus ticket. But Ike found out where she was headed. She was beaten and bought back. We were all so sad for her. He knew that there was only one Tina Turner, but he would threaten her with replacement at a moment's notice. Her self-esteem was just so low.

At a stop in Arizona towards the tour's end, we finally experienced Ike's full fury. I'll never forget that night. We were getting ready for show time in our dressing room as usual. It was a large room just off the stage, in a kind of basement with stairs leading to the stage door. It actually had proper make-up mirrors! We were laughing and giggling, ready for our cue, when, without warning, Ike burst in and just beat the shit out of Tina. We were terrified. The band played our cue over and over as he ripped her beautiful sequined dress off her and beat her in the head and face. Her eye swelled up immediately. The bruising was horrible. We were in shock and I couldn't stop crying. Ike then made his way onto the stage as if nothing had happened. Tina quickly changed her dress, redid her make-up to cover the black eye and bruises and never shed a tear. I fixed my make-up as best I could and, shaking, we headed up to the crowds and the lights. When Tina came out bruised and battered, proud and beautiful, I fell apart. She broke into 'Shake' and 'Fool in Love' and I was a nervous wreck. Somebody gave me a Kleenex to dry my eyes, but Ike kept giving me dark looks. Everyone in the audience could see that she'd been beaten up, but she did that show as if nothing had ever happened.

It was a different time and people lived and thought differently. Men had free rein to treat women how they pleased. Women did as they were told and were totally subservient in most cases. Society expected women to be quiet, self-sacrificing and maternal. To go about the business of raising and nurturing their families.

Of course, some were smarter, using their sexuality to control and manipulate the situation to their advantage. Or, at least, not to their detriment. And there were good men out there as well, who loved and respected their women and I took my hat off to them. But many men I knew called the shots and most women kept their opinions to themselves unless they were asked, which wasn't very often. Too many times I'd watch my mother trying to put her point of view across to my father, to no avail. 'Shut up,' he would tell her. 'Shut up before you make me mad.' Divorce existed, but it was frowned upon. Many women suffered serious abuse, trapped in loveless, spiteful marriages for the sake of their children. Whatever sick behaviour they experienced, they made their excuses and forgave their men. They were conditioned to do so. My mother was like this until the day she died.

I was seventeen years old when I met Ike and Tina and my abusive shotgun teen marriage had already profoundly affected my opinion of men. David did as he pleased. He worked occasionally and ran his little side hustles, while I handled all the domestic duties and worked two jobs. I did as I was told or I got beat up. If ever he was upset he took it out on me. I wouldn't shut up when David told me to and this made life hard on me. I'd learned from my mother that words were my most potent weapon. Physically, however, I was not strong enough.

One reason I've found it hard to trace details of many of my African American ancestors is that life as a slave before the 1860s was unstable. Families separated by the Middle Passage stayed separated for ever once they reached shore. Slaves had no agency over their personal lives. Beyond the violent nightmare of their daily existence, a loved one might be traded away at any given moment. Long-term relationships were encouraged – they added children to the workforce and discouraged runaways – but marriage was largely forbidden on the plantations. The control exerted by the slave masters and plantation owners saw to it that slaves were forced to forget the languages of their African roots and to speak only their master's tongue.

And, of course, women also had to submit to the sexual desires of their masters and were pressured to bear as many children as possible. This was a hateful world, in which black mothers were battling sexism as well as racism. Slaves built America with their blood, sweat and tears, but got none of the economic pie as it was cut and distributed. Abraham Lincoln promised 40 acres and a mule, but they never received it.

After 19 June 1865, known as Juneteenth, liberated slaves were allowed to set themselves up in trades and to practise the skills they had learned as slaves. That was the theory, anyway. Most slaves had to work the land as sharecroppers. Sharecropping gave them access to land, but there was a price to pay. To buy food and supplies at a plantation store, sharecroppers were given credit, a debt to be settled when the year's crop was harvested and sold. This sale rarely generated profit for the tenants and often left them indebted to their landlords, their labour supervised as closely as slaves had been in the old days. African Americans had little say in the decisions of their local community anywhere and in the south, the Jim Crow laws would hold many generations in their repressive thrall. Black families had to be durable to weather all this.

The struggle to survive in such a system, stripped of ancestral identities and support, has created untold anger within the black male psyche. There is no excuse for violence, but I believe it stems from slavery and oppression, the humiliation and the dehumanisation, the frustrations and limitations that black men have for so long been forced to endure.

As for the Christianity forced on us, most kept the faith in it even after the tortures and the lynchings, the brutality of plantation owners and the Ku Klux Klan. My father walked that straight and narrow path and he was hard on everybody, including himself. He was a religious man who did not believe in adultery. Ike was the same but different. He believed in adultery and lived by his wits to grab his slice of the American dream.

Ike was born in Clarksdale, Mississippi in 1931. At the age of eight he was working at the local radio station. Pinetop Perkins taught him boogie-woogie piano and he taught himself to play guitar. His father had been beaten by an angry white mob. The local hospital only admitted whites. Ike's father's injuries turned gangrenous and he died in a tent outside his own home, a horrific thing for a child to witness. Ike became a wild child, selling moonshine liquor to survive. In the late '40s he formed the Kings of Rhythm, cutting his first record at Sam Phillips' studio in Memphis in the early '50s. 'Rocket 88' went on to become famous as the very first rock 'n' roll disc, though Ike was paid just $20 dollars for it and got no credit, because Chess Records pressed it as being by 'Jackie Brenston & His Delta Cats' instead of Ike Turner and the Kings of Rhythm. (Brenston was the singer and saxophonist.)

Sam Phillips took note of the young Ike's talents and employed him as a session musician, a scout and a record producer and he worked with many key names on the Memphis scene. In 1956 he moved to St Louis and in 1957 at the Club Manhattan he met and later married the seventeen-year-old Anna Mae Bullock. Their first record, 'A Fool in Love', was number two on the R&B charts and when it crossed over into the top thirty, Ike changed the band's name to the Ike & Tina Turner Revue. The rest is history. The Revue became one of the most dynamic live shows on the circuit, with the Ikettes inspired by Ray Charles's Raylettes. Just as Ray Charles bedded most of his Raylettes, Ike expected to bed his Ikettes as well. He had as many women as he could possibly deal with.

In a world where women became sex objects, domestic or otherwise, even the wilder ones were often controlled by a man. The whole industry was and still is, mostly controlled by men and few women were granted independence. Meanwhile, Tina put up with Ike for almost twenty years, until her Buddhist faith gave her the courage to get out while she still had the strength to fight back. She picked up the pieces of her life and eventually found true happiness and even greater success.

Back in Arizona, Ike told me between shows that I was going to be fined $50 for crying on stage. I despised him that night. On the bus after the show, I was furious seeing Ike and Tina kissing and touching each other in the back of the Cadillac. I knew she had no choice, but I also felt cheated that I was being fined for caring about her so much. It would be the last time that I cried on stage for Tina Turner.

10

Early '50s (LA)

From Spiritual to Gospel

Slaves sang songs and spirituals as they worked. If you knew to look any deeper, many songs held a secret, forbidden code that would help hundreds to take themselves out of bondage. 'Swing Low Sweet Chariot' gave clues to the Underground Railroad, the route north for fugitives. 'Steal Away to Jesus' referred to the secret all-night religious meetings that the masters so hated and 'Roll Jordan Roll' to the rivers that had to be crossed on the journey. Harriet Tubman, legendary conductor on the Underground Railroad, sang 'Wade in the Water' to give practical warning to runaways to use streams to throw dogs off their scent. By breaking into these songs, she assured those in flight who she was – and that the coast was clear for them to elude their captors.

The slaves were forbidden drums and other instruments on the plantations, so they clapped their hands, stomped their feet and slapped their legs. Call-and-response migrated from West

Africa into the spiritual services to allow a community to share its sorrows, hopes and joys, individual lyrics and phrases expressing personal humanity affirmed in mutual communal support. These were not the degrading blackface parodies of the minstrel shows, which pretended that African Americans had been happy as slaves. The real songs taught us that all should partake in the Tree of Life, that violence is wrong and no one should ever mistreat another. They invoked God's deliverance of his chosen people, as well as a deep longing for freedom, both spiritual and physical. They became the blues and formed the backbone of every American twentieth-century music form, from jazz and rock 'n' roll to hip hop.

My Grandma Stel and her older sister, my Aunt Catherine, set up the Full Gospel Baptist Church. It was our spiritual freedom. At first the congregation were just our closest relatives and we worshipped at my Aunt Catherine's house, close to downtown LA. Most of the men in Stel's family were rowdy and whiskey-drinking, gambling folks whose wives prayed for their souls on Sundays – but some were deacons. On Papa Thea's side, the Coles were also womanisers, alcoholics, even murderers. Strict and controlling, my father was a young deacon who sang in the choir. Unlike his father, he took it all very seriously.

Grandma Stel was the communicator with a big heart and never judgemental. Everyone flocked to her for wisdom and sage advice. She had a great passion for singing. I loved how she would shake her head as she sang. In fact, my entire family sang. We never had any lessons; we just opened up our mouths and there was this amazing sound. Perfect harmony. We didn't have tambourines and drums at our church, just an upright piano, but we still had very fiery services. We would clap our hands and stomp our feet and move together in time. It was beautiful. Like magic.

I loved the choir. Our family coming together in song. The melodies were old and mournful and the hairs would rise on your arms and the back of your neck. Once together, in full voice, the spirit moving among us, we sang hymns; 'Jesus Getting Us Ready for That Great Day' and 'This Little Light of Mine'. I didn't understand the words yet, but I loved this joyful noise we were making. As more of our family arrived in the city, the services expanded. The preacher would light us up and the plate was passed to collect the tithes.

Soon the tithes allowed the church to lease a small building called a storefront. This was a lot closer to our neighbourhood, on 107th Street and Avalon Boulevard.

I would sing my heart out on Sunday mornings, so loud and with such feeling that when the junior choir was formed I became lead soloist. I was still only four years old. I remembered singing my first solo: 'We Are Soldiers in the Army'. The congregation started to shout and testify. A spirit had seemed to move through me. This faith had brought black people through the trials and tribulations of slavery and the rampant racism in America. I wouldn't be happy unless my singing moved the whole church and that's why I sing to this day. I've never been on an ego trip about it; it's just something I love and love to share that comes naturally to me.

I really enjoyed rehearsals. The musical director was a lady named Sister Lewis. What a beautiful black woman she was; tall, very dark-skinned, with a warm smile and the whitest teeth I'd ever seen. She was stylish, everyone adored her and she sure knew how to play that piano. But she was also very disciplined and wouldn't allow too much fooling around. On Sunday morning, we'd line up outside ready to march into the church to our positions in the choir stand.

By the time the pastor started his sermon, the sisters and brothers would be shouting and testifying, clapping hands and stomping feet. Our church was small but mighty!

On Easter Sunday, we sang songs like 'The Old Rugged Cross' and 'Were You There (When They Crucified My Lord)', then we recited the poems and prose that Grandma Stel had written and performed the plays she directed. We kids worked real hard on our parts for weeks, determined to make sure these gatherings were special. We took them very seriously and performed as professionally as we were able. All the girls dressed in pretty Easter bonnets and frocks in organza or nylon. We'd have lovely gloves, white or pink and yellow and wore patent leather shoes. The boys were unrecognisable in their Sunday best; Sears and Roebuck's polyester suits, a hat like their daddy's, clip-on bow ties and shoes polished like mirrors.

At Christmas we performed the nativity plays that Grandma Stel had adapted and sang soulful Christmas carols like 'Silent Night' and 'Oh Come All Ye Faithful'. Boxes of food, clothing and toys were given away for the poor and needy. When we went home, the kids went to bed believing that a white Santa would deliver our toys while our parents and grandparents stayed up half the night. Mama and Grandma would cook and drink whiskey, bourbon and home-made eggnog with the folks from the neighbourhood.

I've believed in God with all my heart and soul for as long as I can remember. However, as I grew older I could see the corruption in religious organisations and the hypocrisy of some of the devotees. As an institution, I began to see that religion had a lot to answer for. Over time, I became suspicious of people trying to push their religion down my throat. It's hard to comprehend the divisions, especially as Christ spent his ministry teaching us to embrace everyone.

11

1965 (California)

My Return to LA

Ike's violence at the Arizona show upset me mentally and emotionally. Soon I would be back home with David. The anxiety of the idea was tempered by the knowledge that I would see my babies again, the idea that I would hold them in my arms again almost too much to bear.

In ninety days, we had visited major cities in the north, south and east of the United States. My young eyes had been opened to the racism inherent in the country. It was in the nation's bloodstream, like a cancer.

I'd learned so much about performing and projecting on stage and after Gloria rescued me from his last assault, Ike had left me alone. I knew I wasn't Tina's favourite Ikette, but I hoped that she respected how hard I was working. Maxine, Gloria and I were great together and the band members had all shown me kindness. I loved being an Ikette. And now we were set to bring the Revue to venues in and around LA. My friends and family would finally be able to see me perform.

I wondered how everyone would respond to the change in me. When we arrived in LA, I went straight to 117th Street. Kevin and Debbie were so happy to see me. Kevin was almost three and I couldn't believe how much he'd grown. I'd spoken to them both on the phone often, but I was taken aback by how far Debbie's vocabulary had developed in my absence. Kevin hugged and kissed me and then ran back outside to play with his new friends, but Debbie stuck to me like glue.

Everybody was excited to hear about my road experiences. After everything I'd been through, it felt good knowing they were proud of me. But Mama took me to one side. 'David hasn't been around as regularly as he should have and he hasn't given money regularly as promised.'

A couple of hours later, when David arrived to take us home, he was driving an Austin Healy sportscar. He never mentioned it in all our phone conversations and I wondered what else he had been up to in my absence. With the kids mostly at my parents or sometimes with his mother, it appeared that he had been living a life of total freedom while I'd been on tour.

I'll admit it, he was looking good. But then, so was I! I could tell he was surprised at that. We had such a strange relationship. He had been forced to marry me and we were only together because of the kids. I never felt that he loved me and more often than not he was cold and heartless towards me. We were both making the best of a bad situation. We lived together, ate and slept together, but mostly he hung out with his friends. Now I'd be home during the day with Kevin and Debbie. And I'd be an Ikette, rehearsing or travelling to perform in and around LA. I had no idea how this would affect our relationship.

Still, I was feeling good about myself. When Ike and Tina played the 5/4 Ballroom and Maverick's Flat, two local Watts nightclubs, my family and friends would come along. The West Coast schedule was more relaxed. We worked less in the week and hit the clubs and the road on the weekends. The new arrangement gave me more time with my kids and I loved it.

David, however, quickly became jealous of my newfound popularity. I'd figured my glamourous new wardrobe and make-up would make him more attracted to me, that maybe *he'd* fall in love with me at last, but instead he just became more insecure. If he watched me on stage and saw the reaction of the crowd, it just seemed to make it worse for him. And whereas in the past he would beat on me for messing his life up and, in his words, being ugly, now he was violent because I looked too good. His jealousy was always at its peak when he became drunk. He would accuse me of sleeping around and all manner of terrible things. Perhaps I should have, but I never went with another man. There was that night, that terrible night, when Ike had raped me, but *I'd* been completely loyal. Aside from David, the only man I'd even kissed was his drug-running friend Leonard and he only kissed me because he felt sorry for me. Yet all that time I was on the road, I assumed David was seeing other women. He had always been free to do what he wished – smoking, drinking and listening to jazz with his friends. I was the obedient, hardworking wife who didn't talk back. I'd started to fight back in the time before

I left with the Revue, taking my cue from my mother – talking back and standing up for myself. Now he was drinking more and getting high all the time. As he became more menacing and frightening, I could feel things would soon come to a head.

Tina also loved being back in LA, being domestic, being a mother, spending time with her boys. My sister Elaine would babysit occasionally and she would always report that they were totally out of control. None of Ike and Tina's babysitters and nannies stayed the course too long. I'm sure Ike had something to do with this.

Meanwhile, the tensions in black LA were set to explode. The summer of 1965 was about to change the lives and attitudes of black people across the US. People had had their fill of the violence they were forced to tolerate from a system that cared nothing for their suffering. The Watts riots would be the first in a string of large-scale uprisings.

Missing the point and unable to fathom the disquiet among the black communities, many complained that the rioters had merely destroyed their own community, that things were worse off after the riots than before. But perhaps only revolution was going to change anything. It was the brutality of the LA police that had sparked the riots, but it was only one of many issues angering the residents, who felt isolated from the immense prosperity of the larger metropolis. The Californian dream had passed South Central by.

By the mid-1960s, the civil rights movement had gained so much momentum in the US, the frustration was sure to spill over. Watts was a tinderbox. The (relatively) minor event of the arrest of a black family by white LAPD officers was the spark that would light the flame.

The National Guard was called in, throwing a cordon around a large part of South LA. Vandalism, looting and arson were commonplace, as was violence against police and unsuspecting white motorists. People chanted 'Burn baby burn!' and 103rd Street, the main business district, was renamed Charcoal Alley. Residents stayed indoors to avoid stray bullets. The air was black with smoke from all the fires. Thirty-four people were killed, twenty-five of them black, more than 1,000 were injured and 4,000 were arrested. More than 600 buildings were damaged or destroyed. Property damage was estimated at between $50 million and $100 million. In the aftermath, Watts looked like a warzone.

It was a frightening time. Those inside the curfew area could be stopped and hassled, even arrested, so I had to collect my children or get them to my parents before dark. I didn't yet know how to drive and was totally dependent on David, who could be very unreliable.

It was an unusual Saturday off from the Revue when David tried to kill us.

While he had spent the day in a quietly malevolent, drunken mood, nothing prepared us for the sudden and brutal way in which he unleashed the spitting Mad Dog persona with the fullest of ferocity. He had been drinking Rainier ale since morning and – I suspect – popping a few red devils as a chaser, but that was nothing new. I was watching cartoons with Debbie and Kevin when, without warning, he flew out of the kitchen swinging a butcher's knife, cursing and threatening to cut my throat and kill the kids as well. It wasn't unusual for me to try to defend myself in these situations by answering back – often to my detriment – but the threat of the knife in front of the kids, who were screaming and terrified, made me keep my mouth shut. I hugged them close trying to reassure them that Daddy wouldn't hurt them. He loved them. He loved us. He didn't normally beat me up in front of the kids. But this was something new. I kept my mouth shut, praying silently that he would calm down. But I had to keep my wits about me for the sake of the children. When the moment arose, I would have to make my escape – and quickly.

And it did. It would have been almost funny if we weren't so scared. A full day of drinking soon saw David in the bathroom, his anger only slightly tempered by his more pressing need to pass water. I waited until he started peeing before I tore out of the apartment to our upstairs neighbours and called the police. I went alone, knowing his anger was directed at me, not the children. I would never have made it upstairs with them.

David was still incandescent when the police eventually arrived. It took more than one officer to kick open the door and tackle him to the ground before he was handcuffed and taken to the station. Kevin and Debbie were unhurt but in shock. We were alive.

I guess I knew that day my marriage was finally over.

For the first time in my life, I was free and in control. It was as if a weight had been lifted. I could enjoy working close to home, in Hollywood, the Valley and up and down the West Coast. Mama was my lifesaver. She really loved Kevin and Debbie and didn't mind looking after them at all. They were good kids, smart and independent and they had friends their own age to play with.

It was about this time that I recorded my first lead vocal as an Ikette. 'What'cha Gonna Do' had a cool upbeat groove to it and also featured Tina and Brenda Holloway, who sings on the track with her sister Patrice. It didn't see a release at the time, but in later years it has become a real favourite on the northern soul circuit.

The Revue also now had a new trumpet player named Gabriel Flemings. The first day he joined, we had a big argument after he stole my seat on the bus – by then I'd learned to mark my territory! I cursed him out, which he thought was funny. We became close and before too long, we were lovers. Although Gabe could be moody from time to time, he was nothing like Ike or David. He was patient and gentle with me and I was finally learning to appreciate sex. It was nice to have a lover on the road. Our union had other benefits, too. With Gabe at my side, Ike knew to leave me well alone.

David was as relieved as I was about our separation. Neither of us had any desire for reconciliation. All the sadness and pain was over, just like our marriage, just like that and I was enjoying my new freedom. My children and I were safe and that was what mattered.

12

1953 (Watts, California)
Raised and Schooled

My formal education didn't start until just before I turned five. The 118th Street Elementary School was located right around the corner and Mama took me for my first day. I remember I was surrounded by all these strange kids, crying for their mothers. I wanted to cry, too. I didn't, but I felt scared just the same.

I was a bright child and picked things up very quickly, first my ABCs, then how to count. Before I knew it I was in first grade learning how to read and write.

I loved to read about Dick and Jane and their cute dalmatian, Spot. There weren't so many white kids at our school – except for Dick and Jane, maybe. I loved all the nursery rhymes and fairy tales, but all the characters were white. There was no black history or cultural stories. The closest we got to representation was *Uncle Tom's Cabin* and *Little Black Sambo*, both of which embarrassed me.

Life was pretty simple until I was seven, but then things really changed. We now had a brand-new little brother, Theo Percy, who we called 'Little Thea'. He was tiny and frail, born with a hole in his heart. If the bathroom wasn't warm when Mama bathed him, he'd start shivering and turn blue. She had to swaddle him in towels and put him close to the heater. We were all in quite a panic about him. It was also important he didn't get too upset, in case he had a heart attack. This meant everyone was walking on eggshells all the time.

These last two births had been caesarean and my mother had had enough. The babies had to stop, so she had her tubes tied.

Ronnie had another operation on his leg, so my parents were making daily trips back and forth from the hospital. Today, I think about how hard it must have been for my parents. Even then I knew that I had to make things as easy as I could on everyone. I was determined to get good grades. I did my homework and helped with my little brother and tried not to take up too much of my mother's time.

After school and homework and chores, all of us local kids got together and had a great time. Everybody liked to hang out at our house with its big front porch, until Mama got sick of all the noise. Mostly we played outside in one another's back or front yards, then, as we got older, we were allowed out into neighbouring streets and to the playground, to play baseball, netball and volleyball. Or we just raced around making as much noise as we wanted to.

Things were always very tense at home and Mama and Daddy argued a lot, mostly about money. But they sure worked hard to provide for their family. At one point they both worked together cleaning offices. I used to go with them sometimes. I liked to use the big industrial floor waxer, which was twice as big as me. I had to really concentrate or it would drag me all over the floor and make the shine all uneven.

Daddy was still very hard on me, but as long as I had good grades and did my chores, I was allowed to play. Still, his temper flared up about the least little thing and he could take his belt out quicker than you could bat an eye. My brother Kenny and I took the most whippings. We'd get beat for nothing really, for trying to explain ourselves, for catching him in the wrong mood, for the usual fights with siblings. What most pissed him off with me was when his opinion didn't sit right with me and I'd say so or roll my eyes upward. None of this helped my confidence dealing with men later in life.

My Grandma Stel helped out where she could, but Poppa Thea just took care of himself. Every Friday he would return home with a fifth of whiskey and two cartons of smokes; Lucky Strikes for him, Phillip Morris Commanders for Grandma. He would open up the whiskey and count his money before giving it to her, who gave him an allowance to party with and took the rest to the Bank of America. This was his ritual. He had a lot of hair, which he fit into these English Cockney caps he wore. Like a Rasta he never combed it, but he would conk it – which is literally frying it with a straightening solution – and take his one bath of the week. Then he would get dressed up to the nines and come out of the bedroom sharp as a tack and totally transformed. He'd pocket his allowance and head out to

Central Avenue to hang out at the blues bars and clubs and get drunk as a skunk.

My Grandma Stel never went with him. They had an understanding. She let him do his thing and he never interfered with her church activities. He was a wild man with no respect for the American system and that included Christianity.

All this time, Grandma Stel had been studying and in 1955 she received her licence to become a real estate broker and a notary public. She would make the bulk of her money between the ages of fifty and seventy-five and was the first in our family to leave an inheritance when she passed away. She was a hard worker, with many dreams and ambitions always successfully manifested. She understood the working of the American economic system very well.

Daddy and Pop had worked together at Restwell Upholstery. Daddy worked long hours but felt underappreciated there. He'd become a first-class upholsterer, a master craftsman. To supplement his income, he took on work from friends and family and, two nights a week, took evening classes in order to get his business licence.

His dream was always to be his own boss and eventually he started his own business, Cole's Upholstery. Meanwhile, when he cashed his cheque on a Friday evening, Daddy too bought a bottle of whiskey or gin, beer and two cartons of cigarettes: Pall Mall for him and Salem Menthol for Mama. He'd stay home and drink with Mama, unless he was on a night shift, or else he'd give her a break and take us kids to the drive-in. This was the only time we had with him. We had to be quiet but we didn't mind; we were watching all the teenagers necking in the cars around us.

California wasn't segregated, but there weren't many white families in our neighbourhood. When I asked my mother about this, she said: 'When black families moved into our neighbourhood all the white families moved out.' But with the influx of blacks the prices had dropped, so whites who weren't racist in nature were moving back to take advantage of all the beautiful homes and suddenly there were more white kids than before at school, including four in my third-grade class.

Toni Sterling was the all-American girl, real cute, light-brown hair, not quite blonde with a shoulder-length bob and bangs, energetic and athletic, super smart and funny. Her mother ran the local chapter of a girl-scout organisation, the Bluebirds. When I brought home all As and Bs on my report card, my parents allowed me to join.

Outside of those I'd seen on TV, this was my first introduction to the world of white families. I really looked forward to the Bluebird meetings, which were held at Toni's house. There were girls from other schools in our group, but only two black girls: Sandy McNeal and myself.

Sandy was a year older than me with long, wavy black hair – the hair we black girls called 'good hair'. Oh, how I yearned for some of that good hair! My hair was what we called 'nappy' – not exactly short, but not long either. To make it straight, Elaine and I had to endure great pain with the straightening comb every Saturday. Mama would wash our hair and when it dried we had to sit by the stove on a chair with two telephone directories to make us sit higher. The iron comb was put on a medium gas flame. As I held my ear down, she would part my hair, put hair grease on the scalp and hair so it would shine. When the comb was hot enough, she would run it through the parted hair. This was agony and we often got burned. If she'd had a beer we were in big trouble – burn marks and blobs of Vaseline everywhere. She then plaited out our hair in various pigtail styles or bangs and ponytails as I got older. On special occasions, she curled it with hot tongs.

We had to be real careful not to get our hair wet when we took a bath, when it rained or even if we played too hard and sweated, because it would kink right back up again and we would need a retouch. All this so we could have straight hair like white girls.

As for the Bluebirds, I loved it all: the blue uniforms and beanie caps, the yellow scarves and Bluebird rings, the badges we earned for selling cookies, community services, arts and crafts projects, camping, athletics and all manner of things. Mrs Sterling was so patient with us. Their house had a different, carefree atmosphere and everyone seemed happy. And I loved when we camped out under the stars, singing songs round the campfire, roasting wieners and marshmallows. Toni's parents would be hugged up close, drinking beer and enjoying themselves. I wished my parents could be happy together like that. I had such a good time, but I knew it was temporary. They made me feel welcome, but I was always aware I was just a visitor to this strange parallel world.

Ronnie was spending more and more time at home now and he had to be real careful not to let his leg become infected. He was learning to walk with a new artificial limb, but it rubbed against his knee. His leg was very tender and he couldn't wear it all the time. Even with just one and a half legs, though, it was amazing what he could do. He could run with his crutches and even ride a bike. He could even dance. He was strictly forbidden to swim, but he would sneak out to Athens Park, wrapping plastic around his amputated leg so the chlorine wouldn't seep through. He would only stay in the pool for thirty minutes, but the water would soften the skin. As he was the one who suffered the damage, my parents only scolded him.

Eventually another operation was necessary. Skin grafts were taken from various parts of his body to cover the amputated knee. He found himself back in hospital for a long time. When he returned, it wasn't long before he was up to his old tricks. There would be no mere scolding this time, I realised, as Daddy took his belt out and ordered Ronnie into the back bedroom. I couldn't stand this, so I volunteered to take my brother's whipping. Everyone stared at me as if I'd gone mad. 'Are you sure?' asked Daddy. Tears were rolling down my cheeks as I looked at Ronnie. 'Yes,' I said. 'I'm sure,' and followed my father into the bedroom.

When I was in fourth grade, Ronnie finally came home to stay for good. By now he had been through some twenty operations, including skin grafts, but the doctors felt he was proficient enough with his artificial limb to attend normal elementary school. At the time, he had the most modern wooden limb available and just from looking, it was almost impossible to tell he had just one leg. He had mastered walking in it and he was so good-looking that the girls all just loved him. He was a great dancer and a real smooth operator, plus his walk was just very sexy. All the guys were jealous and nicknamed him Pimp Jim.

Little Thea was still back and forth to the hospital and clinic. He would be one of the first children to have open-heart surgery, at the UCLA Medical Centre.

I was still the top of my class, bringing home As and Bs and singing my heart out in the choir. But all the whippings I was getting for petty things were making me inhibited and I didn't think I was cute at all. My sister was the pretty one, with her reddish-brown skin – and now she had breasts. I was the darkest one in the family, taking after Grandma Stel, who was very dainty. I was still a bit of a tomboy and had become quite revolutionary, rebelling against any unnecessary criticism. I would talk back to my father when I was being punished. Nothing I did satisfied him. Elaine got all the kisses and the compliments. She got Cs and Ds, but she was still Daddy's little angel.

By now I had also graduated from being a Bluebird to a Camp Fire Girl and had grown very close to Sandy. We were still the only black girls in the group and we just clicked. She was like my big sister and role model, pretty and smart academically.

When she graduated from elementary school, I couldn't wait to join her at Samuel Gompers junior high. I could walk to school with her! She was a real teenager now, wearing straight skirts that showed off her cute figure – plus her mother let her wear lipstick. She and Ronnie told me all about the boys and girls from the various elementaries in South Central LA. It sounded exciting and fun and there were dances at lunchtime once a week and on Friday nights.

Around now Grandma Stel and Poppa Thea moved out into a house on the corner of 117th and San Pedro. Finally, Elaine and I had our very own bedroom and privacy from our brothers. We were both developing quite rapidly, although I was still ashamed about my breast size. Elaine inherited her large breasts from my mother's side, while my small bumps came from my Grandma Stel. I made Elaine promise to tell no one that I was borrowing Grandma Stel's falsies.

13

1966 (Hollywood)

'River Deep Mountain High'

In November, Maxine, Gloria and I appeared with Ike and Tina and the Revue in the movie *The Big T.N.T. Show.* It's the one document of our time together as Ikettes and I've always been really proud of the performance. It was filmed at the famous Moulin Rouge on Sunset Boulevard and we weren't paid a dime. We never got paid for recordings we did with Ike.

On the road, we made $250 a week and paid our hotel bills and food costs out of this. At home, we got just $30 a gig, which was nothing. Plus he was always fining us for something or other. It was unfair and we were getting fed up, but we were too frightened to protest. I was most scared, Maxine a little less so and Gloria would stand up for herself and talk back, even though it did no good. She had known Ike and Tina the longest, so she could get away with it.

Once all three of us missed the tour bus to Houston, Texas and had to catch a plane to make the gig. We did so by the skin of our teeth but Ike still fined us for missing the bus even after we paid for our flights with our own money. We were pissed off and Gloria and Maxine wanted to quit. Maxine told me that Tina wanted to fire me anyway, because Ike had designs on me. I decided I would go along with the plan. I had my relationship with Gabriel and hated Ike, so this didn't faze me.

We resolved not to say we were leaving and just not show up for the next gig. The trouble was, I had two kids to think about. So, on no-show Sunday, I showed up anyway. I felt bad because Gloria and Maxine got me the job in the first place and they were both angry with me. Gloria told me she understood when I saw her years later, but Maxine never forgave me.

Ike and Tina were furious, though it didn't take them long to find two girls to train up. Ike shipped in Ann Thomas from Bakersfield, a concubine who resembled Tina. She was gorgeous and sweet, but she was already totally controlled by him. She could dance a bit, but she couldn't sing in tune if her life depended on it. It got so bad that she got fined if she sang at all (it was impossible to mix her out because we all sang on one mic). Ike had often threatened to replace Tina with Ann. She was no threat but Tina still wasn't happy with her presence.

The other girl they found was Rose Smith. She was also very pretty and she could sing in tune, but, in truth, she wasn't a great singer. Anyway, suddenly I was the lead Ikette and I had to work twice as hard. Almost overnight, singing with the Ikettes had gone from singing in the hottest revue to just being a job.

But the public's focus was on Tina and they didn't seem to care if the Ikettes were singing two harmonies instead of three. We looked good and Ike was still killing it every night with the Kings of Rhythm.

My closest relationship was with Gabriel and on the road I spent my downtime exploring my sexuality with him. Rose and I sometimes roomed together and Gabriel too occasionally, though he'd moan like hell, as he didn't like Rose at all. Ann had her own private room.

Around this time, we learned that Tina would be recording with Phil Spector. Spector was the greatest record producer of the time, responsible for hits by the Ronettes, the Crystals, Darlene Love and the Righteous Brothers. He'd recruited the Revue for *The Big T.N.T. Show* after seeing us play at the Galaxy Club on Sunset Boulevard. Phil had a song he wanted Tina to sing, called 'River Deep Mountain High'. Ike wasn't happy but he gave his consent. He knew that they needed a hit and he knew he had been unable to deliver one. He made a deal with Phil: the recording would be credited to Ike and Tina Turner – but Ike was not allowed in the studio during recording, because he was known to be so controlling.

This was the first time Tina was allowed to do anything without Ike. She was elated and we were all happy for her. Normally her black Lincoln Continental only made trips to the grocery store but now she was driving alone to Phil's house to rehearse. Phil was a weirdo but also a perfectionist and she loved the song. The material she sang with Ike was more raw and funky; this was progressive-pop-orientated, melodic and orchestral. The recording took place at Hollywood's infamous Gold Star Studio. Phil was creating a backing track with at least seventy-five of the best Hollywood musicians for his famous 'Wall of Sound', plus twenty-five backing vocalists. The Ikettes were not invited. Tina laid down a rough vocal then returned a few days later to record the final vocal. Phil worked her so hard she was drenched in sweat. In the end she had to take off her blouse and record in her bra. When she finished late that night, she had recorded the vocal performance of her life.

With Spector's masterpiece on the A-side, Ike was producing the B-side. Rose and Ann Thomas weren't good enough to record backgrounds, so the studio Ikettes with me were Brenda and Patrice Holloway. Brenda was the first female Motown Records artist from the West Coast and I was honoured to sing with these talented sisters.

When Ike finally heard 'River Deep', he was blown away. Everyone was certain it would make number one, but it only reached number eighty-eight. Everyone was crushed. Ike and Tina had wanted it to be their ticket to cross over into the pop and rock market, but the record was too black for white radio and too white for black radio. Times may have been a-changing, but they hadn't changed that much. Nobody had taken account of racist America and Phil shut his Philles label down in protest.

This failure hit Tina hard. She had been on such a high, but now she was forced back to earth and back into the relentless schedule of life on the road. She was back under Ike's controlling influence, seeing his on-tour infidelities play out right under her nose. The presence of Ann Thomas was now a hard pill for Tina to swallow. No threat on stage, she was definitely a threat to the marriage and to the entire harem. Ann Cain especially had a jealous nature. And when Ike got pissed off with one of them, he took it out on them all.

Tina seemed to slide into a deep depression and once again was considering running away from it all. As she never had money of her own, Rose and I gave her a few dollars to buy a bus ticket. Ike always caught up with her, but it was an important show of defiance from Tina. Ann Thomas couldn't sing for shit and, ultimately, Ike knew that without Tina he would be up shit creek.

She made her getaway but made the mistake of telling her mother and the Greyhound wasn't as fast as Ike's Cadillac. He was waiting for her at a bus stop and she was on stage for the next gig. It was obvious that Ike had knocked her around. It was a heartbreaking cycle.

The Kings of Rhythm had a new line-up, hotter than ever if that's possible, with the legendary Soko Richardson on drums and Ron Johnson on bass, Johnny Williams on baritone sax, Gabe on trumpet, of course, and Clifford Solomon still on tenor. Leon Blue had replaced Ernest Lang on keyboards and Herb Sadler was now on guitar, the band's only white musician.

Tina was especially pleased with Williams, who she had a major crush on. He was a mixed-race light-skinned guy and she became obsessed with him. I don't know whether they ever hooked up – I'd like to think so – but his presence certainly brought her spark back. As did the news that 'River Deep Mountain High' had reached number three in the British charts.

After one of our regular gigs at the Galaxy Club, Ike and Tina were really excited to introduce us to Bill Wyman and Charlie Watts of the Rolling Stones. All I knew about them was that they had a hit with 'Satisfaction', which at the time I thought was a cover of the Otis Redding song. In truth, I preferred Redding's version. We had no idea about the British pop scene, but bands like the Stones, the Beatles, the Yardbirds and the Animals were now starting to dominate US music, many with covers of blues and R&B artists.

We learned that night that we were going to England to support the Stones on their forthcoming tour. Rose was ecstatic! She knew everything about them. I was happy that I hadn't quit, but I had mixed emotions as I packed. We would work our way across the US with one-nighters, ending up in New York, then fly to London. I wasn't looking forward to leaving my babies for another ninety days, but they had a stable, secure environment with my parents and I was much happier not living in fear of David. I wasn't sure how long I'd remain an Ikette, but I'd make a decision about that after this tour.

We hit the road that summer, on the way filming a live clip of 'River Deep' for the English chart show *Ready, Steady, Go!*. This is the first film of the song. There have been more exciting versions, as Ike and Tina would perform it with all subsequent Ikettes, but this one captures the Revue the way it was before our first UK tour, featuring Rose, Ann and myself.

14

Mid-'50s (Watts, California)

Dancing Time

At long last, puberty came knocking on my door. I wore a bra, but didn't have much to fit into it. It was 1958 and I would be twelve in October. I'd graduated from elementary in June and would be going to junior high. My best friend was Claudia Doyle. She was quite grown up, with big hairy legs, which the boys thought very sexy. I had small breasts and hairless legs and I was darker than everyone else. Still, I had my share of admirers, though I was still very shy around boys.

That was a good summer. First we were allowed to go to the Athens Park pool to take swimming lessons. I loved to splash around and the local boys loved to tease me. One day they pushed me into the shallow end. It was just a bit of fun, but Elaine told my parents I was messing around with the boys and that was it. Daddy put a stop to it immediately. Elaine was such a tattletale, but this time she messed it up for herself, too. Neither of us learned to swim that summer.

Then there was Summer Day Camp, where we would dance and sing with boys and girls from all over the city. It was very exciting for me. One boy from the West Side was called Shuggie Otis. He was the son of Johnny Otis, the bandleader-DJ-producer who discovered Jackie Wilson, Hank Ballard and Little Willie John. That year he had a huge hit with 'Willie and the Hand Jive' and the family never missed *The Johnny Otis Show* on television.

All the girls liked Shuggie and everybody did that crazy 'Hand Jive' all summer. I too had a silent crush on him, but I was too shy to let him know. I doubt he remembers me, but I had fun with him. I never saw him again. Later he would play guitar with his father and went on to write 'Strawberry Letter 23', which was a psychedelic hit for the Brothers Johnson in the late '70s. But I love his original version, recorded when he was just seventeen, where he plays every instrument.

I also had my first job that summer, ironing Uncle Book's shirts for him and earning fifty cents for each one. Like Daddy, Booker's dress was immaculate. I took in ironing for anyone who needed it. Mama had taught me well and I never left wrinkles. It was a good hustle.

The money I made helped my parents buy any new clothes I'd need for junior high and some of the teenage fashions. With six mouths to feed, the family budget was tight. Daddy gave us a small allowance, one or two dollars a week depending on how deserving he felt we were. Mama stayed home and ran the household like clockwork, eking out the weekly budget she was allowed to the limit. We all had chores and if you shirked your responsibility you found yourself on the end of a whipping.

When school began again, Gompers junior high was everything I had dreamed it would be. We now had seven teachers and seven classes. During breaks, students would gather on a large lawn called the quad, styling and relaxing and checking each other out. I loved school. I was at the top of my class and worked hard to stay there, but there was more going on than just academic learning.

While dating and boyfriends were still out of the question as a pre-teen, I was allowed to go to Teen Canteens, which were the lunchtime dances on Wednesday afternoons and the Friday night Sports Night dances, which began at about 8 p.m. in the gymnasium. Ronnie was there to keep an eye on me and we were well chaperoned, with teachers or grown-ups checking we didn't slow dance too close or get too excited jumping around with our hormones. If a guilty couple were caught grinding too close, someone appeared from nowhere and put a book between them to show how far apart they should be. On Fridays, Mama was there at 11 p.m. on the dot to get me home on time.

To be a teenager at this time was truly special. The music played was fantastic and we hopped, cha-cha'd, slow danced or grooved to all the latest doowop, R&B and Top 100 chart records, to rock 'n' roll artists like Little Richard and Chuck Berry, the Penguins and the Drifters, Elvis Presley and James Brown – and of course Fats Domino, who looked so like my grandfather, who loved him. And with Motown starting in 1959, this was just the beginning!

We had a ball. The girls were dressed as modern and sexy as their parents allowed and the boys would be Ivy League to the bone. There was a whole lotta shakin' and a whole lotta flirting going on, I'm telling you! I wanted a fishtail straight skirt so bad. All the girls were wearing them, but I knew my parents couldn't afford it. My rear end arrived before my hips and Daddy would tease me about my shape. When you're twelve years old, you're trying to handle all these bodily changes and the last thing you need is the people you love making fun of you. He really didn't want me to feel attractive but I was embarrassed all the time. I became good at covering up my feelings so nobody knew about my insecurity. I laughed it off, but all the chaos at home definitely affected my confidence.

School was a great relief from everything going on at home. I was only twelve years old and still finding my way. For the most part, I hung out with the in-crowd, but I always felt on the outside. I didn't think I was ugly, but I certainly didn't think I was pretty. And I was still so shy, so Sandy and her friend Alma Greggs took me under their wing and made me feel good about myself. They were a real positive influence for me and I copied everything they did. Sadly, Sandy was a lot taller than me, so borrowing clothes was out of the question. They were both pretty and feminine and attracted a lot of attention, but they were classy and clever enough to always play hard to get. I had no idea how to act around boys, so I just pretended to be cool.

By now I had blossomed into a well-adjusted, popular, cute and happy little teenager. I had just made the honour roll and was in the top half of my class, my grades were brilliant and Mama and Daddy were both proud of me. I was proud of myself. We walked to and from school laughing and enjoying our youth, without fear of drive-by shootings or drug dealers. I'll always cherish those last days of my innocence.

15

1966 (On Tour in the UK) Rolling with the Stones

I broke up with Gabe the night before we arrived in London. He had joined the Revue from the Joe Tex Band and had protected me from Ike's advances. But musicians on the road are all just sex maniacs with women in different cities. Plus we both had terrible tempers. I caught him in the arms of another woman after our last gig in New York City. It was the last straw and I landed in London a free woman.

We arrived at Heathrow at the end of August 1966. Everything I knew about England I knew from the movies, so I was really curious what it would be like. In the coach from the airport we marvelled at seeing London for the first time. Everything everyone said about the weather was true. It was grey, dreary, cold and dull, with real fog sometimes. The architecture of the old buildings on the Cromwell Road was incredible, though, as we drove to the Norfolk Hotel in South Kensington.

Rose and I had a huge Victorian double room that overlooked Harrington Road. In the middle of the square was an Italian restaurant and for breakfast we would always get a table right up front so we could see everything that was going on. In Hammersmith we'd also seen our first Wimpy Bar. Back in America, Wimpy was a character from *Popeye*, who only ate hamburgers. We had to try them! They couldn't hold a candle to a giant Chilli Cheese Fatburger with everything on it back in LA, however, and this cracked us up.

Close by were two very trendy and happening clubs, the Cromwellian and, behind it, Blaises, both packed and jamming. The music was incredible. It wasn't until then that I realised just how much the English were into blues, R&B and soul. And the bands were all copying American black music. I knew who usually benefitted financially when a white artist copied black music and also that racist payola systems kept black artists off the air and out of the US charts.

On the East Coast, we often shared the bill with other artists, but generally we toured alone. Our audiences were still mostly black but we had played mixed-race venues in Hollywood and the Valley and at white universities around the country. Ike and Tina were known from the big US TV music shows. But, despite the civil rights movement, America was still very segregated.

At home I listened to stations that played a mixture of white and black music, plus the jazz station at 105 FM. The blues were my heritage, but as kids we were more into Motown and Stax. Before I fell pregnant I'd gone to church every Sunday. I hadn't really tuned into the English interpretations of American music at this point, but we were the original Mods long before the English caught on. Still, British music lovers were hip and they looked great.

London was so trendy and the fashion was to die for. We got to shop in the best boutiques and wasted no time tracking them down. Biba was right there in High Street Kensington. Mini-skirts were in. It was Dolly Bird Heaven! Of course, $250 a week doesn't go far, so I really had to juggle. Still, there were no per diems, but at least we could split hotel bills. This was good. I was planning on spending every penny I could. I deserved it.

The King's Road was the epicentre. Ultra-chic shops selling the most amazing furniture and clothing and frequented by aristocrats and hippies alike. Granny Takes a Trip had incredible velvets, elegant Victorian and Edwardian designs and the funkiest embroidered things. All the hip musicians shopped there. There was Art Deco furniture and 1920s clothing, bell-bottom trousers, tights and sparkly gear, feather boas and hats. Anello & Davide in Drury Lane were cobblers to the Beatles. In Carnaby Street, psychedelic outrageousness fused Mod hipness with past, present and future. Here was the youth cultural revolution! Freedom! Oh, freedom!

'River Deep Mountain High' had flopped in the States and we didn't know just how popular it would be here, but our live promotional video was blowing British minds. We would be opening for the Stones along with the Yardbirds, Long John Baldry and then Peter Jay and the Jaywalkers. Everybody seemed hyped up and ready to see us.

I first met Mick Jagger on the opening night of the tour, backstage at the Royal Albert Hall. It was the most beautiful concert hall I had ever seen. It seated 1,000 people and had very sensitive acoustics, so when we hit the stage we blew the roof off the mother. Victoria must have been turning in her grave at the likes of Queen Tina and the Ikettes, plus all those screaming teenagers.

The place went wild the moment our set began. We were on fire. Then Tina took the stage and just blew it up! She outdid herself that night. By the time we did 'River Deep Mountain High', it was just crazy. For the finale, we Shagged off that stage to thunderous applause. It was one of our most memorable shows.

Afterwards, we ran to change out of our wet dresses so we could check out the Stones. When we first met Bill and Charlie at the Galaxy, we'd cracked up at their accents. I had missed them on *The Ed Sullivan Show* and had no idea how big they were. They came on stage and played 'Paint It Black' and the pandemonium was unbelievable. Girls were fainting or rushing the stage to be thrown off like beach balls by the bouncers. If Ike and Tina gave me my first psychedelic experience, this was my second. Keith Richards' low-down dirty blues-rock, Brian Jones' ethnic sound – mystical blues with a touch of Elizabethan magic. Charlie and Bill were incredible. This was some serious hardcore electrifying rock 'n' roll.

As for Mick's strutting version of James Brown's Mashed Potato, he was hilarious, with his gangly white-boy sex appeal, trying real hard to look black – but sticking out his chest and flapping his arms like a rooster in the barnyard. I couldn't stop laughing. He looked like he had been plugged into an electric socket. But he was a magnetic force and his energy was thrilling. The band were loud and I wasn't too sure about his voice at the time, but you could tell he'd listened to a lot of black music. He had a deep feeling for the music he was trying to emulate. I was seriously impressed.

I knew that Elvis had created this kind of excitement in the US, but I had never witnessed it personally. Everyone in the band looked distinctly British and they were all fine, fine, fine. We were shocked! This band were red hot! The Stones to me were and still are the best rock 'n' roll band in the world. It was the beginning of an adventure that would change my life all over again.

The tour was a gruelling two shows a night for three weeks across England, Scotland and Wales. The Stones travelled in huge black Daimler limousines and Ike and Tina in a big Ford Zephyr, while the rest of us did our normal bus thing. Apparently the Stones always had a black support act that they admired on their tours. This way they could mix with the creators of the music they loved, while the black artists found a different, mainly white audience. All of which meant more sales, more royalties and a fairer slice of the pie.

The Stones stood backstage every night and watched us shake our asses, strut our stuff and boogie down. They were getting off on our sexuality and our hot, live funkiness. Mick in particular loved it. He would come into our dressing rooms and we would teach him the dance steps and the funkier groove we felt he needed. He had nearly perfected the Mashed Potato and the Pony. We became firm friends.

All I had to do was look at him and I'd laugh. He was so cute, with those big red lips. I was fascinated by those lips! He had a long waist, which helped him to move in that wiggly way of his. He loved to hear all the black slang, too. His accent was a scream and I think he felt the same about mine. Sometimes I couldn't understand a word he was saying.

It was curious the way we seemed to click so easily. I'd never known a white guy up close. Outside of my time as a Bluebird and a Camp Fire Girl, I had no real experience of whites. And the Rolling Stones in 1966 were certainly no Camp Fire Girls.

Soon I realised that Mick had a crush on me. Bill had the hots for Rose and the two of them would invite us to hang out with them regularly. If they were hanging out at a club, they would send a limo for us and then we'd go back to our hotel or sometimes to theirs. Everybody was shocked. It seemed totally out of character. There were actual newspaper headlines that read, 'Would you let your daughter marry a Rolling Stone?' – and here was shy, introverted me, partying with one of the most notoriously wild white boys in the UK.

Naturally, Ike was pissed about it when he realised what was going on, but there wasn't much he could do about it. As long as we arrived at the gig on time, he had no control over Rose and me. His fines became even more petty, if that's possible. He once fined me $25 for having a run in my stockings. I still hated how he treated Tina and I was starting to feel as if my time as an Ikette had run its course. Maybe I'd leave when I got back to the States, I thought. I still faced the challenge of having no contacts in the business. How would I support my kids?

All the while, Mick and I were just hanging out and having some laughs together. At the end of the evenings, we started exchanging some pretty steamy kisses and I was beginning to wonder what sex with a white boy might be like. I didn't realise Mick was aware of the problems I was facing, but it turned out he already had a plan.

In Glasgow, he and Bill arranged for Rose and me to travel with them to the next show in Newcastle. Ian Stewart, the Stones' road manager, packed our gear in with theirs and Rose and I were waiting inside the Stones' limo when they did their final runner off stage. Then, when they left the theatre, the fans went wild. They threw themselves onto the car, screaming, kicking, punching and crying. I was frightened and immediately regretted not taking the tour bus. Rose was shaken up but excited. In America, black girls didn't ride around in limos with white boys. This was scary. In the eye of the storm, the Stones seemed accustomed to it, but sometimes I think it frightened them a little, too.

As the limo headed south toward the border with England, we drove past Gretna Green. It was known as a place where a couple could get married without their parents' permission and had a kind of romantic reputation as a destination for underage eloping couples from south of the border, where the laws were more prescriptive.

'It's okay to go out with coloured girls,' someone said and everyone started to laugh, 'but you can't take them home to meet your mother.' I could feel their laughter and my hackles raising all at the same time. 'And you certainly can't marry one!'

I guess it was meant to be amusing, but I went OFF. I was all the way back in Watts in full-on Mary Cole defensive mode, cursing them all: 'Fuck all you motherfuckers!' and then I told them what they could do with their Gretna Green.

My outburst only made them laugh harder. They were killing themselves and quoting some English gameshow host called Hughie Green and shouting, 'Take the key, open the box! Take the key, open the box!' I started to think they were all insane and I was genuinely frightened. When I looked to Rose for support, she just sat there, looking uncomfortable, so I carried on cursing. And when I looked to Mick, he was laughing along with all the others. It was so disappointing. I thought he was my friend. Whatever it was that was so funny, I didn't see it. In fact, I thought they were being very rude. Under my fear, I was furious. I couldn't wait until the journey was at an end.

It was a long drive to Newcastle, but I'd calmed down by the time we arrived at the Station Hotel. Rose and I were both pretty shaken and we agreed we'd just stay in our room and wait to see what happened.

We didn't have to wait long. Someone knocked and there was Mick with a smile on his face. 'I'd like to apologise for what happened in the car,' he said. 'We didn't mean any harm. You took it all so seriously that it made us laugh even more. We were only taking the piss,' he said, very amused. 'What does 'taking the piss' mean?' I asked. 'It's the English way of teasing.' I was still angry: 'It wasn't very funny to us! Back in the States we call that kind of talk racist! I'm not used to being around white guys and I felt very uncomfortable. I was frightened!' He assured us that no one had meant any harm. 'Come have dinner with us,' he said as he continued to laugh and gave us the suite number. We thanked him. He gave us both a friendly hug and me a juicy kiss and left.

In the suite, there was a dining area set up. The room had been filled with toys and I couldn't help but think how much fun Kevin and Debbie would have had if they were here. Someone had arranged a movie projector so we could watch a film after dinner. Having come from a life on the road that meant sharing a room at a Holiday Inn or finding a tree to pee behind, it felt like a different world entirely.

Rose loved every minute. She was more sophisticated than I was and more used to moving in integrated circles. I was more withdrawn. This was an elegant dinner: starters, main, dessert and wine. We talked about the gig and the day – though no one mentioned Gretna Green. I don't remember much about the movie, but it was a nice way to finish the evening. When Mick suggested we leave and go to his room, it seemed very natural.

I had never had a white guy as a friend, let alone as a lover, so when he undressed me and his white skin connected with my brown skin, it felt exciting. He was a gentle lover and he had no inhibitions. This was a first for me! I had never been satisfied like that! This was hot and heavy and romantic, reciprocal in every way, warm and satisfying. I forgot all about being shy. I felt like I was in a dream. I had crossed a line I had never imagined crossing. I was making love with a white boy – and not any old white boy, but the world-famous singer of the Rolling Stones!

I was first to wake. Mick was still sleeping. It was strange being next to him. He was very fair, with blond eyelashes. But then he reached out for me and it was ON again. I was glad I'd pinned my wig on. I wanted to retain the Ikette image he had fallen for.

Everybody had been shocked when we left with the Stones, so I'm sure there was gossip that day in the Ike and Tina camp. Mick arranged for us to be taken to the theatre in a cab rather than the limo. As bad luck would have it, we were five minutes late for soundcheck, so naturally Ike fined us $25 on the spot. Everybody wanted to know what was going on, but we kept them guessing.

I knew Tina was aware Mick fancied me, but I think she was shocked I was spending so much time with him. She couldn't wait to find out what was going on. Black guys had always been interested in white women, but back in the mid-'60s, an American black woman hanging out with a white man was taboo. This relationship was turning me on to new thrills and I was surprised at my own daring. Plus I liked Mick. I needed some fun and romance in my life. This was my first adventure on my own and I was determined to enjoy it. In three weeks I'd be back in the States.

When the Stones arrived, Mick came over with one of his great raspberry-lips kisses. I would've hated it if he had tried to hide that we were together, so I was pleased it was no secret. From then on I slept with him every night.

When we were together, we talked about each other's lives. I told him about my children and a little about my life in Watts before becoming an Ikette. He asked me about Ike and Tina. I told him about the harem and Ike's violence. I also told him that I was planning on leaving when we got back to the States, but I wasn't exactly sure what I was going to do.

He was honest with me and told me about breaking up with his girlfriend, Chrissie, the sister of the very famous model Jean Shrimpton. He asked how long I'd been singing. 'Since I was four years old. I grew up singing gospel music in the church with my family.' I described growing up in the Baptist Church and we talked about soul and R&B. He was fascinated when I told him the blues he was so passionate about was the music of my parents and all the older generations. I'd grown up watching the elders party to B. B. King, Bobby 'Blue' Bland, T-Bone Walker and Jimmy Reed. I was less familiar with deep legends like Robert Johnson, Son House, John Lee Hooker or Elmore James. To most kids of our generation this was old folks' music! But here I was in England learning even more about these pioneers from some skinny, pretty white boy.

On our off-days, I didn't see Mick. This didn't bother me. I'd be heading back to the States shortly and he surely wasn't taking a black woman home to meet his mother. Actually, I was having a ball. I hadn't dared think this would be anything more than hanging out. Even Ike couldn't put a damper on the fun I was having.

The Revue was fast-moving and exciting from beginning to end. But the finale required precision and one second's mistiming could be disastrous. At the show in Bristol, on a darkly lit stage with a flicker light going, Rose misjudged and ran into a grand piano off stage, breaking her arm. The rest of the tour she had to do in a cast. She received lots of sympathy from everyone, plus a few mentions in the press that she was really happy about.

Backstage that night, I had noticed this very pretty blonde girl, a famous English pop singer called Marianne Faithfull. She had travelled from London with the Stones' photographer Gered Mankowitz. She was very polite when we were introduced. Mick had already booked me a room at the hotel, so I thought no more about her.

After the show we went back to the hotel as normal, for dinner and a movie. That night it was Roman Polanski's *Repulsion*, starring Catherine Deneuve. I knew nothing about either of them or about any European films. This whole European world was new to me. But everyone was looking forward to it and there was a definite buzz.

I wasn't really surprised to see Marianne and Gered back at the hotel. I saw Marianne and Mick flirting and people seemed hypnotised by her presence – plus she had a strong resemblance to Deneuve. In the film a girl has a fear of men and turns completely psychotic when her sister leaves her on her own. She starts having weird sexual hallucinations and she kills two guys after they try to hit on her. The first she beats to death with a candlestick, the second she kills with a razor, before hiding their bodies under a bed. It all seemed a bit sick to me, but I was more focused on the moves Marianne was making on Mick. When everyone retired to their rooms, I realised only Mick, Marianne and I were left. She and I played a little Mexican stand-off for a while, until I realised what was up and returned to my room. I had no claims on Mick and I wasn't stupid. I just wished he hadn't booked my room. It was the first time that I had dealt with a situation like this. My time in England was introducing me to a lot of first experiences.

16

1961 (LA)

The Summer of 1961

My high school adventure was gearing up to begin. Up until now, my father had been real strict about staying out late and dating and I was looking forward to a summer of freedom and putting my all into dancing. This was going to be the most exciting time of my teenage life!

A popular soul group, the Olympics, had a hit with a record about a dance called the Hully Gully. At the only private party I'd gone to, when I was about thirteen, I'd done a pretty wild Hully Gully where you stood in one spot and shook your shoulders from side to side. I was so enthusiastic that my dance partner got the wrong idea. First he got excited, then he was all up on me and my brother had to snatch me off the dance floor. Even so, I couldn't believe it when he told my father. I wasn't allowed to attend private parties any more. My actions were entirely innocent, but once again I found myself accused of sending out sexual signals. Meanwhile, my three brothers spent most of their time lying about getting laid. And obviously as a man my father knew how boys' filthy minds worked, which meant I always stayed under suspicion. But the truth is, sex was the farthest thing from my mind. When it came to boys, my father had put the fear of death in me. I was very uncomfortable around the opposite sex and I still had no confidence in my looks.

I'd moved into the ninth grade now and at least Daddy had let me have a boyfriend. I can't even remember how I met him. To have impressed my father, he probably had some connection with Ronnie. His name was James Higdon and for some reason Daddy liked and trusted him. So did I. I was thirteen and he was maybe seventeen, but still Daddy let him drive me home from school occasionally. These were contradictions to my father that always confused me.

James was tall, dark and handsome, with a big smile full of strong white teeth. He taught me about petting, hugging and cuddling, but he was always a perfect gentleman. Sometimes things got a little hot, but he never tried it on. He said he didn't want to betray my father's trust in him, which made me respect him a lot. He was kind and gentle with me. He had an older girlfriend named Gwen and I think he was having sex with her, but I don't recall feeling jealous. I was too young to be bothered about it really. I just enjoyed laughing and talking with him. He had a custom-made '52 Chevy called the Pink Lady, freaked off with a funky manifold low to the ground that sounded deep and throaty, the way custom cars ought to. That short low-riding trip from school to home was the hippest thing that I was allowed to do. He would walk me home and as I stood on the porch and he stood below he would give me the sweetest kisses I'd ever had.

Then, right before my graduation, he went and held up our local Jack in the Box in a burglary and was sent to Soledad prison. He served time with black revolutionaries like the Soledad Brothers and always wrote me beautiful letters. He was looking forward to resuming our friendship when he got out of jail, but I was devastated.

No one realised just how much I was affected by things at home. No one seemed to entertain the idea that you could have a roof over your head, clothes on your back, shoes on your feet and food to eat and still not be happy. An opinion meant a whipping, so I kept my mouth shut. Elaine told Mama anything I told her and I couldn't confide in Mama because she always told Daddy. My Grandma Stel was the only person who seemed to understand me, but I wasn't mature enough yet to know how to have an open relationship with a grown-up.

I'd passed all my tests with good grades and was looking forward to buckling down at high school and going to college. I loved learning to type and Daddy wanted me to be a legal secretary, a highly sought-after role for a young black woman in those days and a lofty enough ambition to please everyone. I had good secretarial and business skills and was sure I wouldn't have a problem. I hadn't thought any further than that.

As a reward for making the honour roll, Daddy gave me permission to have my first teenage house party for my best friends (but no alcohol). I was so excited!

The night started off great. Everybody looked fashionable and cool and we were dancing, eating and laughing. Ronnie had been allowed to invite some of his friends from high school, which made it exciting for us junior high school graduates. They were so suave and sophisticated and such hot dancers. Then the party crashers arrived. By around 11.30 p.m., the house was packed with strangers bringing in alcohol. Everything was getting out of hand, until Daddy pulled the plug to stop the party early. I'd hoped he would let it go on until past midnight. Still, it was a big success and we talked about it for weeks.

Then came my first Hunter Hancock Record Hop. KJLH was the hippest black radio station of the time and this was *the* event to be at. Every Friday night Hancock visited a different high school and the one at John C. Fremont High was known to be the best. All the finest, coolest, hippest guys on campus would be in attendance. My girlfriends and I were so excited to be allowed to go. We would all be freshman at Fremont in the fall and couldn't wait to get a preview.

The first person I clapped eyes on was David Arnold. Every other girl had their eyes on him too and I was shocked when he asked me to dance. He was such a great dancer and he liked the way I moved. Like singing, dancing freed my soul. It took me high above all of life's mundane problems.

That summer was all about Chubby Checker and the Twist. David had its energy down perfectly, hands and hips in perfect motion. He was so fine!

Once we started twisting together, it was obvious we had something going on. All I remember about that night is that we danced the Twist, then the Cha-Cha-Cha, then the Mambo, then the Hop – and finally we slow danced. We danced! I have no memory of conversation, but I gave him my phone number when he asked. I had been allowed to receive visits and calls from boys since graduation. I was on my way to being a full-fledged teenager and I loved it.

I lived in Watts and David lived in Slauson Village, but that summer David came calling regularly. When it was warm, the porch was our fun hang-out and, as long as we stayed in the front yard, Mama didn't mind David visiting during the day.

David was a good kisser. What wasn't so easy was getting him to stop. I was totally infatuated, but I also didn't really trust him. David was also about four years older than me and charmed my parents into giving him permission to visit in the evenings. I wasn't allowed to go out with him but he could visit me at home. I think the reason my parents were so protective of me is that they felt I was older than my years. But I don't understand why they let older guys court me. It was asking for trouble.

Meanwhile, I looked forward to the record hops. I rode to them in Ronnie's car and he was on notice from my father to look out for me. My brother took this seriously and David knew to be on his best behaviour. But Ronnie was pleased I was having a good time and became good friends with David. Plus, despite his leg, he gave everyone competition on the dance floor.

The Fremont campus seemed fifty times bigger than the one at Gompers and I'll never forget my first day. I already had the low-down on high school etiquette from Sandy and Alma, but it was so much better than I'd imagined walking in the massive quad area, with students from different communities all across the city milling to and fro. The guys from the Slauson side of town took great interest in us girls from Gompers. The Slauson girls were pretty, but also tougher and rowdier. They didn't like us getting all this attention. Everyone looked so sharp, just going to school. The Mods in England had no idea!

David lived just a few blocks from Fremont High. He'd already graduated but hadn't started college yet, so he regularly met me after school and we would hang out before I journeyed back to Watts with Ronnie. Our kisses were getting more and more intense and he was so good-looking! He was also becoming impatient with my not putting out.

Most of my girlfriends had steady boyfriends now and I was the only one who hadn't experienced sex yet. David kept suggesting I ditch school and come over to his house when no one was home. But I had never ditched school before. To keep him happy I decided I'd skip music appreciation, a class I could easily make up. David would meet me after lunch and we'd go to his house, listen to records, pet and kiss and touch, stuff like this. I wasn't planning on sex. I had to be back at school in time to ride home with Ronnie. I thought I could hold out. I was dumb and naive.

I met him outside the school and we walked to his house. Once there he took me to his bedroom. There was nobody around. I knew this was wrong. I knew I should insist on leaving. The kissing began. I was scared shitless but David was wasting no time. Everything happened so fast. Before I knew it he was on me and in me. 'Stop! David! Stop!' I screamed. It hurt. And then it was over. My virginity was down the drain.

I was so embarrassed. Also, I was scared, as he hadn't bothered with a rubber. My brothers always carried rubbers. Not David. He wasn't thinking about me at all. He only cared about his own satisfaction. He was so pleased with himself. In fact, he was overjoyed. He'd made his conquest! And I was so disappointed in myself. 'Did you like it?' he whispered.

As we were leaving, David's mother walked up the pathway. David told me she probably hadn't seen us and we tried to leave by the back door. It was too late. She was in the house. She had seen us and she was furious. We were busted. She asked who I was and David lied. He said we were just passing by so he'd shown me where he lived. She didn't believe him and asked my name. 'My name is Pat Cole,' I answered meekly. 'If I ever catch you in my house again when I'm not home, Pat, I will call your mother.' I apologised and got out of there quickly.

Normally his mother didn't come home until much later, David told me. 'It was just bad luck.' Bad luck! The whole afternoon had been bad luck. No more ditching school for me. From now on, I'd only see him as I headed home from school with my brother or at Sports Night or during one of his visits to my home. I was doing so well in all my classes and I was looking forward to my first football games and track meets. I wasn't about to let David mess things up for me. Little did I know, he already had.

17
1966 (London)
Opportunity Knocks

One day late in the tour Mick invited me for lunch at his flat, in a beautiful mansion block on the Marylebone Road. It was the first time I had been there. Afterwards we walked in Regent's Park and talked about our problems. His relationship with Chrissie Shrimpton had ended badly when, shockingly, she tried to commit suicide. I also knew about his fling with Marianne Faithfull, but I was only in England for another couple of weeks and it didn't bother me. We had an understanding and no one had ever been this nice to me. I was very happy with my newfound freedom.

Ike was now openly hostile with me, giving me a hard time and fining me regularly. He seemed almost jealous that Mick and I were close. But I wasn't here working my butt off to have him siphoning off my wages for stupid reasons. I knew I would never make good money as an Ikette.

Mick told me that Stones manager Andrew Loog Oldham wanted me to stay in England after the tour to record for his independent label Immediate Records. I was shocked! I loved London, but staying there was a daunting prospect. I told Mick I knew nothing about the music business and had never thought about a solo career. Mick knew I was sick of Ike's constant abuse of his women and that I was thinking of leaving when I got back to LA. 'Staying in London had never crossed my mind,' I said. 'Well, you should think about it and let me know, because Andrew really likes your voice and would like you to record for him,' Mick said. 'It will take at least six months to get a record out,' he replied, 'and you'd have to be around to promote it.'

In LA, I'd have the support of my family, I explained. But I'd have no savings and no means of supporting myself here. 'I think that you should consider the offer,' he said. 'If you decide to stay, I'm sure everything else can be worked out. Andrew and I will both produce the album. Call your mother. See what she says. Decide from there.'

I couldn't believe what he was offering me. I felt the same excitement I had when Tina suggested I go to Fresno. I loved London – but could I handle it? Maybe this was just what I needed. It was evident that he and Andrew believed in me. Maybe I should start believing in myself?

I called my mother and told her about the offer. I explained that I had no idea what might happen. 'Your daddy's not here,' she said. 'I'll have to speak to him and see what he has to say.' My mind was racing. If joining the Ikettes had been a big decision, this was on a whole new level.

The next day I spoke with my father. 'Your mother and I have prayed on this and decided to give you the six months,' he said. 'We know nothing about the entertainment industry, but we do know you have talent and we wouldn't want to stand in your way. It seems that God is opening doors for you and you've done well so far to make life work for you. We can help with the kids, but you'll be a long way from home and you'll be on your own.'

In tears I thanked them for having faith in me. I told them that I still had a meeting with Andrew to iron out all the details. 'I wanted your permission first, before I even considered the offer,' I said. 'I'll call you after the meeting and let you know how it all went.'

I'd never spoken to Andrew beyond cordialities. As the Stones' personal manager, he had helped catapult them to fame and had been responsible for their bad boy image. He was a huge fan of Spector's 'Wall of Sound' and right now, like everyone over here, was trying to recreate it. The English also loved American girl groups, so I was in the right place at the right time. In fact, Mick had already produced Jimmy, Rose and me singing on tracks by the British R&B singer Chris Farlowe, including a version of the Four Tops' 'Reach Out I'll Be There'.

Andrew now confirmed everything. He promised to support me in every way while the recordings took place. He would be responsible for the bulk of the album and Mick would be a contributing producer. I was excited but also filled with anxiety. When the Revue returned to the States, I would be staying in England on my own. Who could I trust? I knew nothing about the business, nothing about making records, nothing about nothing.

Mick seemed really genuine to me, but in reality, I didn't really know him. I had grown up in a very segregated society, with no real experience of living among even white Americans. Six months away from my children, family, friends, everything I knew and living among British whites in another country and another culture – this was a BIG step! What if Mick and Andrew turned out to be as bad as Ike? There were so many unanswered questions. And I didn't have a lot of time to make up my mind.

I prayed on it. I talked more to Mick about it. He promised he would be there to support me, but he also warned that his commitments to the Stones had to come first. I decided I had nothing to lose and everything to gain if I stayed. I called home and told them what I'd decided.

'If you think that it's the right thing to do, do it,' Daddy said, 'You know that we're here if you need us.' I told them how much I loved them and thanked them for the faith they had shown in me. If things didn't work out for me, I would be home in six months. And if they did, I would come home and get the kids.

My last gig with the Revue was at the Ram Jam Club in Brixton. I brought all my luggage in a taxi and hid it in a storage room, making sure no one saw how much there was. I kept everything to myself except for my ex-lover Gabriel. He recognised this was a once-in-a-lifetime opportunity. He promised not to tell a soul and wished me well.

The club was packed and it was a great gig but I found it hard to concentrate and performed on automatic. While I was on stage, the Stones roadie Ian Stewart and recording engineer Glyn Johns packed all my gear into their car. After the gig I said goodbye to everyone and told them I would meet them at the hotel. They assumed I was off to my last secret rendezvous with Mick. Then Ian and Glyn whisked me off to Epsom in Surrey, where they both lived. We arrived in the middle of the night and I was introduced to Glyn's fiancée Sylvia and Stu's wife Cynthia.

Around 4 a.m., I received a very irate phone call from Ike. 'Bitch, is you crazy?' Probably someone in the Stones camp gave him the number. Maybe Gabriel had blabbed. 'What the fuck do you think you're doing leaving in this way?' He was screaming. He had one Ikette who could barely hold a harmony and one who couldn't sing at all. I shakily told him that shouting would do no good. He was cursing like a mad man and calling me all kinds of names: 'Yuz a crazy bitch! You might be separated from David, but you're still legally married! You got two small kids back home, what are you going to do about them?' This was none of his business, I said. 'You don't know nothing about the business!' he told me and he was right about that! 'Mick Jagger don't care nothing about your black ass! You are a fool!' He went on and on, with many threats. 'I'll find your ass before morning and you'll definitely be leaving with us.'

'I'm sorry to leave without notice but I'm taking this opportunity and there's nothing that you can say to convince me any differently.' And I hung up the phone. I couldn't get back to sleep, terrified he'd show up any moment. After hours of second-guessing myself, I fell asleep and didn't wake until noon. I phoned the hotel to check if Ike and Tina had checked out. They had. I relaxed and spent my first day in England among strangers, praying that I had made the right decision.

18

1961 (LA)

Pregnant

Although we lived some way from each other, Daddy still let me see David. When you're fifteen, your mind works differently. I was an infatuated teenager; everything was about who's cute. But still, I was beginning to see David's dark side. I was four years his junior. He was a man, satisfied he'd made his conquest.

His mother Mae was from Louisiana, a light-skinned Creole woman with that elegant mix of French and African beauty. Mae's mother had been a stand-in for Dorothy Dandridge, the black Hollywood actress. Hollywood makes demands on black women and I suspect that all the partying and hustle is the reason Mae had fallen into prostitution in her younger days. She had eight sons, all told. Eight Arnold boys and they all looked alike, although I don't know how many of the Arnold boys shared the same father. Half were very light-skinned and the others were brown-skinned. David's complexion was much lighter than all his brothers and he had a lot of hang-ups about this. He also hated his mother. Perhaps I should have taken that as a warning sign.

David had no interest in schooling but he had learned some things. For one, he was a prolific cat burglar. He was light on his feet, very strong and athletic. As a result, he was always dressed in the finest clothes. At first he told me his mother had bought them, but I later learned he had a knack for charming older folks. In the foster homes he was placed in, he gained their trust and learned the secret hiding places they kept their money and jewels.

As he got older, David did some juvenile time early on, but he was smarter than his brothers and never seemed to get caught after that. Still, his street name was Mad Dog, which should have set off big-time warning bells. I was pretty naive, I guess. Plus my family life, high school and church meant I had plenty to keep me distracted from his shortcomings. In any case, I was a kid and in my eyes he could charm the birds down from the trees. I liked the romance of us being together. In short, I enjoyed having a boyfriend. Still, I was going to learn eventually, there was good reason people called him Mad Dog.

One thing I've learned after a lifetime of making mistakes is it can take a long time to really know somebody. When you're fifteen, your hormones are starting to cloud your judgement, just at the moment you are opening your heart to someone new. You never consider that the person, this stranger you are opening up to, might have a damaged history. As a teenager looking for acceptance you often don't realise you're being lied to. You take everything at face value. It's impossible to understand the traumas others may be dealing with when you don't even understand yourself.

Two months passed and I'd missed my periods. They had always been like clockwork and Mama had a check-up system, which she called a 'show', because we had to show her the blood on our sanitary napkin. Luckily for me, Elaine was always irregular and, that November, her time was almost in sync with my own. When Mama asked to check my 'show', I simply presented one of Elaine's soiled napkins. I know it sounds nasty, but desperate times call for desperate measures.

When I told David, he pulled an instant disappearing act and I was on my own. I was terrified. My father had put the fear of death into me if I ever became pregnant. His threat went around and around in my head.

Come December, Elaine's irregular period hadn't arrived yet, so this time I used fresh liver, wiping it over a towel for my show. Mama couldn't tell the difference so, come January and February, I did the same thing again. I hated having to be so devious, but I just couldn't bring myself to tell my parents. My breasts, which had always been so small, were now filling out my bra. Also my belly was beginning to show. I was going out of my mind. When I confided to my sister, she assumed that I was joking. I was sleeping more and more and took to staying in our bedroom.

My secret was taking its toll. At home after school, I wore a loose white shirt that hung over my Levi's, which was the style of the moment. But at gym class we had to wear our gym blouses tucked in. I tried to wear mine outside but I was pulled aside by my gym teacher. I was scared and embarrassed. I started to talk in my sleep. I knew I wouldn't be able to lie to my mother much longer.

One day, a school monitor entered my classroom with excuse slips for another girl and me to go to the nurses' office. I let the other girl go in first and asked her what happened when she came out. She said they checked your heart and took your blood pressure and I was relieved.

In the room, the nurse asked me to open my blouse. Slowly, I unfastened half the buttons so she could hold the stethoscope to my heart. 'Patricia,' she frowned. 'I need you to undress completely.' She was watching me closely now, eyeing me like I was a criminal. 'You have been called in today because we suspect you are pregnant.' Immediately I started weeping. She asked how far gone and I told her four months. She called my mother immediately.

The truth was finally out, but I felt no relief. Finally, four months too late, I understood what my parents had been so afraid of. One bad choice had changed the whole direction of my life.

When she arrived, Mama began hitting me and cursing me. I was crying uncontrollably. 'Your father is going to kill you! How could you do this to us?' I had brought shame to my family. Tears were streaming down my face. Meekly, I followed my mother out onto the beautiful front lawn and into the car. As the car pulled away for the dreaded drive home, I said my final goodbye to my beloved John C. Fremont High. I would never return. I never got the chance to say goodbye to my classmates. In the short time I'd been a high school student, I had been a popular and well-liked achiever – and now I was the disgraced talk of the school and the community. The grapevine moves fast.

As my mother predicted, Daddy wanted to kill me. I was prepared for that, but not his disgust and disdain. That made me wish I was dead already. When I told him the child was David's and that he hadn't wanted to see me since I told him, I could see the tears forming in his eyes. 'You won't be having an abortion,' he said, his voice shaking. 'And the child won't be put up for adoption,' he said. He was devastated. 'Now go to your room,' he told me. He didn't want to look at me. But I knew this wasn't the end of the matter.

When Mama called Mae George, she said she hadn't seen David for a couple of days, but she snitched me out for the day she caught me sneaking out of her house with David. When David didn't show up by the next evening, my parents called the police. Given our ages, he could be arrested for statutory rape.

I was taken to the police station and quizzed about our relationship. How many times had we done it? Where? When? Which positions? Did he use a condom? (Evidently not.) When had I last seen him? It felt like such a humiliation. I didn't know where he was. In fact, it was slowly dawning on me that I knew very little about him and his long juvenile record. The David Arnold I knew and the real David Arnold were two quite different people.

By the time he was found one week later, I wanted nothing to do with him. I had been such a fool. He had shown me he had no feelings or respect for me – and I had none for him now. I was scared and confused. Daddy's plan was to force him to marry me or have him sent to jail. Marriage had never crossed my mind. I just wanted to be someone's girlfriend. But David had dragged me down to his level, which was nowhere. He was a street thug messing around with young girls – and I had fallen for him hook, line and sinker. By going out with him, before high school even started, I'd lost any chance of a normal relationship with boys my own age. My dreams, all my ambitions, were shattered.

'I'm so sorry for everything. David doesn't love me and he's not a nice person.' Daddy agreed. He had talked with David and he understood exactly how cold and selfish he was. He forbade me from having anything to do with him. After the child was born, it was agreed that I would go back to school and get my diploma. I was delighted with Daddy's sudden change of heart. David disappeared from our lives and I began the next four and a half months of pregnancy on my own.

As punishments go, this was the worst I could ever have imagined. No more Sports Nights now, no football games, no track meets, no shopping with my girlfriends, no innocent dates at the movies. Under the new regime, no calls or visits were permitted. I was not allowed out of the house. I became a virtual recluse, which was fine with me; I was so ashamed. I helped my mother with all the chores and spent most of my time in my bedroom. My belly had blown up overnight and soon I was feeling my baby move inside me.

My friend Padodee's mother Josie Forest was friendly with my mother and organised a baby shower at our house. I was pleased my father allowed me to have it. All my girlfriends came and I got so many nice presents. Everybody was shocked to see my big belly. I let them feel the baby moving and they were amazed. I'd been the last of us to explore my sexuality, but the first to fall pregnant. I was not a good example as far as their parents were concerned, however, and this was the last time I saw them together like that. After the shower, they were all forbidden to see or call me.

Nevertheless, life went on and I embraced my new status as best I could. I was still a baby myself, a short, petite young girl, an unwed teenage mother with a huge belly. As my body changed, so did I. And so did relationships with my family, my church and my community.

To shame your family was as bad as being a drug addict or criminal. Tongues were wagging and the hypocrites had a field day. I missed choir, but soon stopped attending altogether. Daddy could have, but he didn't force me to go. In a way, I was grateful that his shame took precedence over his sense of duty to the church. And all the while, I was losing my identity. I was terrified, had no idea what to do. I cursed myself. A first child should be a happy event, but the situation in which I found myself was making no one happy.

It was too late now, but my parents would never have considered me having an abortion. Terminations were illegal, in any case. Besides, they didn't have the money to quietly send me away and support groups were unheard of.

I realised I'd blown it big time. My friends were all getting on with their lives while I spent hours in my room with my gifts, imagining them dating and going to parties every weekend. I was so sad and pitiful, Ronnie convinced Daddy that maybe it would be good to get me out and see friends in a controlled environment.

He took me to the annual City Track Meet. This was a big deal and I was so excited. I wasn't even worried about people seeing me eight months pregnant. I saw a lot of people I knew. They all said that they missed me and to let them know when the baby arrived, which was nice even if they didn't mean it. I also ran into David face to face. The coward. He barely spoke to me and acted as if he didn't even know me. He was enjoying his life while mine was ruined.

The baby was due at the end of July. People were always so keen to tell me how painful childbirth could be, but I refused to show any fear. Whatever happened, however the birth played out, I was determined that I would rise to the occasion. Even so, every tiny twinge from my belly made me think labour was starting. I just wanted it to be over with so, to get things moving, I decided I would jump off the front porch. This seemed like it had started my labour pains, so we went to the general hospital. After checking me over, they sent me home. The doctor told my mother I should only come back when my contractions were less than ten minutes apart. I'd hoped I would get away with an easy time, but my baby was in no hurry to be born. Ultimately, it would be another couple of days before my cervix opened. I had no understanding of what was happening and just wanted someone to put their arms around me and comfort me.

In the event, 1 August 1962 would be one of the longest days of my life. Labour kicked in early that day but my parents didn't take me to the hospital until early evening. I was in agony all day, my hopes of a painless labour dashed. I thought that I would surely die. The pain was excruciating. Never in a million years did I think anything could hurt so much. And I was getting no sympathy.

There were no antenatal clinics or birthing classes back then and there was little to prepare you for what was to come. There were no Lamaze classes in those days and family was not allowed on to the wards. When I was finally admitted, I was sure that I had died and gone to hell. All I could hear was women screaming and crying out to God to help them. I was on my own.

My mother had agreed to me having a spinal block, but I wouldn't get it until the contractions were in the final stage. I was put in a giant crib. Was it to keep women from falling on the floor from the pain? I was in agony when I grasped the real reason: the bars gave me something to grip on to. The young white doctor assigned to me turned out to be an angel. He was so compassionate and did his best to explain to me what was happening in my body. Apparently the baby's head was large and I was young and so small, so it was taking a lot longer than usual for me to dilate. He let me hold on to him when I was having contractions and I never got the chance to thank him for letting me dig my nails in. I must've scratched him up real bad. I never saw him again.

At 6.30 a.m. on the morning of 2 August 1962, my son, Kevin Lamont Arnold, arrived, weighing in at 7lbs 6oz. He was a healthy baby boy – with a very big head. I was in labour for thirty-six gruelling hours and they needed forceps to deliver him. I had to have a lot of stitches and could barely walk, but he was the prettiest thing I'd ever seen and I soon forgot all about the pain.

He was so beautiful and I just poured my love into him. I had experienced physical pain that no man can ever imagine and brought life into this world. I now had a real live baby boy to dress up and play with and I didn't care what anybody thought about me.

Now, however, I had to get my life back on track. I would enrol in school in January for the winter semester – it was too soon for September. I would prove to my parents that I could still make a success of myself. I'd be a good mother and take my responsibility seriously.

I'd given him a grandson, but Daddy was still simmering and I constantly had to tiptoe around him. Theora Cole was serious: if he promised you a whipping, he never forgot. I knew that it was just a matter of time before the anger came out. But my parents did love Kevin and were as proud of him as I was. And after months of Mama and Daddy keeping me under house arrest, I was finally allowed visitors. Suddenly it was okay to visit Pat – they just couldn't hang out with me. Not that we had anything in common any more. My life had changed completely.

One friend who defied her parents and came to see me anyway was Erma Kent. Erma is and always was cool. She was the delinquent daughter of Theora Cole's worst nightmares and I first met her in junior high. She is still my oldest, dearest friend.

Aside from me, Erma was the only girl in my group who lived with both of their parents, but she started ditching school way back in seventh grade and had acquired a pretty wild reputation. At fifteen, she was already ahead of the curve. Gorgeous and light-skinned, she had big, sexy eyes, a very elegant nose and luscious lips. Erma knew how to work it. She also had a great sense of humour. She was a survivor who didn't care what anybody thought about her.

It was nice having someone my age being real with me and she was also very compassionate. I even defied my father by walking her down to Imperial Highway and San Pedro after one visit. This was only halfway between our houses and I thought I could make it back home before Daddy and I almost did – but he drove past me a block from the house. It was just the excuse he needed to let out all his pent-up anger on me. I came into the house and took Kevin out of the stroller and put him to bed. Next thing I knew Daddy had picked me up and threw me down in the stroller. I'd been fortunate to fall belly down across the width of it, which hurt like hell but broke my landing. He wasn't finished, though. He unfastened his belt and let me know exactly how he felt about me leaving the house without his permission. It was the closest I came to hating him.

19

1966 (Surrey)

Life in Epsom

Had I lost my mind? Here I was in a house in Epsom full of English people I didn't even know. Was I letting my emotions rule me again? Was this just infatuation?

Or was it like the last time I took a chance? Pat Cole: high-school drop-out in an abusive teen nightmare marriage with two young children and zero confidence – becomes an Ikette! Pat Cole: shy, sweet, innocent Ikette trapped in the Revue – becomes a solo artist in another country! In each case I had fled with people I knew nothing about. The unexpected seemed to rule my life.

Glyn Johns says now: 'I got Andrew interested in you, not Mick. Ian Stewart said to check you out, he thought that you were an amazing singer and he felt sorry for you. He said, "There's only two Ikettes that can sing and this girl is fantastic." He thought the whole thing you were going through with Ike was revolting.

I told Andrew you had an amazing voice and that's how you got your record deal. It was Stew who drove it all.'

The house in Epsom, a single-storey bungalow, belonged to Ian Stewart. Stew was a really sweet guy, very shy, extremely honest, with a lovely sense of humour. He could play serious boogie-woogie and rock 'n' roll piano. In fact, he had been one of the original Stones, but he didn't have the look that Andrew felt the band needed, so he was demoted to road manager and off-stage pianist. He was more than a little bitter about this and I had the feeling he didn't like Andrew much. Nevertheless, he had stayed on as the band's most loyal and trusted friend and confidant. He plays on many early Stones recordings, but his self-esteem had been damaged. If he'd ever wanted fame, it was clear he wasn't interested any more. He wasn't exactly handsome to me, but he was quite cute. He had a very square chin that made you think of a lovable Popeye. He was so kind and very protective of me. I suppose his experience with Andrew meant he could see the dangers that lay ahead of me.

It was a lovely little one-storey house that they called a bungalow. Stew shared it with his wife Cynthia, who was Andrew's personal assistant. She had a very aristocratic nature and a sarcastic kind of humour, which I found hard to understand. I worried she was smiling in my face but laughing behind my back. But this was just my paranoia and insecurity. She was lovely and took me under her wing.

Glyn Johns and his girlfriend Sylvia also shared the house. Both seemed to be from upper-middle-class backgrounds. Glyn was an extremely talented engineer, working with the Stones and other major artists. He was lovely, a very good-looking, hunky guy and we got along really well. He had a flash E-type Jaguar with the licence plate LP1 and he too had his own axe to grind about Andrew. It turns out he had been the original Stones producer before Andrew arrived.

Sylvia was a blonde Mary Quant type, a very pretty English rose. She was pleasant but also distant with me. I suspect everyone felt that Mick and Andrew had upset their routines.

Epsom is renowned for its horse racing track on the Downs. It was miles from London and I spent most of my time alone. Cynthia and Sylvia worked during the day, Stew was away with the Stones and Glyn mostly just slept before going to the studio in the evening. On the rare occasions it wasn't raining, I explored the village. I seemed to be the only black person there and with my long wig and flashy showbusiness look I stuck out like a sore thumb. After about a week, I began worrying that maybe Ike was right. But here I was. I had to hold the line and see how things would play out. I wished I was in London, though.

The Stones were touring Europe and Andrew was with them. Mick called now and then but I didn't see him. I really knew no one else in England. Mick's affair with Marianne had been brewing long before I came on the scene – or so I was now reading in the music papers. She had been discovered by Andrew and Mick and Keith had then written her first hit, 'As Tears Go By'. I'd never known Chrissie Shrimpton and though she was obviously stunning, I never felt threatened by Marianne. Mick and I were just good friends with no obligations, but I was still beginning to feel a little neglected. I was under no illusion that he would ever commit to a black woman, but I was concerned about my situation. I was determined not to let my heart get broken again. I was fed up spending all my time alone, but I tried to stay positive.

Over time, homesickness crept up on me. Cynthia, Sylvia and Glynn were all very nice, but I didn't want to become a burden. So, I did my best to settle in and adapt to all these strange new customs. For example, shops closed so early, at 5 p.m. on the dot, with 'early closing day' one day a week when they closed at 1 p.m. for lunch and didn't open up again. Bizarre! Back home a grocery store stayed open twenty-four hours a day and definitely didn't close for lunch. It seemed so strange to me. Didn't the English like to make money?

Also strange was the number of meals a day: breakfast, lunch, tea, dinner and supper. Tea and supper were kind of like formal snack times. I thought this was real cute.

Of course, it rained all the time. I wasn't used to everything being so damp and grey. In LA, a rainy day meant a day off. We would even stay home from school because of the rain and the few who went in just played rainy-day games. This perpetual rain was different, though. I could feel myself becoming lazy and morose. I was bored of books, so I started travelling to London by train to wander around Piccadilly Circus, Leicester Square, the West End, Carnaby Street and Bond Street. Mostly I just window shopped and saw movies because I had practically run out of money. No contract had been signed and I didn't want to ask Andrew for money. I was suffering in silence and feeling very insecure. Perhaps when Mick came home he would advise me.

I was such an innocent Christian girl. I hadn't been schooled in the art of hustling. Everyone was trying to make me welcome and comfortable, but they were all so formal. I didn't feel that I could confide. Probably they were just as frustrated as I was. I was trying not to be a problem but my introversion made it easy for no one. I just didn't feel comfortable. My inferiority complex was making it hard to adjust.

On Saturdays, I went shopping with Cynthia. There were no big supermarkets in England yet, so we went to a greengrocer for fruit and vegetables, a butcher for meat and a bakery for freshly made bread. The bread was delicious. We'd also buy cakes and biscuits, which we call cookies in the States. Back home biscuits are like hot dinner rolls and we eat them for dinner with mashed potatoes and gravy.

Then we went to a dairy for fresh milk and eggs. These were amazing, nothing like the homogenised supermarket milk and battery eggs back home. Then a little local store for staples and canned goods. It really was an education!

I loved these trips, but I hated how people just out-and-out stared at me. It made me go further into my shell. I should've just been black and proud, but I was just a stranger in a strange land.

On our return, Cynthia would make a great lunch. On Sundays, we had a traditional English roast dinner followed by puddings and delicious custard. Then everyone took a nap! We were completely out of sync. I had spent the week on my own, climbing the walls, waiting for something to happen, while they had been working hard, looking forward to their lazy weekend. They were snoozing and I was desperate for some excitement.

One time Glyn showed me some European currency. I thought the Italian lira was so beautiful, Glyn gave me a 50,000 note as a souvenir – he didn't know I was nearly broke. I accepted this graciously, planning to take it to the bank and exchange it for something I could use. I was the first in line the next morning at the National Westminster Bank foreign exchange department. I handed over my lira, expecting at least £100 for it. I was devastated when the cashier handed me about 20 pounds. I felt sure she'd made a mistake, but she assured me she hadn't. Embarrassed, I walked home and cried like a baby. Still, £20 was better than nothing.

Eventually I explained my situation to Cynthia. She called Andrew immediately and demanded they sort money out for me. He did so straight away. I had just been too shy to ask. My father taught me to never obligate myself unless I knew what the situation was. This had saved me from being controlled by Ike Turner and I wasn't going to change my approach here in England.

At last, the Stones were back in England. But when Stew arrived home he told me Mick had left for a post-tour holiday. He'd be in touch in a couple of weeks. Why hadn't he told me this himself? It was embarrassing to have to hear it from Stew. The others felt bad for me. No one would tell me the real reason Mick was not around, but the music press knew and I soon found out. He was on holiday with Marianne. They were telling the world they were in love. I heard Ike's warning again: 'Bitch, Mick Jagger don't care nothing about your black ass.' Everyone did their best to cheer me up, but it didn't really help.

To make matters worse, I missed my period. This freaked me right out. I'd been on the pill with Gabriel, even though it didn't agree with me, but I'd run out on the tour and had taken a couple of chances with Mick. I couldn't believe it. The last thing I needed was another child, let alone a baby by Mick Jagger. He was living it up with Marianne somewhere in Morocco and here I was pregnant by another Leo. Fertility-wise, Leos were definitely bad news for me.

Perhaps some would have seen this as a financial opportunity, but I was still only nineteen and already had two kids. I had not stayed in England just to be caught up in a rock 'n' roll scandal. No matter how it looked to others, I knew Mick and I were genuine friends. I didn't want to spoil our connection this way.

I felt that Cynthia was the only person who could help. She located Mick for me. 'Mick,' I said, 'I really hate to tell you this, but I've missed my period and I'm pregnant.' He asked if I was sure. 'I'm a couple of weeks late and there's no way that I can have another baby. I don't want this to interfere with our friendship.' We both decided that an abortion was the best solution and I wasn't going to wait until he came back to hold my hand.

I was really scared. But abortion was legal here. Cynthia made the arrangements and the termination took place within days. I was booked into a hospital in Kingston and it was over in a day. I received a huge bouquet of flowers from Mick, who called every day to see how I was and promised to see me as soon as he returned. He obviously felt bad, though not bad enough to cancel his holiday. Not that I asked. I was devastated.

20

1963 (Watts, California)

Pregnant Again

I scarcely noticed that everyone I knew was having fun, getting on with their regular teenage lives. My life now revolved around Kevin, my perfect baby boy. Following his birth, we lived in a world of our own, while I immersed myself in becoming the best mother I could be. I'd bathe him, dress him and change his diapers. I used to say, he had to be the cleanest baby ever. He was so good! I loved to fix his formula and feed him, hold him in my arms and play with him. I thought that he looked like me, but it was undeniable he had inherited David's good hair and big head. I was addicted to him. I felt so glad to finally meet him – and to have him out of me!

Kevin brought new joy into the house and the whole family loved him. If I was the wanton delinquent, everybody loved and spoiled Kevin. I sometimes had visitors, mostly just being nosy, but I just got on with my new life. I was proud of how I was coping.

Coming right with Theora Cole meant cash and David knew this. Obviously he'd heard through the grapevine how beautiful our boy was and how well I was doing, but still I was shocked when he arrived out of the blue. He had a nerve. He apologised at least and when I reminded him about how he'd blanked me at the track meet, he explained that he'd been startled to see me pregnant and hadn't known what to say. I wasn't about to pretend to be nice. He had been selfish and cruel. 'Why are you here now?' I asked. He said he just wanted a chance to see his son. Kevin was asleep, so I reminded David he couldn't see the baby unless Daddy allowed it and Daddy wasn't home right now.

David returned later after Daddy had come back and they had a long talk. He had a job now at the new LAX space-module restaurant and the two of them agreed he'd give my father $25 a week to cover formula and other expenses. I had no say in this. My life was turned upside down but David had sacrificed nothing. And now, for a paltry $25 a week, he was back in Daddy's good graces.

Nobody cared what I was going through. I still couldn't communicate openly with any of the adults in my life. Despite all the time I'd given to the church, nobody came to talk to me in a spiritual way.

David was still fine, well dressed and arrogant, with that mischievous glint in his eye. As agreed, he made regular payments and that meant regular visits, but I knew he hadn't changed at all. But, as a result of his cowardly behaviour, I *had* changed. And I no longer trusted my father's judgement.

That winter I enrolled at George Washington high school. It was outside my district, but they accepted unwed mothers. I finished early, around 2 p.m., and Mama looked after Kevin until then. None of my friends were there and at first nobody knew I had a son. When word got out, I didn't really care. They all seemed so childish to me. My head was not really in the tenth grade but I still did well. I was smart academically and I worked real hard to catch up on what I had missed.

David continued to make his unannounced visits. But I could tell he wasn't just paying attention to Kevin now. He looked better every time he arrived and I was looking pretty good myself. Daddy had made a big mistake. Didn't he realise how dangerous it was letting him back in so easily?

Soon David was stealing kisses on the sly. I made the mistake of letting him pick me up after school and drop me off at babysitting. Despite everything that had passed between us, we started to get close again. He appeared sorry and began to open up more about his behaviour and I took his regret at face value. I knew very little about his life in foster homes. His mother was trying to make amends for the mistakes she'd made as a young woman, but he hated her and blamed her for everything. He was such a charmer and, slowly at first, I began to feel sympathy for him. I was still a lonely young girl and I didn't know how to control my emotions.

Sex didn't have to lead to marriage and the pill was all the rage for single women. People knew that 'nice' girls did it. They even enjoyed it. The church was totally against the pill, but it empowered women to make rational choices about how many children they wanted. I should have been on the pill. Sexually active teenage girls could get it from clinics, but I needed my parents' consent. Despite the stable door being open and the horse having already bolted, my daddy the deacon believed it encouraged sex outside of marriage. I had already sinned. He was not going to allow any more sin under his roof. Mama and I had no say.

My parents didn't want to put thoughts of sex in my head, but David had other ideas. One thing led to another and he assured me he would wear a condom. Three or four times later, David didn't wear his raincoat and came inside me.

When my period didn't come this time, I could hear my daddy's voice ringing in my ears: 'A hard head makes a soft ass.' My parents had just begun to trust me again. I felt such a fool. I could have kicked my own ass! What the hell was I supposed to do now? Would David be there for me this time? Somehow I doubted it.

True to form, David, who had spent all this time trying to charm me and gain my sympathy, had none of his own to spare. He blamed me for being stupid. I reminded him it was his idea.

I decided to speak to Myrtis Smith, Uncle Book's latest girlfriend. Myrt was in her early twenties, younger than most of his women, and she knew all about street life. I wasn't about to keep this to myself for four months this time. She was a little wild, but very friendly and sensitive towards me. She drank bourbon like it was going out of style, but I felt I could trust her.

'Myrt,' I pleaded, 'I've missed my period and I may be pregnant.' She was sympathetic and gave me some quinine tablets.

When my period didn't come in a few days, she said I might need an abortion. A new fear gripped me. I knew nothing about the procedure or the risk; all I knew was the word. But I had to do something. Naturally, David thought an abortion was a fine idea. Myrt said we had to be careful that my uncle didn't find out. I told her my lips were sealed.

David and a friend drove me over to Myrt's house, where she would perform the abortion. She packed a lot of gauze inside me with a sterilised coat hanger and told me I'd start bleeding in a couple of hours. It hurt like hell and I'll always remember the atmosphere in that car as David's friend drove me home. I was so ashamed of myself and in a lot of pain. I was naive the first time – but this time was total stupidity. As cowardly as ever, David looked relieved to be off the hook. That's what he thought, at least.

I tried to act as normal as possible when I arrived home, but that was asking a lot. I started bleeding, supposedly a sign that something was happening. I prayed that I would abort. I had violent stomach cramps but then the bleeding stopped. Myrt couldn't understand what had gone wrong. 'I'll have to do it again,' she told me. I answered straight away: 'There is no way that I'm coming back and going through that again.' It looked as if I was still pregnant. What if I had damaged the baby? I was frantic. She said taking more quinine tablets might work.

I took so many over the next twenty-four hours that my head started to ring. But God was not answering my prayer. There was nothing that I could do. I knew that there would be no adoption. I could hear the shotgun ringing in my ears. I knew Daddy would insist that David and I get married.

I told David that I would have to tell my parents. I asked him to come over and be with me, but he did his famous disappearing act again. I would have to tell them on my own. I was terrified that I'd harmed the baby and perhaps even damaged myself as well.

Daddy and Mama were livid. Their disappointment and disgust broke my heart and I resigned myself to whatever fate awaited me. Whatever was coming, I figured I deserved it. After that it was like a re-run of my pregnancy with Kevin, police and all. A warrant was put out for David's arrest. He was twenty and I was still a minor, so it was jail or marriage for him. Daddy was insisting on a shotgun wedding.

I never told my parents that it was Myrt who performed the abortion. I was so angry at myself. I was taken to the doctor for a check-up as the police searched for David. They found him about a week later. He was laying low in Compton with people he knew in one of his foster homes. It was decided that we would get married the following Saturday. The ceremony was to take place downtown, at City Hall. Appointments for the blood tests were rushed through.

There would be no invitations sent. There was no joy surrounding the marriage of Theora and Mary Cole's oldest daughter Patricia Ann. The only witnesses were Mama and Mae. No grandparents, brothers, sister, close family or friends. Even Daddy didn't come. It was such a sad day. No loving kiss, no reception, no carrying the bride over the threshold, no honeymoon. David and I were moved into the spare bedroom at my grandparents' house. We had no say.

My wedding night was a nightmare. I was abused verbally, mentally and emotionally and then we slept with our backs to each other. There was no affection and no desire. He said I was too ugly to look at and I cried myself to sleep. It was the start of two years as the wife of David Arnold. Two years of hell.

21

1967 (UK)

Back to London

I'd had enough. I hadn't seen Andrew or Mick for weeks. Cynthia saw Andrew every day and Mick spent all his time with Marianne. I'd promised my parents that if nothing happened in six months I would come home and my time was running out.

I packed my bags and caught a train to London. At the Immediate offices, I insisted that Andrew or Tony Calder find me somewhere to live in London. I said I was bored and lonely in Epsom. They'd been kind enough, but I felt like I was getting in the way. Besides, they shouldn't have to feel responsible for me.

Tony was Andrew's partner and he handled the business side. I didn't really know him – not that I knew Andrew either really. Tony introduced me to Stephen Inglis, who worked in promotions and suggested I stay with him and his girlfriend Cathy Barou in Fulham.

Stephen was very stylish and hip with a lovely smile and an electric energy about him. I liked him straight away and drove with him in his Austin Mini through the West End and down to Fulham, talking and laughing with him about Swinging London. His flat was in Parsons Green, in an old Victorian house, on two floors. It had wooden floors that squeaked spookily and they said there was a ghost that sometimes pulled the loo-chain in the middle of the night. Or perhaps they were winding me up. It was definitely cold and that toilet seat was freezing first thing in the morning. Plus the toilet paper was like wax paper and you had to rub it between your hands to soften it up.

Cathy was short and pretty with long mousy brown hair in a fringe, another perfect Mary Quant dolly bird with a hip London accent. She and Stephen were very easy-going. They liked to smoke hashish and we would just chill out and have a good time. They were very up on the London club scene and we went to all the trendy late-night music-industry haunts: the Cromwellian, Blaises, the Scotch of St James, the Marquee and the Flamingo. Instead of just singing in clubs, I was enjoying nightlife for enjoyment's sake for the first time. London was swinging and I was swinging with it. This was more like it. This is how it was supposed to feel, to be young and free!

A few weeks passed, however, and I began to feel antsy again. Cathy and Stephen were planning to move to a new flat in Ladbroke Grove. Andrew and Tony were giving me money to live on and drawing up my contract. Once it was signed, I would begin recording.

Meanwhile, I hung out with Stephen and Cathy, often at the Bag O'Nails. Its owners also had the Ram Jam Club, scene of my last show with Ike and Tina. Two brothers, Rik and John Gunnel, ran the club. They also owned the Gunnell Agency, which booked the great soul bands, including Geno Washington and the Ram Jam Band, Georgie Fame, Zoot Money, John Mayall and many more. It was in the Bag O'Nails that I met Ronnie Jones.

Ronnie was an ex-American serviceman who had stayed in London. His band, the Blue Jays, were also with the Gunnell Agency. They performed all the soul classics and he was a great singer. Sometimes I sang with him. One gig stands out in my memory: the first I did with them outside of London. It was up north in Stockton-on-Tees, at the Kirklevington Country Club. I was nervous as hell. Ronnie introduced me to the crowd as an ex-Ikette, but despite my time in the Revue, I had no idea how to present myself. I could hear Tina's voice in my head, offering encouragement and though she'd never know it, she gave me the confidence I didn't know I had. Everything I knew, I knew from my time with Tina, so I let go of my nervousness and simply let rip. The audience loved me.

With so much time on my hands, I was increasingly disappointed in Mick. I hadn't seen him for a very long time now and things were moving far slower than I had hoped. I was single and free and this was fun, but I was also homesick and missing my children. I had responsibilities that no one else my age here seemed to understand.

One time I called my mother and asked about the kids. She told me they were fine: 'They're really growing and they miss you a lot. They're always asking when you're coming home. They don't have a clue where London is, but they know that's where you are.' I told her about adjusting to the ways of the British people, about how white people were different in England and about how long it was all taking.

Then I spoke to the kids. When I hung up I cried. I missed my family. I knew I'd never be able to talk to my mother about this new life I was living, not about the hashish or the brandy or rum and Coca-Cola or my affair with Mick and certainly not the abortion. Even if she came over, she'd only understand some of what I was going through. This is when I realised how alone I was. I had no idea when I'd be home. I just had to be patient.

After what seemed an eternity, Mick finally called. Our friendship was based on laughter and a lot of hot sex and though his affair with Marianne was now a full-blown relationship, he hadn't abandoned me. He was very honest with me about her and I knew she knew about me. This was the Swinging Sixties, when everybody had more than one lover. I was learning so much from Mick about British culture and about this new rock 'n' roll lifestyle. No woman in my family had ventured this far from our roots and I was grateful for this opportunity. I hadn't asked him for anything.

I wouldn't have this much freedom once I brought my kids over, that's for sure. Nor would I have had this experience back in the States. In fact, as naive as I was, I'd have been eaten alive.

22

1963 (Watts, California)

Under the Gun

Patricia Ann Arnold!

After David and I were married, we were forced to move in with my grandparents. My little brother Theo missed me so much that he ran to the end of the road every morning to see if he could see me.

My whole life changed overnight; not just my name. I had new in-laws I didn't know at all, I was sixteen years old with a six-month-old boy and expecting a second child I was praying hadn't been harmed by an attempted abortion.

My mother-in-law became a dear friend. Her family hailed from New Orleans and she loved to cook gumbo and shrimps and rice. Her skin was flawless. She said it was because she drank lemon juice in water every morning. Her husband was a kind, quiet-spoken man. They loved to drink and spent their weekends doing just that.

As for David, he still resented his mother for placing him in foster care as a child. His hatred made it impossible for him to love anyone else, but he could never forgive her for abandoning him. It made me realise how little we know as teenage girls. If your parents don't let you date a boy, you see it as cruel. You can't see they're trying to protect you from making mistakes they probably made themselves.

When she was young, David's mother had lived a fast life, which had turned her young sons into petty criminals. She loved David most of all and tried to spoil him, but he preferred stealing to anything she bought him. He robbed his parents and treated them like shit.

By contrast, my Grandma Stel was always there for me. She never judged me and always encouraged my inquisitive mind. She concentrated on her real estate business while I cleaned and cooked. She wasn't the greatest cook in the world, but she taught me the basics.

With David it was a different story. If things were hard before, they were twice as much so now. We had our own bedroom and with my grandparents out working, nobody but the child in my womb witnessed his daily cruelty. He was careful not to do anything in front of Kevin, but otherwise I became his punching bag. My first pregnancy had been extremely emotional, but at least I wasn't dealing with David's temper.

There was no communication. He would wake up, get dressed and disappear. He still worked at the airport, but I didn't know his working hours and he never told me. Most of the time I was just glad he was gone. When he returned, late, he was high on marijuana and always smelled of beer. He'd climb into bed and turn his back to me. When no one was around he'd knock me about. I was every ugly black bitch to him and in his eyes I had stopped him going out with prettier young women. I could do nothing to please him. If my happiness ever crossed his mind, he never showed it.

From my experience of Mama and Daddy, however, this was just how husbands were: they beat on their wives when they didn't like something they said or did.

David was sullen and silent most of the time, but he was also a horny young man with husband privileges and after a while he started having sex with me. But it wasn't romantic sex. He never cared if I was satisfied and it only happened when *he* wanted it. He could put on a charming-guy act around other people, but he had no real respect for women. Yes, despite all this, I was still in love with him. I thought that maybe in time he would love me, too.

Debra Elaine Arnold was born at 6 a.m. on 17 November 1963. She was named after my favourite Hollywood movie star, Debbie Reynolds and my sister Elaine. I was in labour for twenty-four hours, which was short compared to Kevin's thirty-six and at 7lbs 4oz she weighed less, too. I feared she'd been damaged by the attempted abortion, but she was perfect. David and I may have had our differences, but we made beautiful babies.

It was after we brought Debra home that things came to a head between my grandfather and David.

Papa Thea suspected I was being knocked around and then David went too far and started beating me in our bedroom when

Papa Thea was at home. My grandfather went crazy. He threatened to kill him if he laid another hand on me. After that, he told my parents that we would have to start looking for our own place.

I was not looking forward to living alone with David, so things became even more strained between us. The little money he was earning wouldn't take us far, so I found a job in Eagle Rock at Taco Tom's, a Mexican fast-food joint. It was a shit job but we needed money to move. There I learned how to make the best tacos, burritos and enchiladas. To this day my family asks for them. Even David loved them.

The manager was playing me for a fool, though, leaving me to do all the work while he banged the other girl in the back room. David suggested I start to skim a few dollars from the cash register while they were doing their thing. A few times I did, but I had no desire to become a thief. Finally, I got pissed off and threw all the lettuce, tomatoes and cheese at the manager before quitting on the spot.

David found us a two-bedroomed apartment in a fairly new block on Century and Hoover Boulevard and we moved in and set up house. I knew little about decorating, but David was very artistic. He was a talented burglar as well as a junk store addict and before long we had created a nice environment for ourselves, cosy and groovy. Daddy made us a living room suite that was modern and practical and we collected as much furniture, cookware, dishes and other home comforts as we could from family and friends. Debbie had inherited Kevin's crib, so we bought a bedroom suite, a bed for Kevin and a dresser for the kids' room.

We both loved music, but he was a jazz fanatic. We had a good record player and could do whatever we wanted. It soon became the hangout place for all of his buddies.

To make some extra money, David started selling bags of weed and soon felt it was more lucrative than a straight job. He thought I should be working to bring in more money. But how the hell was I going to work and take care of the kids, not to mention all the responsibilities living away from my family for the first time in my life, with no car? I'd really made things hard for myself.

David had a friend, Lonnie Baker, who lived around the corner with his wife Liz and their twin sons Taronnie and Tazonnie. Lonnie and Liz were very much in love and making a go of their marriage. They didn't fight, but they were struggling to make ends meet. Liz was great. She was so cool and also very sexy, with great big tits and a delicious southern accent. We became super tight and our kids played together all the time.

Our husbands were making similar weed runs and us girls would get together sometimes and drink beer and smoke a reefer and have a good laugh. But they were all a little worried about me, because of how David was behind closed doors. I had acquired my mother's gift of hiding my fear by talking big and cursing. But I was still terrified, never knowing when he would go off on me. I hated when he got drunk. He could not hold his liquor and was very aggressive and violent.

Life was definitely not easy. Everything seemed very unbalanced. I was just seventeen and the unhappiness of being married made me feel trapped. Neither of us really had a clue. He had no plan to go back to school and while I had the brain to do this, I had neither time nor the encouragement. A job would bring money into the house and then I could at least pay my mother or whoever to look after my kids.

A friend of mine, Frances, worked downtown at a clothing factory, the Sally Shops of California. She told me that they were hiring in the office and as I could type over 100 words a minute and was good at filing, she got me an interview. I was underage, but they hired me anyway. I was so happy to be earning decent money. Frances also helped me get a part-time evening job at the Helms Bakeries factory where we sat at little machines separating the egg whites from the egg yolks for bakeries and flicking the bad eggs so they didn't get mixed up with the good ones. The job was pretty mundane and required no brains at all, but it could be fun at times. Until you caught a rotten batch of eggs. Then I'd have to go to the bathroom to throw up.

Soon I had established a daily routine: I got up early in the morning and dressed the kids. Frances picked us up, I dropped them at my mother's and collected them around 4.30, took them home and fed them, then put them to bed to be ready when Frances picked me up again for our night jobs from eight until midnight. Our daily routine brought us really close together and we had lots of laughs. The Sally Shop job was really cool and we would get discounts on clothes and sometimes lunch in nice places. Working in an office with other women was doing me a world of good and it was nice to be independent. By the time I got home every night, David and his gang would still be getting high and listening to jazz: Miles, Mingus, Monk,

Horace Silver and Sun Ra, plus the great vocalists like Billie Holiday and Sarah Vaughan, strong and revolutionary music reflecting the pain and the beauty of the black experience. We tuned into KGFJ, to local soul and R&B radio stations and to FM 105, which is still the local jazz station to this day, blowing classic jazz for our times and I immersed myself in our extensive record collection: from Marvin Gaye to Gladys Knight, Dionne Warwick to James Brown. These artists provided the soundtrack to my turbulent and abusive teen marriage.

I didn't have to spend too much time around David and his buddies when I got home. Usually I was too tired. Sometimes I would come home to find wall-to-wall black guys in my house eating my food. They would be wasted on Rainier ale and weed and playing silly and dangerous macho games like hot foot, where if somebody nodded off they stuck lit matches in the soles of their shoes. If I said anything it only started a fight and I was too exhausted to face any of his drama. He didn't care that I had to wake up early, but I was so tired I would just pass out despite the noise they made.

David still had an outrageous temper, though, and now I didn't have Papa Thea around to protect me. I learned how to tiptoe round his mood swings, realising what Mama had been going through all these years. All the ass-whippings from Daddy had prepared me for this maniac. I was seeing my family daily and he was smart enough not to hit me in the face.

Earning my keep and being the best young mother really helped my self-esteem. I was becoming bolder by the day. I even started getting the occasional lick in, determined to leave scratches where they'd be seen. The more I worked, the stronger I got. I was learning to stand up for myself. I was damned if I was going to just take shit off David the way my mother did with my father. My unexpected rebellions shocked him a couple of times and he was starting to realise that I had a mind of my own. He definitely began to pick his moments more carefully. Once I threw a pot of chilli beans at him that only just missed and the battle scars he sported became a little embarrassing for him.

He was always attracted to me sexually, though he'd keep me on ration, which pissed me off. Plus some of the brothers who witnessed his abuse liked me. Once, when David was away on one of his Mexican runs, Leonard, who organised the drugs, propositioned me. I turned him down, but I did let him kiss and feel on me a bit. It felt good to be hit on after enduring so much.

I was still only seventeen years old.

PART 2
A Fresh Start

'And don't get lost in de wilderness.'
– 'Go Down, Moses'

23
1967 (London)
'The First Lady of Immediate'

Tony had found me a flat in Bryanston Mews East, an elegant little cottage with a lovely roof terrace and Georgian antique furniture. Everything was dainty, delicate and feminine, a doll's house perfect for a petite little lady like me. I loved it! My babies and family were 6,000 miles away, but Mick's flat was nearby and I felt safe and secure.

Shortly after I signed to Immediate, however, the Stones split with Andrew. Allan Klein, a seemingly shrewd American businessman, took over. He had been Sam Cooke's manager, helping him start his own label. Mick, who had studied at the London College of Economics, was very impressed. Klein would end up owning the rights to the early Stones catalogue – and ripping off the Stones, the Beatles and Phil Spector.

I didn't let this worry me. Mick still felt that Immediate was a good place for me and besides, I had no one else to advise me. Andrew and Tony sorted out my living, clothing and pocket expenses. They had full control of production, publishing and my career. Advances had never even been mentioned. Was Mick even aware just how naive I was?

Gered Mankowitz had taken beautiful pictures of me for the label, looking more like a twelve-year-old than my actual nineteen years. In a brainstorming meeting with Andrew and I regarding what my stage name would be, he suggested 'P.P. Arnold': 'You were this little girl with this big bluesy, gospel voice,' he remembers, 'and I felt that it would be quite gimmicky. When people first hear your name they wouldn't know if you were a guy or a girl!' I had always just used my married name with Ike and Tina. A few male artists used initials – B. B. King, O. C. Smith – but it was unusual for a woman. In hindsight, I wish that I'd used my family name, that my parents had been credited, not the Arnolds. And 'P.P.' has always been embarrassing, for obvious reasons. I tried changing it in later years, but by then, P.P. Arnold was already established in the minds of the public, so I kept it.

Gered and I hit it off straight away. He was a curly-haired Jewish boy, a little overweight, confident and fun, very trendy and artistic, with a studio in Mason's Yard in the West End. He saw how shy I was and thanks to a genuine kindness and his expert use of light and shadow he captured the essence of my soul at that time. I see all my fear and pain wrapped in innocence and hope every time I look at the great shots he took.

Andrew at this time was already very successful, a Svengali, living a lavish, wealthy, outrageous lifestyle. He was incredibly good-looking, with ginger hair and was always immaculately turned out. He had an amazing Phantom V Rolls-Royce with dark-tinted windows and he rode around smoking joints rolled by his equally elegant, Edwardian-dressed chauffeur Eddie. That car was a party on wheels, with a fitted state-of-the art sound system and a bar full of booze. He never went anywhere without his little black bag full of amphetamines and barbiturates.

His father had been an American airman of Dutch descent. During the war, he was shot down over the English Channel, so Andrew never met him. His mother Celia was a nurse dogged by intrigue, with one lover mysteriously murdered in his Rolls-Royce. In the early '60s he worked for Mary Quant and did press for various rock 'n' roll acts and finally for Brian Epstein. He saw the young Stones at the Crawdaddy Club in Richmond and understood immediately they would be huge. He took over their management, proclaimed 'lock up your daughters' and signed them to Decca Records.

When Marianne's early singles charted, he and Tony had formed Immediate, creating the model for the many independent labels that followed. Tony didn't really fit the predominant modern Edwardian Dandy image. He was short and wore the kind of dark spectacles that brainy people wear. He had a Julius Caesar look about him. To be 'camp' in those days was very trendy and sexy. Andrew was the King of Camp, but Tony couldn't quite pull it off. He always talked in hushed tones as if he was in on some secret joke and I was very uncertain about him. I felt he was a bit sneaky, but I got on with him and his girlfriend Josie, who also worked at Immediate. The label had acts like Fleetwood Mac and the Small Faces and there was a big buzz going on. I arrived innocently into the middle of all this.

I was their first female signing and now things started happening real fast. My inspirations were soul singers like Mavis Staples and Mary Wells, Brenda Holloway and Patti LaBelle – and of course Tina Turner. I'd loved Aretha Franklin ever since I heard her sing 'Never Grow Old', recorded when she was just fourteen. She and Billy Preston, who I knew, had taken gospel standards and given them a modern, progressive feel. In 1960, the very young platinum-haired Etta James had recorded 'All I Could Do Was Cry' – I loved her sound, too.

It goes without saying that London was very cosmopolitan. There was racial separation, but this wasn't evident to me among the youth, especially in the music scene. Pop music seemed colourblind if anything: blues, R&B, rock, even elements of jazz. Everything definitely seemed more fresh, youthful and open. Back in the States, black stations didn't play white music and white stations didn't play black music. It was great to be somewhere where everything was everything, so to speak.

Immediate Records offices were located at 69 New Oxford Street, next door to Dick James Music and around the corner from many music shops, coffee shops and studios in Tottenham Court Road and Denmark Street. I loved going to the office. There was so much energy and excitement and I still couldn't believe that I was a part of what was happening there. The label was full of creative, progressive ideas. Everybody was excited about me as well. There was a definite family vibe, with so many great artists, songwriters and producers creating a kind of Tamla

Motown in-house situation. It was here I first met Steve Marriott and the Small Faces. Steve and I hit it off instantly; it was only natural that we would record and collaborate together at some point. As the first female signing, I became 'The First Lady of Immediate'.

The moment I signed, Andrew got me into the studio and I took to recording like a fish to water. The sessions were aimed at producing a full-length album and he had a concept in mind. I would listen to material he suggested and between us we would decide what to do. He never forced anything on me and I allowed him to guide me. His confidence in me gave me confidence in myself.

We started by experimenting with the Spector girly sound. We first tried a Spector/Goffin/King composition that Marianne had recorded: 'Is This What I Get for Loving You?' We put my vocal over the pre-recorded backing track, but it didn't feel right. The next was a Spector/Mann/Weill song called 'Born to Be Together', arranged by Arthur Greenslade. I loved it then and I still love it now.

The first release was an up-tempo British soul track, 'Everything's Gonna Be Alright', written by Andrew with David Skinner and Andrew Rose. There were so many great songwriters around. It was released in February 1967 and though it failed to chart, it would become a northern soul anthem in the '70s. The B-side was 'Life Is But Nothing', a real-cut-your-wrist sad blues track written by Andrew Rose, with a very beautiful, classical Greenslade arrangement.

After 'Everything's Gonna Be Alright' failed to chart, we really needed a hit, so Andrew brought in producer Mike Hurst, formerly of pop-folk vocal trio the Springfields (Dusty Springfield with her brother Tom). Mike was also producing the second album by one Steven Demetre Georgiou – who the world knew as Cat Stevens, but we all called him Steve. Steve lived above his father's Greek restaurant, which was right around the corner. *Matthew and Son*, his first album, had been massive and his song of first love gone wrong would become the jewel of my album. I related to it straight away; it was as if he had written it especially for me. 'The First Cut Is the Deepest' was basically my life story and it was perfect for me. Cat Stevens never released it as a single because he always said he considered my version to be the definitive one.

'The First Cut' was released on 6 May 1967 and stayed in the charts for ten weeks. It wasn't the huge hit it deserved to be, but it became a classic.

Mike says that Andrew's chauffeur brought me to a trial session, probably at Decca, 'and you arrived stoned', which was 'Andrew's control technique, getting his artists stoned and therefore pliable', but Mike insists that was never his way of doing things. He says I could barely sit on the stool and he made the chauffeur bring me back when I was clear-headed. But that was not *my* way of doing things. Eddie Reed, Andrew's chauffeur, wasn't someone who could be ordered around and I was certainly never too stoned to sing. I liked to hear every nuance when I interpreted a song, which helped me to improve my sound. I would always sing along with the orchestra so they got a feel for me. I do remember rehearsing with him being a nightmare. He was a nice guy, but horny as hell. He would actually chase me around the room and I was constantly fighting him off. But the recordings turned out beautifully. Mike's brilliant production gave me a big Spector sound of my own.

Around this time, I inherited the Blue Jays from Ronnie Jones, who had relocated to Italy. Being on the soul circuit with him had given me a good fan-base and being a former Ikette didn't hurt me either. The next big break was a UK package tour headlined by Roy Orbison and the Small Faces, beginning on 7 March 1967. Jeff Beck had pulled out after just two days and we replaced him.

I couldn't afford all the Blue Jays, so I only took the rhythm section, who called themselves Four of a Kind: ex-John Mayall guitarist Roger Dean, drummer Colin Davey, Chris Dennis on keyboards and Pat Donaldson on bass, who later played with Sandy Denny and others. As Colin remembers it, the set included 'Heat Wave', 'You Keep Me Hanging On', 'Dancing in the Streets' and 'The First Cut Is the Deepest'. After us came the Settlers and Sonny Childe's T.N.T., with the Small Faces closing the first half. Paul and Barry Ryan would open the second half, backed by the Rob Storme Group and then Roy closed with his band the Candymen.

The tour also gave me the chance to get closer to my label mates, the Small Faces. Little like me, adorable and full of beans, they were London-born East Enders with raw Cockney accents. Kenney Jones was shy and sweet, Ronnie Lane and Ian McLagan were lively and fun and Steve Marriott was clearly the leader. They were super-trendy, super-cool and super-cute – but

Steve was the cutest. He had the charisma and the confidence, the engine that powered their creativity.

We were all roughly the same age, a little younger and a little shorter than many of our peers. I was instantly comfortable with them. They were all very dapper, reminding me of my brothers wearing what we called the 'Ivy League' style back home and they were talented singers.

The Small Faces were happy liggers who loved to get high, hang out and make music. We loved being a part of Immediate. Its motto was 'Happy to be a part of the industry of human happiness' and it was a slogan that we all believed in – though sadly the label let us all down in the end.

As a child, Steve's grandmother had played Ray Charles records to him and he'd fallen in love with Ray's soulful, gospel blues sound. He was the most soulful English singer and musician I'd met to date. Steve put his heart into everything he played and sang; his feeling and expression was real. I loved singing with him and we had a great sound together. He was at the Italia Conti stage school until he was thrown out and had been the original Artful Dodger in the Lionel Bart stage show of *Oliver!*. He loved early Motown, Little Eva, Lorraine Ellison, Aretha Franklin, Otis Redding, Sam and Dave and Booker T. & the M.G.'s. Luckily for Steve, he worked in a music shop, because this wasn't easy music to hear on UK radio at the time, except via the pirate radio ships.

As it so happened, he had just moved into a flat on Devonshire Place, a hop, skip and a jump from my own Bryanston Mews flat. He invited me over and this was the beginning of a long-lasting friendship. He was such fun. Mischievous and cheeky, with an abundance of hyper-energy, we spent many great evenings smoking, laughing, jamming, singing together and listening to soul, R&B, blues and rock – as well as a little extra-curricular sexual activity.

This wasn't just a physical connection, although we were definitely attracted to one another. Steve's vocal style was raw and emotional and it blended perfectly with my natural gospel style. From the outset we had a deep soul connection and spoke about recording together. We instantly became soul brother and sister.

Steve was the only Englishman that invited me home to meet his family back then. That's how beautiful and real he was. He didn't introduce me as his girlfriend – though we were already fooling around a little – but as his mate. His mom and sister were both called Kay and he had told them all about me and how tight we'd become. That meant so much to me. His family have always been kind to me. He was and still is my dear friend and soul music soulmate. I miss him and his great talent dearly. We did a lot of growing up together.

One evening Steve asked me to come down to Olympic Studios. It was an electrically charged, stoned, cosmic evening. The band's new track was 'Tin Soldier'. Steve recorded his great vocal and then he and I laid down those historic backing vocals. People sometimes ask me if it's about me, but, as far as I know, he wrote it for his girlfriend Jenny Rylance.

Steve and Ronnie did write 'Afterglow' for me, but then decided to keep it for themselves. They wrote another song for me, which would become my third top-forty hit. Alan O'Duffy was the engineer on this session: 'We cut a track that Steve had written for Patricia, "If You Think You're Groovy", and she blew these guys from east London right over. It was very much like working with your hero, as Patricia effortlessly musically cruised through the track. I don't think she realises to this day how much Steve, Kenny, Mac and Ronnie seriously rated her.'

Andrew didn't feel Four of a Kind were right for me, so I needed to pull a new band together fast. Mickey O., my driver at the time, suggested Keith Emerson as a possible musical director. Keith had just quit the V.I.P.'s and it was evident when we met that he was a great player. He told me straight away that he no longer wanted to be just a side man, so I agreed he'd have his own spot opening up my show and he agreed to put a kicking band together for me. They were bassist Lee Jackson and drummer Ian Hague (later replaced by Brian 'Blinky' Davidson). He also asked guitarist Luther Grosvenor of the V.I.P.'s, but Grosvenor was turning them into Spooky Tooth, so instead he went with an up-and-coming seventeen-year-old guitarist called Dave O'List.

As Keith remembers it: 'I was white, but apart from Dave Brubeck the only records I listened to were by black artists. I don't recall any racist bullshit back then. Most musicians regarded black artists as the real deal and I had no reason to doubt it when I showed up at Pat's mews house in London. She was a cheeky impish girl and still is. She had a Fender Rhodes piano in the front room. I'd never played one before. She played me "First Cut Is the Deepest" and I wondered how on earth I could fit into all of this. Pat just said, "Get a band together. Here's a load of records, learn these." They were mostly Wilson Pickett, Bobby "Blue" Bland. She said my band could play whatever we wanted until she came out thirty-five minutes later!'

Keith says I asked them what the band were called and no one had any idea. Steve had introduced me to the Lord Buckley album *The Nazz*, Buckley's name for Jesus (as in 'of Nazareth'). I liked the sound of Nazz and I loved the British saying 'nice one'. My accent made it easy to combine the two. Keith remembers that he groaned: 'P.P. Arnold and her Nice – what? But Pat loved it. Sometimes clubs got the name wrong and listed us "P.P. Arnold and the Mice"!'

We were a great combination. At first the music press only said things like 'ably backed by her four-piece', which peeved them a bit, but as their reputation grew, this would soon change. It was obvious they were a musical force in their own right, building up a progressive sound that would be recognised as the birth of prog rock. We toured the country alongside the Small Faces, Jimi Hendrix, the Who, the Kinks, David Bowie, Cream, Blind Faith, Pink Floyd, Jeff Beck, John Mayall, Peter Green's Fleetwood Mac and many others.

Andrew was also taking notice. He set up a gig for them without me at the 1967 Windsor Jazz and Blues Festival, to see how they would go down. I told them I didn't object to them doing their own set. I'm told that Andrew supplied them with some explosive fireworks, to be set off as Fleetwood Mac played in the main tent, so all the journalists and punters would come to check out the noise and excitement. Roadie Baz had put joke-shop smoke powder into the Leslie organ which billowed out as

Keith broke into 'Billy's Bag'. This proved they could do it on their own.

It probably didn't hurt that my friend Sandy Sarjeant, a funky and creative dancer on *Ready, Steady, Go!* who was dating Ian McLagan, was on stage with them scantily dressed in a leotard, with flowers strategically covering her private parts. She also danced the night I was performing with them on the festival main stage and we released doves of peace. Then they played all our remaining dates before I had to return to the States, as my work permit was set to run out.

The First Lady of Immediate was nearly finished. Mick was meant to produce half of it and despite the split with Andrew and being busy with touring and with Marianne, he had not abandoned me. He scheduled time for us to cut some tracks and persuaded me to write some songs. I had never written a song in my life and he gave me no advice, but I prayed and the spirit gave me words and melodies out of nowhere. Before I knew it I had three songs about me being fed up with being let down by guys: 'Treat Me Like a Lady', 'Though It Hurts Me Badly' and 'Am I Still Dreaming?' Most of my lovers had been musicians and you know what musicians are like.

Mick and Marianne were now in Wales with the Beatles and the Maharishi – but true to his word he returned for these sessions to produce the final tracks. I sang my songs to him and he used everything I came up with. I had surprised myself with my ability to write and collaborate with him. The tracks he produced were raw and original and I loved working with him. I had no idea of my own potential but, like Andrew, he had shown real belief in me. It was as far from life on the road with Ike Turner as one soul could travel.

The sessions were at Olympic Studios. Andrew suggested using the Nice, plus indestructible session guitarist Caleb Quaye (who later played with Elton John) and Madeline Bell and Dusty Springfield. I sang my ideas to the musicians and it all came together. Keith Richards and Charlie Watts played on 'Am I Still Dreaming?' and the brilliant Nicky Hopkins on 'Though It Hurts Me Badly', with Mick playing guitar.

My second single was 'The Time Has Come'. Written by Paul Korda and released on 5 August, it had good reviews, but Immediate was having distribution problems and it barely scraped into the UK top fifty at number forty-seven. I did lots of promotion in Europe and it was a big hit in Italy, where Patty Pravo covered it as 'Se perdo Te'.

My third single came out in January 1968. It was 'If You Think You're Groovy', written for me by Steve Marriott and Ronnie Lane, with the Small Faces performing the backing. It too was highly regarded, but it stalled at number forty-one.

Three months later came the album, including all my singles to date, plus 'Something Beautiful Happened' (also by Paul), 'Born to Be Together', a wonderful version of Billy Nicholls' 'Would You Believe' (Billy's version was released much later), 'Life Is But Nothing', 'Everything's Gonna Be Alright' – and the three songs Mick produced and encouraged me to write.

I look back on all this with pride. We were all so young, gifted and full of life! I was touring the length and breadth of the country with the Nice. I was performing all over Europe. I had been adopted and accepted by the British public alongside singers like Marianne Faithfull, Billie Davis, Cilla Black, Lulu, Sandie Shaw and Dusty Springfield. The media loved my petite, powerful projection. At *Disc and Music Echo*, Penny Valentine had christened me 'The Chocolate Button'. I hated it, but any publicity was better than none at all. I was finally being recognised as an artist in my own right.

24

1967 (London)

Sex, Drugs and Rock 'n' Roll

I loved my house in Bryanston Mews and I was seeing Mick often. He had so many artistic friends – musicians, artists, photographers, designers, aristocrats. I felt very out of place and tended just to observe. I wasn't one of his intellectual black American lovers. They came later. I wasn't his first black lover either. He knew I was a real soul sister from Watts, LA and he also knew I was very innocent. I think he was intrigued by me. He was helping me learn to live in an integrated society. I was becoming a revolutionary icon without ever even thinking of myself as being revolutionary.

Still, it could be disconcerting. Once I went out to dinner with Mick and maybe ten others to a popular Knightsbridge fish restaurant. It was an elegantly laid table setting, but what were all these forks and knives? Three forks and two knives (one shorter and flatter than the other), plus another smaller fork and a spoon at the top. This was nothing like a soul food stop. Refinement came as second nature to everyone else and I remember feeling very unsophisticated. I was so embarrassed, particularly as Marianne was seated at the table with us.

She and I were as different as night and day. Her father was a British military officer and a psychology professor. Her mother was a ballerina and a baroness. She had Jewish roots but was also connected to the Habsburg dynasty. Her great-great-uncle had been Leopold von Sacher-Masoch, whose novel *Venus in Furs* gave us the word masochism. Her parents divorced when she was six years old and she lived with her mother in very reduced circumstances. As a child, Marianne had suffered bouts of tuberculosis. She was quite arrogant about her background and very proud to call herself half English and half Austro-Hungarian.

Given that I was a descendent of slaves, it's really no wonder I found her so different. My parents and my grandparents had been sharecroppers. In fact, Marianne and I had a lot in common. I had a strict Baptist upbringing and she was a convent-school girl. We were both teenage mothers and teenage brides. Both she and I had been discovered and launched by Andrew Loog Oldham and we were both Mick Jagger's lovers.

Like me, Marianne also had serious insecurities. We were both sexually active from a young age and very passionate. But where she became rebellious and outrageous, I was still shaking off the fear of God. And I had to think about my reputation. Mick often talked about how hung up black girls were. Maybe he was right, but I was finding this whole sex and drug scene a little scary. I was willing to experiment and to initiate some sexual adventures of my own and I liked smoking hashish, but I had no interest in any of the other drugs. This was considered very square. Mick was okay with it, because while he dabbled, he was no out-of-control user.

Marianne had her own flat with her son Nicolas. I did my best to visit Mick when she wasn't around, but one night she arrived with an American girlfriend and joined us in bed. Before I knew it I was in the middle of an orgy, with these two soft white blonde girls all over me. This was my first lesbian experience. It all happened so fast that I could only go with the flow. Mick was in heaven but Marianne was more interested in me. I had always been a good kisser and so was she. I tried to let myself go but I was also uncomfortable. Mick sensed this and sent the others to another bedroom. I spent the rest of the night with him, then went home to ponder what had happened.

He was unlike any man I had ever dealt with. He was the first guy who seemed to really care about helping me and although he wanted me to be more adventurous, he didn't force it. He felt Marianne could be a good friend to me. She was very beautiful of course and for a while we were caught up together in this heated ménage à trois, but ultimately it was Mick that I was infatuated with, not her.

In some ways, she and I did become closer. I loved shopping with her. She taught me to shop beyond my means, at Harrods and the boutiques in Beauchamp Place and helped me put together the *First Lady* image. Deliss was a very elegant French boutique, where the amazing shoes I wore back then were made, as well as the beautiful iridescent long orange dress I was photographed in.

Somehow, however, I'd become the 'other woman' and it was a feeling I hated. I felt out of my depth and didn't yet understand the power I had as a black chick from the States. Each of us pretended not to be intimidated by the other, but girls will be girls and I think the envy between us was beginning to simmer. The relationship started to feel uncomfortable; there was a plantation feel about it, like I was a plaything, only there to entertain the two of them.

I also had my own thing happening. One night at the Bag O'Nails, my guitarist Roger Dean told me that an American guitarist was in the club asking if he could jam with the band. I had seen this brother earlier, surrounded by girls and lapping up the attention. He was really out there, with wild hair and a very funky, hippy look about him. I told Roger to tell him he could jam at the end of the second set. Well, this brother came on and just ripped it up. He blew everyone away. I hadn't seen his like before and I haven't seen it since. He was merging blues and rock 'n' roll with a cosmic psychedelic flair that seemed to come from another world. This was the first time I met Jimi Hendrix.

He was so magnetic and he had a crowd of girls who were drawn into his orbit. Earlier, I was gossiping with a girlfriend and joking around that this new guy thought a lot of himself. I had a nerve! As if I wasn't also lapping up all the attention I was getting! Of course, Jimi and I hit it off right away. I was homesick by now, so it felt so good to meet someone from back home. I'd got into the habit of pretending I was alright, because

I didn't want people thinking I was ungrateful, but when I was feeling blue, I had no one who shared my experience. He was shy too, but he knew exactly what he wanted, who he was and where he was going musically. He encouraged me to open up and go with the flow. He too was going through transition, this amazing black brother from a similar background on a similar journey. His timing couldn't have been better. He was a gift from the universe. A godsend. Plus he lived in Montague Square, right around the corner from my flat in Bryanston Mews East. Surely this was no coincidence. I guess it was only natural that we became lovers.

At the time, the top British guitarists were Eric Clapton, Jeff Beck and Jimmy Page – but Jimi's lifelong immersion in the great bluesmen put him light years ahead. He *was* the blues. According to him he'd even worked briefly with Ike and Tina at some point and we cracked each other up relaying stories. Tina and Jimmy Thomas insist he was never in the Revue, but his stories all rang true to me! In New York he had worked with the Isley Brothers and for a short time with King Curtis. A girlfriend of Keith Richards, Linda Keith, had recommended him to Andrew Oldham and to producer Seymour Stein. But they didn't connect with Jimi's music and both passed on him. So, in early 1966, Linda tried again. She introduced him to former Animals bassist Chas Chandler. Chas brought Jimi to London and changed the spelling of his name. In London he formed the Experience with Noel Redding and Mitch Miller and the rest is history.

Jimi's flat soon became the party epicentre of Swinging London and he would escape to my house when he needed peace, tranquillity and some good old down-home loving. I was always excited when I answered my intercom and it was him. His presence totally filled my little home and I would laugh at how big his feet looked coming up the stairs. We talked about our new lives on the British music scene and compared it to segregated America. We shared a lot of laughs and a lot of sex. Now Mick wasn't the only one with two lovers, but I kept all this on the down-low and only people close to us knew.

I was enjoying my new-found freedom. Steve Marriott and I were also becoming close and he lived nearby as well, on Devonshire Place. Everything seemed to be happening in close proximity.

I was working hard and playing hard. Everyone assumed that all black American girls were tough and super-hip, so despite my insecurity I pretended to be Miss Super Cool. I was the exciting new black girl on the block, with the pick of lovers all around me, so why was I so lonely? Mick and Jimi knew how shy I really was – and so did Eddie Reed andrew's chauffeur and right-hand man. Eddie drove me everywhere and knew all my secrets. He was gorgeous and funny and really sweet.

I knew all this would change once I brought my kids back with me to England. They were the reason that I couldn't let myself get too wild. But I had changed a lot. Before I had smoked grass and drank occasionally; now I had my own rolling machine and my tipples were rum and Coca-Cola and Rémy Martin brandy. A drink and a smoke relaxed me and I was more fun to be around. I was having a fling at being a single, successful pop star.

Perhaps some things were getting out of control, but I seemed to be winning, so I didn't complain.

To promote 'The First Cut Is the Deepest', I'd gone out via tugboat to the pirate radio station Radio Caroline, which was located on a ship offshore, to do a live broadcast with DJ Tony Blackburn. Coming from Watts, this was my first time on a boat and the ride out was rough and I was seasick. I was taken to Tony's cabin to rest before my interview and I wound up vomiting all over his bed. Tony was very nice about it and after drinking lots of water and coffee, I did my interview. Pirate radio was made illegal shortly after that, which was a shame, because they were the best stations in England for pop, rock and soul music.

Around the same time, I was booked to play several Immediate package tours with the Small Faces, including television in Germany, Holland, Switzerland, France and Spain. Steve was a nervous flyer and would only ever board a flight if he'd gotten wasted beforehand. I wasn't that keen on it myself but it had to be done, so I just visualised a safe journey and a safe landing. If we ever hit any turbulence, I would hold Steve's hand in mine and try to comfort him.

Beat Club was a German music programme filmed in Bremen. My first appearance was on 24 June 1967, promoting 'The First Cut Is the Deepest' alongside the Small Faces, the Kinks, Twice As Much, Lulu and Cat Stevens. The presenter was another Caroline pirate DJ graduate, Dave Lee Travis. My friend Sandy Sarjeant was a regular dancer on *Beat Club* and sometimes when we flew to Germany she would accompany us. It was nice to travel with another woman. Instead of always being so accommodating, I should have demanded it.

With the Second World War still a relatively fresh memory, many Brits made no secret of hating the Germans. Music had been helping heal the wounds ever since the Beatles had played in Hamburg, but some of the musicians did everything they could to make things hard for the film crew and the hotel staff, by insulting as many Germans as possible. Not that this put any of the groupies off. If anything, they seemed to enjoy the abuse hurled at them.

It was all quite riotous at times, although I wasn't the only one who didn't participate in the madness. David Bowie, who at this point was still finding his feet and was several steps away from the stardom he'd one day achieve, seemed to find the whole scene a little too much. On one occasion back in our hotel after a TV show in Amsterdam, at a reception with lots of food and drink, the other guys were being their usual boisterous selves. I was trying to mind my own business amid the anarchy when, out of nowhere, David grabbed me. He held on to me real tight, like a frightened child.

He wasn't attacking me in a sexual kind of way; it was more like an emotional outburst, like he was reaching out to me, but I was really shaken. Billy Nicholls walked me back to my room to make sure I was okay. This was before David became a big star. He always travelled with his manager and never seemed happy. Even then, he seemed as if he was on another plane to all the other pop stars. I later wondered if he shared my feelings of isolation and my own fear of everything that was going

Left: Patricia Ann Cole: six months old and ready to face the world.

Right: My mama, Mary.

My daddy, Theora, and Uncle Book.

Performing as part of the Ike & Tina Turner Revue in *The Big T.N.T. Show*, 1966. I am the middle Ikette, behind Tina.

Singing my heart out on *Top of the Pops* in 1967.

On stage with the legendary Small Faces on France's *Bouton Rouge* TV show, 1968.

On my wedding day, 5 October 1968, smiling alongside my manager and new husband, Jim Morris.

Such a happy bride receiving a kiss from both my groom, Jim, and the best man – my dear friend Barry Gibb of the Bee Gees.

Looking very sophisticated in a studio portrait from 1969.

Above: Circa 1970, starring in Jack Good's *Catch My Soul*, a musical version of Shakespeare's *Othello* set in the American Wild West. I was Bianca and P. J. Proby (centre) was Cassio.

Left: My former partner and collaborator Calvin 'Fuzzy' Samuel, pictured here in 1972.

My beautiful
daughter, Debbie.

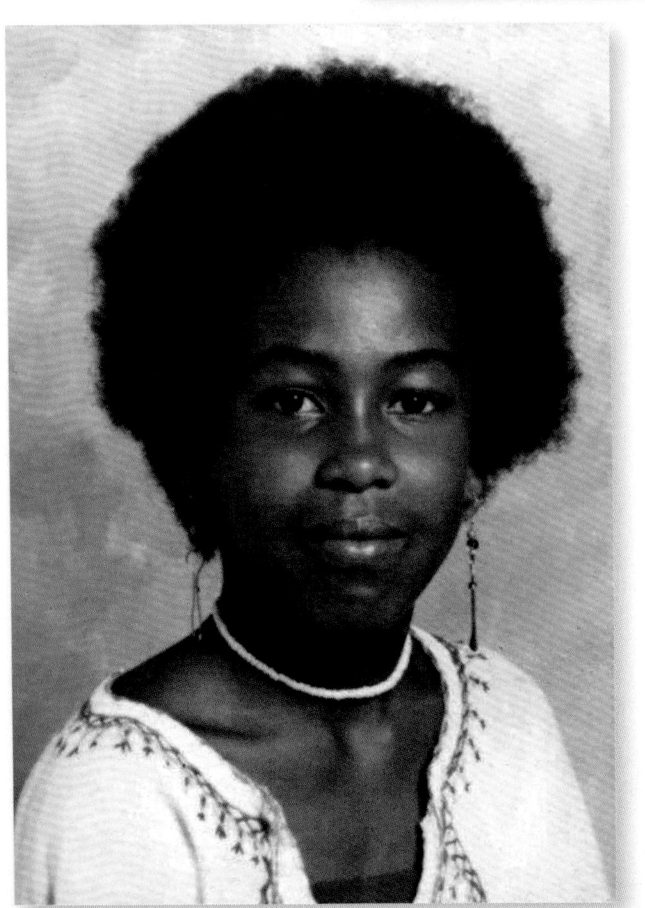

Debbie aged thirteen.

Left: Kevin and Debbie as children, looking happy in their school uniforms at Alderney Street.

Right: With my sister and fellow soul survivor, Elaine.

Left: The family elders. From left to right: Grandma Stel; Daddy; Mama; Big Mama Mattie Mae.

Right: A beautiful day with my family. Theo, Larry, Mama and Daddy are on the left of the shot; Grandma Stel and Kenny are on the right.

Posing with Andrew Lloyd Webber, Richard Stilgoe and Frances Ruffelle at a dress rehearsal for the musical *Starlight Express*, 1984.

Celebrating *Starlight Express* with my wonderful sons, Kevin and Kodzo. I am so thankful for them both.

Standing outside my former home, Hoplands, in the Cotswolds

on. Everything felt so strange to me. I was from such a different culture and I hadn't learned how to fake it. It was hard enough just hiding my low self-esteem and I can see now just how damaged I was.

I honestly think David was the only one in that room who could see all this and felt compassion for me. The next day at the airport we avoided each other. We were both embarrassed. Not knowing how to communicate my feelings, I just left it. I don't think he knew what to say either.

By contrast, the Small Faces were a randy lot, prone to humping anything that moved. This really put me off, as did a trip to Dr Robert of Harley Street. He discreetly treated everyone's Love Generation STDs with doses of penicillin and had a side hustle in amphetamines, but I was starting to be a bit more careful about free love. I still hung out with Steve, but the sparks were no longer flying in the bedroom.

In September and December, I was on *Beat Club* to promote 'The Time Has Come' and then 'If You Think You're Groovy' and 'Tin Soldier' with the Small Faces.

Back at the hotel after one of these *Beat Club* performances, Andrew had arrived just back from LA hanging out with the Beach Boys and the Mamas and the Papas. We were all excited to see him and decamped to his room. Entertaining as ever, he was in his element and we hung on his every word. He then broke out his little black bag and passed out what I thought were uppers. I wasn't really into barbiturates, but I would take a benny (Benzedrine) if I felt tired and we'd been travelling since the early morning and then recording all day.

We went to our rooms to get dressed to go out to dinner and in the elevator with Sandy, I pushed the button to go to our floor and the next thing I knew we were turning flips and giggling our heads off. We kept pushing the buttons and the lift kept going up and down. Nobody else could use the lift and the buzzer was ringing. I don't know how many times we went up and down but, finally, miraculously it stopped on our floor and we got out. Sandy was laughing her head off. Between her fits of the giggles, she explained what had happened to us: we had taken LSD. They had all taken acid before and were really into it. I was totally freaked out and got really scared. I told her I wasn't leaving the hotel while tripping. Back in my room, the hallucinations began for real. I realised I didn't want to be alone and ran to Sandy's room to deal with the vibes. She was with me but really I was on my own, as everybody as everyone is when dealing with their own trip.

Later, on our return to Andrew's room, still in our lysergic haze, the weirdness continued. He opened the door in a long white robe, looking like Jesus Christ and in a malevolent voice yelled at us, 'GO AWAY!' We were all stunned and terrified.

Downstairs, our guides for the evening had flagged taxis down for us. What a sight we were, in our crêpes, satins and velvets, with bells, beads and flowers in our hair! We were tripping out of our minds, flying the hippy flag high in the middle of conservative Bremen. Off we were driven, not knowing where we were going to eat. The taxis seemed to be going round and round in circles. We'd stop occasionally, but no one would let us come in. Partly, I think, because of how we were dressed, but mainly because we were acting so crazy. The guys were cursing and slagging off everyone who was refusing us entry. Each time we were turned away we had to find more taxis. Finally, a restaurant in a more bohemian part of town let us in. It seemed to take us hours to order food. Coca-Colas kept appearing and disappearing on the table. It was total madness.

The next thing I knew we were in a discotheque. The music was incredible. You could feel the music in every part of your body. In your fingertips, in the hairs on the back of your neck. I danced and danced until sunrise. I remember finding myself on a patio and feeling so beautiful and peaceful as I came down off the acid. At some point that night, I had let go of all my fears. In all the chaos, I had managed to find myself in a way that I had never experienced before. It was truly a beautiful thing. But I also remembered how Andrew had behaved. Maybe it was a moment of LSD-assisted clarity, but I realised that Andrew was going through a tough time. I had picked up an incredibly negative vibe from him when he screamed at us to go away. I don't think that Andrew realised that I had never taken acid before or that I didn't know that it was acid. I thought it was an upper. I took it willingly and I enjoyed the trip, but it made me suspicious. I had genuinely loved Andrew. I put him on such a high pedestal. He had changed my life and I'll be forever grateful for his belief in me and the way in which he was able to mould me into the artist that I never dreamed I could be. Our relationship had been built on trust. I never really knew how to communicate with him intellectually. My shy inhibitions had perhaps made it difficult for him to communicate with *me*. Either way, I knew I was out of my depth. Ultimately, I felt he was a bit disappointed in me.

Maybe it was a foreshadowing of what was to come as, within weeks, Immediate went bankrupt and Andrew and Tony went to ground.

Looking back at my time at Immediate, I can say it was a pleasure to be part of it all. I was 'happy to be a part of the industry of human happiness', but I'd worked my ass off for very little in terms of money and the experience left me feeling a little sore. We'd placed all our trust in Andrew, thinking he was so smart and above the fray. But, like the rest of us, he was young and just as vulnerable to the drug culture of the time. We were all getting ripped off in the '60s, including Andrew.

25

1967 (LA)

Back in the US

The time finally came for me to return to LA.

Right before I left Europe, I was booked on the very first colour TV show in Berlin alongside the Jimi Hendrix Experience and many other artists. We were still a thing and would meet up whenever we could find a gap in our schedules. I was looking forward to seeing him. The night before the show, we were pretty loved up and excited about the couple of days we would have together. The show was filmed in a large indoor stadium and it was packed solid. German groupies were all over Jimi and when I went to his room afterward I found him very occupied with one of them. I was furious! Why, I don't know – I had never been jealous before. I stormed out and ran straight into the arms of Noel Redding. Revenge never leaves a good taste and Jimi was not amused. He spent the rest of the night pleasing as many German girls as he could. Sadly marred by these rock 'n' roll events, that was the last time I would see Jimi.

With an early morning flight to LA, I had no chance to say goodbye. The twelve-hour flight was both exciting and exhausting but I was angry with myself. I regretted my stoned evening with Noel and leaving on bad terms with Jimi. But I wasn't going to let this spoil seeing my babies and all my family and friends.

I'd been away for nearly a year. I was P.P. Arnold now, a solo recording artist with a hit single and my first solo album nearly completed. I was an independent young woman exploring my sexuality and newfound freedom. I had crossed racial barriers I'd never dreamed I'd cross. What everyone would think of my new identity, I wondered?

As I made my way to the baggage area, I caught a glimpse of my kids. They ran to my open arms crying, 'Mommy! Mommy! Mommy!' Mama, Elaine and Theo were all there to meet me and we all hugged one another and cried tears of joy. It was beautiful and overwhelming.

In the car back to 117th Street, Radio KGFJ was playing all the new sounds that hadn't made it to England yet. This wasn't the BBC fusion I'd got used to, of R&B, rock, blues and soul. I was back in the US, where music was segregated into black and white.

At the family home the entire neighbourhood was waiting. I had bought a lot of duty-free liquor, so the party was on. Everybody was intrigued by the slight accent I'd picked up and all the British expressions I now used unconsciously. Daddy was checking me out for hidden signs of what I'd been up to in Europe. Despite everything, it was so good to see him.

Everyone loved my London look and they were all into the British rock 'n' roll scene now. I was shocked to realise everybody was dropping acid and tripping out, while lots of my girlfriends had fallen into drugs and prostitution. They all thought I was a wild, psychedelic rock chick now, but really, many of my friends were breaking on through with far more committed zeal than even I had.

While I smoked hashish and took the occasional upper or downer when I needed it, I was not into acid or hard drugs. I loved being a part of Swinging London, but I hadn't lost sight of my purpose. Being a pop star was hard work: recording, touring, endless cycles of promotional interviews and television.

But I had to keep myself in check. All the drugs and groupies and the constant fast-lane party life had been a little scary for me. Back in the UK, Marianne was being dragged through the press. All her noble ancestry hadn't helped to save her. What chance would I have had as a black American woman? I would have been dropped like a hot potato if I'd let myself get that out of control.

The English music scene was moving fast and all the drugs weren't helping, that's for sure. But the last months had been an opportunity for me to have fun as a teenager for the first time – albeit a teenager with many responsibilities.

I was grilled all night about my adventures. When they realised he was my close friend, they asked me all about Jimi. I turned them on to the Nice and the Small Faces and they wanted to know if I knew Twiggy. Elaine and my girlfriends loved my wardrobe and like a fool I gave it all away. It was my way of sharing my new experience and lifestyle.

Tony Calder called me from LA to help finalise my divorce. I invited him to celebrate with my family and have some of Daddy's famous Texas BBQ and Mama's mouth-watering potato salad. Few white men ventured into that neighbourhood alone back then, but here was Tony – arriving in a limo of all things! – bravely joining the party. With his English accent and his role in my success, he won everybody over, even Daddy.

My parents eagerly asked him about my financial security.

Immediate was doing well and a larger flat had been found for me in London, with a nanny to help with the children and chores. As with Ike and Tina, I now see that my trust and optimism were entirely rooted in hope, not definites. I should have asked for all these verbal assurances to be backed up, but I didn't and that's on me. I hadn't told my parents everything, either. They weren't worldly and they didn't understand this new culture, but they did know all about being ripped off. I wish they had warned me against some of the dangers. I just honestly – naively – believed that I could make things work.

Tony took me to a Hollywood lawyer and I filed for divorce on grounds of domestic violence and abuse. I might still be using his name, but David wasn't going to benefit from my success. He didn't contest. He was happy for me to pay for everything and like an idiot I released him from child support. So, in the end he got away with never taking any real responsibility.

It was lovely to be home, but I couldn't see a future for myself here. I wanted my kids with me and I didn't stop to think how much I was uprooting them. Mama had grown especially close to them and was not happy that they'd be so far away. My heart broke for her a little. Without everything she'd done to help me, none of this would have been possible.

Kevin and Debbie were excited about flying and about London, but I'd be 6,000 miles away without family close by. I hadn't thought about the cultural adjustments or my clashing responsibilities. I just picked up their passports and packed their things. The truth was, I was just as much a child as they were. All the while, the world around us was getting much fiercer.

I only knew a little about the Black Panthers – the Black Panther Party for Self-Defence, to use their full name – founded in October 1966 in Oakland, California by Huey Newton and Bobby Seale to protect African American neighbourhoods from police brutality. Newton and Seale were from Louisiana and Dallas respectively and they too were part of the great African American Migration out of the south to the West Coast, their forebears slaves and sharecroppers. The Black Panther Party had formed to agitate for the basic right to armed self-defence for African Americans in the United States, arguing that violence and black nationalism were necessary and justified when fighting for freedom: 'by any means necessary,' as Malcolm X said.

Martin Luther King, who preached non-violence and wanted people to join together for integration, was quick to condemn America's involvement in the Vietnam War. Back in 1963, at the time of King's 'I Have a Dream' speech, the key groups organising the sit-ins and freedom rides of the early civil rights movement were all non-violent, but after the Watts riots in 1965, divisions had opened up. Malcolm X still stressed self-determination and self-defence, but he also expressed a new willingness to work with civil rights leaders. In 1965, he was assassinated.

Against this backdrop of escalating tension and unease, a division opened up between the older and younger generations. There was frustration everywhere – and the drugs scene and even the mini-skirts weren't helping. I had gone to England as a young black American woman, loyal to the civil rights movement changing my country. Now I was a part of the carefree rock 'n' roll revolution, a full-on youth explosion, its movers and shakers all so young and idealistic. I was finding out what it meant to a free-spirited teenager after all. But at what cost?

26

1967 (London)

With Kevin and Debbie

My new flat – *our* new flat – was in a high-rise apartment building in Clifton Road, Maida Vale, near Little Venice and the canal. It was a bit dark and not ideal for Kevin and Debbie with no outside area for them to play in, but I was determined to make it work. The weather was cold and rainy most of the time and they were accustomed to playing outside with the neighbourhood children. Our nanny Elena was from Czechoslovakia and didn't speak English well, but I bought them lots of toys and when the weather permitted we took them to Regents Park.

Mick came to meet Kevin and Debbie. He would visit from time to time, but we couldn't hang out like we used to. The kids were adjusting and, if I wasn't working, I wanted to spend every minute I could with them.

My new driver was Kenny Pickett, one-time singer and songwriter for the Creation. He'd split from the band following a dispute and now worked for Andrew. While I was away, Andrew had quietly stolen the Nice away from me and signed them to Immediate. I had always known they would go their own way. They would be missed, but I was happy for them.

I was recording new tracks and Kenny was driving me to and from the studio in a nice Jaguar. Through him I met the young British blues and soul singer Rod Stewart, who was not yet established as a solo artist. He'd worked with Steampacket and Long John Baldry and was co-lead vocalist with Beryl Marsden in Shotgun Express, with Mick Fleetwood and Peter Bardens. His Sam Cooke imitation was spot on and I loved his voice. His one single, Mike d'Abo's 'Little Mis Understood', had been a flop, but Mick thought it might work to put Rod and I together to record an Otis Redding/Carla Thomas-type duet.

Mick was now very tied up with Marianne, whose vibe towards me was very changeable. I was still infatuated with Mick, but I recognised that she was his main consort. We'd enjoyed threesomes from time to time, but I was never into her on a purely sexual level. Sometimes she could be cruel and I think she knew I was only doing it to satisfy Mick.

Jimi, meanwhile, was back in the States promoting *Are You Experienced*. He had taken off big time over there. Steve was with Jenny, who worked at the fashionable boutique Quorum selling op art textiles. He and I were still close. We fancied each other but sexually we weren't really suited. Rod had lived for a few years with Jenny before she and Steve got together. Now Rod started spending more time with me. It was such an incestuous scene.

Rod and I would hang out with the Small Faces from time to time. One evening, high and happy, we decided to pay Mick a surprise visit and maybe persuade him to jam with us, so we trooped over without calling ahead. When he opened the door and saw us all in the hall, he freaked out, because he'd just returned from tripping on Primrose Hill with Marianne. He later said that he'd never realised how short we all were, except for Rod towering hilariously over us.

Mick and Marianne had moved to Cheyne Walk, but they were also looking for a country home and they invited me and the kids for a day out somewhere near Hampshire, to view a house with them. We set out in two limos, one for Mick and Marianne and her son Nicholas, the other for us and Michael Cooper, their friend the photographer, probably best known for the cover of *Sgt Pepper's Lonely Hearts Club Band* and the 3D photo on *Their Satanic Majesty Request* cover. Michael had been present when Mick, Keith and Robert Fraser the art dealer were all busted on drugs charges at Keith's 'Redlands' home. He was very sweet with me and seemed just as shy as I was with Mick and Marianne's aristocratic circle.

Still, it was a perfect sunny day for a drive to the country. Stargroves Manor was an enormous Victorian house with its own grounds and surrounded by acres and acres of land. We were all eager to explore – except Debbie, who didn't like its vibe. I had to lag behind and comfort her and for a moment I was angry that she was keeping me from enjoying the afternoon with my friends. But they were just strangers to her and she was only a baby. She didn't give a damn about Stargroves; she just wanted to be with me. This was the first time Debbie and I had been alone since I brought her to England and she just wanted to hold my hand and walk with me, so that's what we did.

As I walked through the grounds with her, I reflected just how far from our culture we were. How the hell was I here, by this historical mansion? History means different things to different people. In the seventeenth century, just as my ancestors were being sold into slavery, here on the other side of the world, the folks who lived in houses like this had made that world. A world that said it was okay to buy and sell a person, that one man was worth more than another. Was it just my feelings for Mick that had brought me here? Suddenly it felt so alien and I understood Debbie's discomfort at our surroundings. I felt ashamed and I was pleased when it was time to return to London.

On the way back, we stopped at a quaint little pub off the motorway and sat in the garden for high tea: smoked salmon sandwiches, scones with preserves and clotted cream and of course tea. Marianne was in one of her 'Lady of the Manor versus the Ghetto Mistress' moods and began bitchily comparing my Watts roots with hers as daughter of a baroness. I was in no mood to put up with this and simply ignored her. I didn't want to get into an argument in front of the children. I was hungry and refused to let her spoil the afternoon.

Back at Cheyne Walk, I was surprised when Mick rushed Marianne into the house to a waiting doctor, who gave her an injection. This may have explained her behaviour. She needed her drugs and was having withdrawals.

I'd already noticed a growing, scary vibe to the London scene, which could get dark and quite heavy. Anita Pallenberg, who had been Brian's girlfriend, was now with Keith. I found them very weird and intimidating together. He was always nice to me but now that he was with Anita I couldn't connect with either of them.

I knew I had to separate myself from this escalating drug use. I was cool with pot, but if Marianne wanted to be an addict, she was close to home, she was English and she had family she could leave Nicholas with. If I became an addict, I could guarantee nobody would give a damn. So, I had to keep my act together. Mick was always considerate with me and we would still see one another from time to time, but I didn't see Marianne again for many years.

I was happy that Kevin and Debbie were adjusting. When I wasn't travelling, I did all my recordings at Olympic Studios in Barnes, normally in the evenings, so I was able to spend most of my time at home. I had a nice big new upstairs flat now, in Twickenham near Richmond, with three bedrooms and lots of light, plus a large garden where the children could play.

Even the kitchen was spacious. It was a Victorian mansion house converted into two very large flats and the landlord's family lived downstairs. They were called the Gambles and they certainly seemed open-minded about black families. I think that my celebrity status intrigued them and at first it was the perfect location, being so close to where I was recording.

I was also now hanging out with Rod the Mod, as everyone called him. We were looking forward to recording together and it was nice to be befriended by a vocalist I could jam with as I tried to find my own voice. We had a lot of laughs and the sex was cool. He was very cute back then and we were both were passionate about soul music, but he was also extremely arrogant and could be a spoiled brat if things didn't go his way. He drove an MG Midget sports car and was very prissy about his leather gloves and all the gear.

Around this time Andrew was looking for a new touring band for me. Sam Cooke's nephew Sonny Childe was an American singer returning to the US. He'd inherited a soul band called T.N.T. from another soul man, ex-boxer Freddie Mac. The band comprised Billy Adamson on drums, Mike Vaughan-Jones on keyboards, Phil Kenzie on saxophone, Eddie Phillips on bass and Ernie Hayes, a very soulful Stax-influenced R&B guitarist who often worked with Steve Marriott.

As before, I'd inherited a soul unit from a fellow American who was unhappy with his lot in England! Ernie was really lovely – quiet, sensitive and kind. He was very laidback, smoking a lot of hashish and reading *The Hobbit* in the van on the way to the gigs. Eddie had been the guitarist with the Creation, my driver Kenny's old band. The rest of the guys all got along and once again I was fortunate to be working with smoking-hot musicians who seemed to respect me as an artist.

In the meantime, my landlord Mr Gamble was having second thoughts. His fantasies of renting to a pop star were becoming a nightmare. Initially, the pop world seemed glamorous to him, but he hadn't taken into account how different it was from his own. Overnight, the Gambles became nosy and intolerant: 'Could you not play your music so loud? Could you be a bit quieter when you're going upstairs late at night? Was that Mick Jagger visiting you? Wasn't he arrested for drugs?' It was more trouble than it was worth.

I liked Twickenham, but to be honest it was a bit far from Central London and I hadn't had a chance to integrate into the local community. Another move was due, but I wasn't expecting what happened next.

Rod and I woke in a daze about 7 a.m. to find three policemen and a policewoman in my bedroom. We had come in at around 3 or 4 that morning and hadn't got to sleep until 6 a.m. Rod was scared shitless, but I was furious! It was obvious that Mr Gamble had called the police and then let them in with his keys. Buck naked, we were both ordered to get out of bed to be searched. I had no intention of cooperating. Insulted by their intrusion, I stood up in the middle of the bed in all my naked black womanhood. I could see Rod was embarrassed by this, but I was defiant: 'You want to search me after waking me in my bed? Can't you see that I'm naked?!' I knew they were looking for drugs and flung back the covers to show there were none in the bed. Rod found his trousers and was taken out of the room. The policewoman stayed in the room. 'How did you get in my house and where are my children?' I asked, getting more and more angry. After being searched, I wrapped myself in my dressing gown and insisted on being allowed to see my children. By this time I was wide awake and starting to worry.

The policemen were searching my whole flat. It was a close call. All I ever did was hashish, but luckily on this occasion I had none and no paraphernalia either. Nor did Rod, though he seemed more worried about being caught in bed with me and what his family might think than about my children, who were crying and upset. Elena was trying to calm them down and Rod was totally freaked out. He hadn't begun to think of what might have happened to me had anything been found. It wasn't that long since the Redlands bust, which is what I imagined inspired Mr Gamble. He wanted me out of the flat and if I was detained he'd have a good excuse to break the lease. But nothing was found, thank God, and the officers left after giving me a warning about late-night noise. They didn't have to worry. Just the thought of me being busted and deported was enough to bring me to my senses. As soon as they left, I called Immediate and insisted they find me another home. I was also not amused at Rod's selfishness, either, though it seemed that all of my lovers exhibited this same trait.

27

1968 (London)

Clarendon Road

The new place Immediate found me was a brand-new townhouse in Clarendon Road, in a very affluent and fashionable area just off Holland Park, with its playground and Japanese garden full of peacocks and squirrels. I was over the moon! There were high-class restaurants and shopping destinations nearby, plus Hyde Park and Notting Hill Gate, as well as the amazing market in Shepherd's Bush. I couldn't get out of Twickenham quick enough.

The townhouse was spacious and had a small garden, perfect for the kids to run about in. It was the third move in less than six months, but it was great to be back in central London. Now I could register Kevin in school.

I wanted to live as normal a life as possible. But my growing profile made it harder and harder for that to happen. I believed I could juggle career and motherhood, including recording and travelling to and from Europe for promotion, but my main support system was on the other side of the world and it wasn't as easy as I'd imagined.

Kenny Pickett now introduced me to more of his musician contacts. Kim Gardner was a bass player who lived in west London and he acquainted me with his neighbour Ronnie Wood, who everybody called Woody. They had known each other as teenagers and when Rod left Steampacket, he and Ronnie had joined the Jeff Beck Group. These were cute, funny guys and brilliant musicians.

All four were good mates and frequently hung out at my house. I was the only one with my own pad back then as they all still lived with their parents. I was trying hard to keep my new freedoms separate from my responsibilities as a mother, so while everybody smoked hash, I didn't allow it until the children had gone to bed. Our bedrooms were at the top of the house, so the kids weren't affected by this night life.

Kim was very funny, with a warped sense of humour. Ronnie was very quiet and shy. His girlfriend Chrissie, who was another very pretty English rose type, stuck to Ronnie like glue – and I could see why, as he was so fine! They adored each other. Completing this close-knit group were James Morris, who everybody called Jim and Ray Mayall. Jim had a good grasp of how the music business worked and everyone liked him.

Ronnie and Chrissie were homeless at the time, so I put them up for a while. Woody has claimed he lived at my house with Jimi Hendrix, but Jimi wasn't even in London at that time, so this isn't correct, but Jimi's dog Loopy did live with us. Loopy was a lazy dachshund Jimi gave to Woody and Chrissie. The kids adored him so I agreed that he could stay, too.

Kevin was now enrolled at the local primary school and Debbie at a local nursery, but it wasn't like the close-knit neighbourhood culture they knew from home. Still, they were happy and everybody loved them. They had both grown up listening to the best soul and R&B music since they were babies, including Little Stevie Wonder and the Jackson 5. Kevin would entertain my friends by imitating them, while Debbie was just sweet and funny. She was always laughing and they were both picking up an English accent.

My relationship with Rod, however, was falling apart; we seemed to argue constantly. We had a lot of laughs but there was also a tension between us. His arrogance reminded me of David and he was selfish and tight. When we nearly got busted, I realised he was also a coward like David. And he was so scared and embarrassed at being found naked in bed with a black woman!

After a particularly disastrous session recording 'Come Home Baby', an Otis Redding/Carla Thomas cover for Immediate, we had our final argument. We were driving in his beloved MG and as we approached the Shepherd's Bush roundabout, we stopped and I jumped out of the car and that was it. Another tempestuous relationship had come to an end.

Meanwhile, Woody was often away in Europe with Jeff Beck and Chrissie and I had started to clash. She was an aspiring model with a haughty air about her, plus she was lazy and not very generous. I was sharing my house, my food and my life, but she'd buy things and put them in a cupboard for her and Woody only. I'd never lived with that mentality. I remember she freaked out once when my nanny at the time borrowed her pancake mix. We argued about it and when Woody returned from the tour, he and Chrissie moved out. It's been said that I kicked them out, but it was a mutual decision. We had lots of fun, but sometimes it was stressful. I always felt I had to entertain everybody. Drinking and smoking hash so much was still new to me and my paranoia was mounting. They were all old friends and I was ultimately the foreigner who didn't really have a clue.

While I loved being a part of Swinging London, I still had my boundaries. The club in Covent Garden everybody was going to now was called Middle Earth. I was more Mod than hippy and it wasn't my favourite place, as I wasn't into just sitting on the ground tripping. It was around this time I met Alexis Korner, the founding father of British Blues. Paul Jones and I would sing gospel and R&B at the local gigs Alexis organised. I really enjoyed working with both of them and I loved singing with Paul. It didn't bother me that we never got paid.

One gig I played with Alexis in particular stands out in my mind. Organised by Viv Broughton, it was a tribute to Dr Martin Luther King concert in April 1968 on the steps of St Paul's Cathedral, with Julie Felix, Jon Hendricks and Philly Joe Jones. To sing my own music on the steps of this historic cathedral in tribute to Dr King was both memorable and touching. I remember climbing the stairs to the Whispering Gallery and listening to the echo of my voice going round and round and round.

Alexis lived pretty close to me in a flat in Queensway and I was often there rehearsing. He was a lot older and I was fascinated by his encyclopaedic knowledge of black Americans and the Blues. I had heard the Blues all my life and I was familiar with quite a few of the significant artists. My Uncle Book gave me my first two albums, Bobby 'Blue' Bland's *Two Steps from the Blues* and Nancy Wilson's *Today, Tomorrow, Forever*, but the first record I bought for myself was 'My Guy' by Mary Wells. My siblings and I were totally into doowop, R&B, soul and Motown, but I never bought blues records for myself. I knew the artists Alexis spoke of and some of their hits, but I didn't know the music the way he did. I'm embarrassed to admit that coming to London in the mid-'60s greatly improved my education in the music of my own ancestors.

Alexis had grown up in France. He was as European as you could get, a Jewish-Greek-Turkish mix who even looked like a mixed-race black man, with his dark skin and curly Afro-style hair. His first band was Blues Incorporated, with blues harmonica player Cyril Davies and – at one time or another – Charlie Watts, Jack Bruce, Ginger Baker and Long John Baldry. All the up-and-coming blues enthusiasts followed his lead. As a music journalist and broadcaster, he knew every American R&B and blues artist who came over. He was really cool and incredibly hip. His wife Bobbie, daughter Sappho and two sons, young Nico and Damien, were all lovely, very creative and very talented.

One Sunday afternoon, Alexis and Bobbie came to visit me in Clarendon Road. Alexis had taken it upon himself to convince me that I should loosen up a bit and thought that if I took acid I might not be so uptight. I tried to explain to him that I was fine just smoking pot. I think he also sincerely felt acid would help me vocally, allowing me to be more creative and understand the music better. The discussion became heated and I got paranoid and asked him to leave. Maybe I was just more square than everybody else, but I had no family around me, so if I went off the rails, who was going to look after my children? I didn't like Alexis pushing me into something I wasn't open to.

Our confrontation left me feeling upset, as I genuinely liked Alexis and enjoyed working with him. My resistance to drugs was starting to separate me from my friends, I thought. Sometimes the situations were just silly, as with Woody and Chrissie or with Rod and me parting, but this fear of getting deeper into the drug culture was different – first with Mick and Marianne and now Alexis. But I understood that it wasn't the right direction for me. I loved music and I loved to sing – that came naturally to me and I didn't believe I had to be off my head to be able to feel. The one experience in Bremen had been enough.

28

1968 (London)

Angel of the Morning

After Rod and I split up, Jim Morris came round more and more. He was chauffeur and right-hand man for Robert Stigwood, who represented Kenny and Kim's band the Creation. Unlike everyone else, Jim never arrived empty-handed. He'd bring me flowers, wine, nice smoke and take me out to dinner. He was a real gentleman, with class and style and he always brought something for the kids, too. Everybody else expected me to entertain them, but Jim seemed interested in me as a person. If we weren't working, we'd all go to the movies or the park or he'd take us for long drives in the country in Stiggy's beautiful white Bentley coupe with its black convertible top. He was very together and dependable and we soon became lovers. For the first time in England, it seemed someone was interested in me and only me.

T.N.T. and I were now working the circuit and I was happy with how everything was going in England and Europe with the Immediate package tours and television shows. Everything seemed to be on the up. I had built up a loyal following with a great band, I had many new friends and the opportunities poured in daily. The kids were coping with their new surroundings just fine and I had a nice boyfriend. Yet, despite all this, I was homesick; I missed my family's humour and Mama's cooking, so I tried to keep my vibes alive by cooking good soul food when I had the chance. Jimi was doing his thing back in the States and I missed him. Things were going well for him; he had cracked the international market and had become a counter-culture superstar.

From time to time, I would see my friend Madeline Bell. She was the hottest backing singer in town and had come to London from America in 1962 with the Alex Bradford Singers, in the gospel show *Black Nativity* and now lived and worked with Dusty Springfield. We occasionally worked some sessions, which I loved and when we got together she was always a hoot. It was the beginning of a lifelong friendship. We had that black American bond and understanding and I adopted her as the big sister I never had.

Meanwhile, Ike and Tina Turner were also back in England, once again touring with the Stones with some new Ikettes: Ann Thomas, Paulette Parker and Claudia Lennear. Even before the tour Claudia had got my number from somebody and was calling me excitedly and often. She was particularly interested in information about Mick. Long-distance phone calls weren't cheap back then and I could tell she was on a mission.

Jimmy Thomas came to visit me with Paulette, who he was seeing, along with Claudia and other members of the band. I was really glad to see them. I cooked and we all ate, drank, laughed and gossiped about the latest happenings in Ike and Tina world.

I had hoped to be able to see Tina to explain why I left like I did, I guess to get her blessing. I also wanted to see Ann Thomas and Rhonda, but Ike was not having it. He didn't like the other Ikettes visiting me either, probably because he didn't want them getting any ideas about jumping ship as I had.

Claudia was a beautiful girl and she did connect with Mick and the English music scene. When she left Ike and Tina, she joined the Leon Russell Band as backing vocalist with Rita Coolidge on Joe Cocker's Mad Dogs & Englishmen tour. She later acquired a record deal with A&M Records and in 1973 made her only album, *Phew*. She's often said to have been the inspiration for Bowie's 'Lady Grinning Soul', after their meeting.

Rumour had it that Mick also wrote 'Brown Sugar' about her, although here things get complicated. Once, in LA in the late '70s when I was lunching with Marsha Hunt and our mutual friend Linda Livingston, Linda told us that she'd heard that Mick had written 'Brown Sugar' about me – a dubious distinction when you now read the lyrics with 21st-century hindsight. I just laughed, but this didn't go down well with Marsha, who claims that it was written about her.

It's common knowledge that the song's original title was 'Black Pussy'. It's about a southern white plantation master and his slaves. They have no choice when they are summoned 'just around midnight' and to me it's all quite crude and nasty. Certainly, Mick had a lot of black pussy long before he wrote the song and I never heard him say who he wrote it about.

Who knows? I have long since learned that people are going to speculate. Of course, Mick had relationships with both Claudia and Marsha, but we had been lovers long before that. Mick was my first white lover, back when interracial relations were taboo. In fact, the very first song that I ever wrote, 'Though It Hurts Me Badly', was about the secrecy of our relationship.

Meanwhile, Jimmy Thomas was impressed by how the British public had embraced me as P.P. Arnold. We'd been friends since the day of my audition with Ike and Tina and now he wanted to move to London to pursue a solo career. Jim and I collected him from Heathrow a few weeks later and he stayed with me for a while at Clarendon Road while he sorted himself out.

I didn't have much time off. I had a lot going on looking after my kids, working hard and trying to understand what was going on at Immediate. Jim made me feel relaxed and he was good with Kevin and Debbie as well. He really adored me. I had never been adored before and it was nice.

My schedule was relentless, though. Not only was I yo-yoing up and down the country, crossing paths with other bands at the Blue Boar motorway services on the way back from another show, but it was also time to record my second album for Immediate, what became *Kafunta*. Most of the compositions on the first album had been originals and ambitious as this second one was, with its four internal linking segments ('Kafunta One' through to 'Kafunta Four'), it probably had too many cover versions, including 'Eleanor Rigby', 'Yesterday', 'As Tears Go By', 'God Only Knows', the Bee Gees' 'To Love Somebody' and the great Chip Taylor's 'Angel of the Morning' and 'Welcome Home'. In fact, the only original was my own song, 'Dreamin''.

Chip Taylor's most famous song is arguably 'Wild Thing', written for the Troggs and immortalised by Jimi Hendrix, while 'Angel of the Morning' had been recorded without success in 1967 by Billie Davis (I've read that I sang background on this version, but if I did I have no recollection of it). Andrew had brought in the respected session musician John Paul Jones (soon to be in Led Zeppelin) to do the arrangement on my version of 'Angel', so I was definitely hoping that it would be a hit for me. In the end, it turned out really well.

When he created the gorgeous sleeve image for *Kafunta* – ethnic and psychedelic – Andrew outdid himself. The plan was to recreate the image for TV. First there was the photo session at Gered Mankowitz's Mason Yard studio and after that we were going to the TV studio to perform. I was styled in an angelic white gown, with hair and make-up by Leonard's famous salon. The hair was absolutely beautiful, blue and yellow stacked on a wire frame and very tribal indeed. And the make-up was so ahead of its time, with ostrich feathers for eyelashes. The image was heavenly; I looked like an African angel. And then we all remembered that they'd be filming in black and white. I was devastated!

'Angel of the Morning' hit the charts on 13 July 1968, the very day I flew to Bremen to perform it on *Beat Club*. It stayed in the charts for eleven weeks. I was so happy. I didn't know it then, but it would be my last performance on this legendary show, as well as my last hit single for Immediate.

Disappointingly, 'Angel' got nowhere in America. Merrilee Rush would have the hit there. Nevertheless, things were going really well for me – except that as an American citizen I still had a problem with overstaying my work visas. I could move back to the States again, but really I needed to be in England to promote *Kafunta*. My label, management, agency and work were all here too, as were my children's schools. Life was getting complicated.

I thought one solution might be to get married and one night I was talking with Jim about this predicament and to my surprise he proposed. While it seemed like a proposal born out of pragmatism as opposed to wild romance, we did have a very loving relationship. I liked and greatly trusted him, but, still, marriage was a big step and I was only just divorced from David!

His family were all lovely to me, but his parents weren't ecstatic about the idea. Jim was his mother's baby boy and I was sure she hadn't planned on a black American soul-singing daughter-in-law with two small children in tow. In hindsight, we weren't really mature enough to take into consideration anything outside of our present situation.

Jim was making decent money with Stigwood, 'Angel of the Morning' hadn't done badly and *Kafunta* was about to be released, but one thing I've learned in all these years is that in the music industry you never know what's going to happen. Chaos is always a factor. You can be flying high and feeling recognised one minute and then suddenly everything changes. All that you put your faith in will crash to the ground and you find yourself spiralling downwards, understanding nothing.

Things hadn't been the same with Andrew since that night in Germany on acid, though it had never been easy communicating with Andrew at the best of times. I was already dubious about Tony and I had no idea what was going on at Immediate. As it turned out, things weren't too good. He had invested so much in me that I'm sure my lack of trust annoyed him, but Steve Marriott had also fallen out with them. Perhaps Andrew felt I was being ungrateful? In reality, I was just young and scared.

Either way, communication suddenly ceased and Andrew and Tony went underground. Immediate went bankrupt and I was without management or a label or any guidance whatsoever. I continued to work, though and my agent, Barry Dickens, still believed in me. I was his first artist to have a hit record. We smoked together sometimes and always had a good laugh, but I had no clue where I was going or what I was going to do.

29

1969 (London)
Here Comes the Bride

Immediate was bust and I naively imagined I could still promote *Kafunta* and any further singles taken from it. I was wrong.

Jim was very supportive, as was his good friend Barry Gibb. The Bee Gees were enjoying a lot of success; 'Words', 'Massachusetts' and 'I Gotta Get a Message to You' were all smash hits. I was a huge fan. Barry and Robin had written 'To Love Somebody' for Otis Redding, but when he died in the plane crash they went top forty with their version. Mine was one of the early covers and Barry really liked it. This was humbling to me, as Nina Simone and Janis Joplin had also recorded their own versions. I was in illustrious company.

We became close friends with Barry and his young new girlfriend Linda Gray, a striking raven-haired former Miss Edinburgh. They were a perfect sexy-looking couple, both very warm and friendly – he with his down-to-earth sense of humour, she with her lovely accent. They were very much in love, but the relationship was causing problems with his manager Robert Stigwood and the Gibb family.

Stigwood was a theatrical agent and manager who'd met the brothers when they returned to England from Australia and he'd turned them into the biggest male vocal group since the Beatles. Born in the Isle of Man but having grown up in Australia, they were talented songwriters with a publishing catalogue already worth millions. They'd had number ones in Australia and the UK as well as major hits in the US. The world was theirs for the taking.

As twins, Maurice and Robin had these amazing harmonies, which reminded me of the tight family sound between me and my siblings. Robin was introverted and shy and very competitive with Barry about who sang best lead. Sibling jealousies were a major factor in their disputes. Robin had the most beautiful, hauntingly sad vibrato sound, which touched your heart and made you want to cry, but to me Barry had the strongest voice. He was the group's backbone: the oldest, the most talented and creative, the most charismatic – and most definitely the best looking.

Maurice on the other hand was very funny, with a bizarre sense of humour. Unlike his brothers, he was a real party animal, but he was likeable and always friendly.

Barry and Linda moved into a beautiful house in Eaton Square and Jim and I would visit them there. I loved hanging out with them. Barry would play his acoustic guitar and sing the song ideas which ran through him like water. When Jim told him of my predicament with Immediate, Barry immediately started writing songs with me in mind. He loved my voice and very much wanted to produce me. He also had a strong-sounding plan to make it a reality. The plan didn't go down well with the other brothers, however and for a time it put me right at the heart of some heavy politics. Still, it felt like the chance to work with a great artist and it seemed that luck was back on my side again.

First, though, I had to sort out my visa problems and Jim and I had finally decided to get married. With all these upheavals, I sent Kevin and Debbie back to LA to spend time with the family. School was out for summer and children under twelve could safely travel alone back then, so while Kevin and Debbie were chaperoned on their flight to LA, Jim and I set about making my next professional move.

Barry planned to interest Robert in managing me and bring the project in-house with RSO Productions, whose roster then included the Bee Gees and Eric Clapton. If this paid off, my solo career would be back on track. RSO was released via Polydor in the UK and Ahmet Ertegun's Atlantic in the US – the musical home of Aretha Franklin, my greatest musical inspiration.

Barry and I worked together on the songs he had in mind. Ahmed Ertegun was visiting London and Barry and Linda invited him to a dinner party at Eaton Square, along with Robert, Jim and I. Stiggy had no idea about Barry's plan and I was so nervous when he and Ahmed arrived. After dinner, Barry pulled out his guitar and we performed some of the songs. Stiggy was not amused, but Ahmed was very impressed and suggested that he sign me up. Very uncomfortably, Robert told Ahmed that contracts were already in the process of being sorted out. I knew Robert had only agreed because he saw Ahmed's interest and he was still very unhappy about Barry working with me.

Barry assured me that he held all the cards, however. Putting Stigwood on the spot was part of his plan and it had the desired effect. Robert sent the contracts over the very next day. Once again there was no advance. Robert was now to handle my business management and (under his guidance) Jim would handle my personal management. Ultimately, this arrangement worked out badly: we had no kind of close creative relationship and didn't have a clue how to relate to one another.

Meanwhile, another move was in the offing. Jim and I had decided that living in the heart of the capital was disrupting our family life, so he'd asked a friend, Perry Press, estate agent to the stars, to look out for a house outside London big enough to include an office and PA for him. Everyone seemed to be buying or renting manor houses in the country and Perry found us a Georgian manor house in the Green Belt on a twelve-month lease at just thirty guineas a week in a beautiful little Surrey village called Tilford, about 30 miles outside of London. It was called Horsley House and it had twelve bedrooms, a large reception hall, a gorgeous dining room, a sitting and a living room with a seated alcove looking out on ten acres of garden, connected to a large study that was perfect for Jim.

The owners paid for the upkeep of the garden and it all came with stables and two horses. The owners would pay for them too, but we could ride them. There were actually two kitchens – the second for the live-in servants that we didn't have, plus a little self-contained flat for our nanny, Angela, who was also the stable girl.

Seven bedrooms was more than enough for our family and we decided not to use the top floor at all. But there was also a ballroom on a lower floor, which we thought could be perfect for rehearsing the band and for parties. The house was beautiful, but we were living in cloud-cuckoo land to even consider living there. On top of the rent, it cost at least £50 a week to heat the damn place. And then there was food for everyone, family clothing, travel to and from gigs and Jim's live-in personal assistant. A huge Aga in the kitchen did save some electricity, but I have to laugh when I remember the big oil tanker pulling up the drive to top up the oil-fired central heating. It was all such false optimism, but, then, such is the way of innocent youth. We imagined that my new label and management would work out and I would continue to have hit records and success, but even the industry didn't know where it was going. I should've stayed put in Clarendon Road. It was a perfect refuge and many people will still have good memories of the times we shared there. I'd made a few mistakes since bringing my children to live in England with me, but moving to Horsley House was the first really bad one.

It was now autumn. I was earning some money with live appearances, but my visa was running out fast and the wedding needed to be thrown together quickly.

Gita Renick – girlfriend of Jim's friend Ray – worked at the Fulham Road Clothes Shop, which belonged to up-and-coming fashion designer Zandra Rhodes and her boss, Adrian Hughes, approached Zandra about designing my wedding attire. Zandra took my measurements and created a very funky white satin overall wedding ensemble, with a lovely Chinese linen jacket and 'Fulham Road Clothes Shop' stamped through the textile.

We were married at Guildford Town Hall and had a small reception at Horsley House. Barry was Jim's best man and Linda was my bridesmaid. A few close friends attended, along with Jim's family, but once again none of my family could be present to witness my special day, not even the children or Elaine, who was going to fly back with them to help me out.

I realise now how caught up I was in this very bizarre journey. The whole idea was absolutely mad: this young late '60s inter-racial couple living in a traditional Georgian manor house in the heart of English nobility, with a housekeeper and a cook, a gardener, horses, stables and a stable girl who was also a nanny.

Jim and I were both from working-class families, but the music industry had given him serious delusions of grandeur. He was set on being a millionaire by the time he was twenty-five, but he was no longer even Robert's chauffeur, so his only source of income came from managing me. I had similar delusions. We were out of our league and headed for disaster.

Jim's mother had been totally against his marrying a black woman and this was indeed a shocking thing in 1968 Britain. His father Jock was a Scottish socialist and I think he liked the fact that we were upsetting the status quo. His sister Rita and her husband Ron just thought that we had both lost our minds.

It turns out, they were right.

30

1969 (Surrey)

Horsley House

I was so excited to collect Kevin, Debbie and Elaine from Heathrow with Jim. I hoped they would like the whole English countryside experience and I prayed that my sister would be happy with us. But I had an ulterior motive. The notion I had, that she would simply arrive and disappear all my worries, was unfair, naive and unrealistic – and very selfish of me. I'd had a couple of years to adjust to England. She was coming straight from Watts to rural Surrey and it was a shock to her system.

At first she loved the house and the children ran around taking it all in. They weren't used to separate bedrooms, but with a night light they were fine.

The gardens were beautiful, with snowdrops, bluebells, daffodils, tulips, hyacinths, carnations, petunias, pansies, roses and lilies. The smell of herbs was intoxicating, especially the lavender. There were shrubs hanging over the lawns, herbaceous borders everywhere and all manner of trees leading into the woods, including oak, maple, wild cherry and birch. The ponds were full of goldfish, frogs and newts that Debbie loved to bring inside in her hands and show me for a laugh. Both the kids liked the local school, which stood on the village green among shops and pubs and were the first black children to ever attend. Indeed, we were the first black people ever to live in the village and Jim and I the first inter-racial couple. But really we were asking for trouble and living way above our means and needs.

The servants could tell I was uncomfortable giving orders and they took advantage of this. I should have revelled in my authority, but the cook was really rude and took the piss and I always had to be on her case. It was also obvious that Angela knew very little about being a nanny, though she was fine with the horses and the kids loved learning how to ride the ponies.

We'd often visit Jim's family in West Drayton. They'd warmed to me and loved the kids and visited us from time to time, too, as did Barry and Linda. Barry would bring his guitar and play things that he was working on for me. There was always music in the house.

Gita Renick had recently split up with Jim's friend Ray, so we now hired her as Jim's PA/secretary. She was company for Elaine, helping out with domestic chores and they went out walking with the kids and took them to the movies occasionally, becoming really good friends. But for the people of Tilford, we remained an oddity. There were stares and whispers wherever we went. It made me super-paranoid and my smoking didn't help me adjust or fit in. The kids were oblivious to all this, thankfully, and had settled in well at school. Elaine and Gita didn't seem to mind either. Horsley House was very secluded, so I didn't really get out to mix with the locals, which at least stopped me being stared at. And, while our lifestyle was very far removed from neighbourhood customs, it was totally ridiculous that we were living there in the first place.

On one occasion, Jim and I were out doing a gig when my good friends from the Flirtations – Viola Billups (aka Pearly Gates) and sisters Ernestine and Shirley Pearce – tried to pay us a surprise visit at the house, along with Stevie Wonder, who was seeing Ernestine at the time. I was so upset that I missed meeting Stevie. I'd have to wait another year until I had that opportunity again.

It was also around this time that Marsha Hunt recorded a cover of the Dr John song 'I Walk on Guilded Splinters' for which I was asked to sing backing vocals. Because I was unavailable, I passed the session to Elaine and she did a great job. Then, a little after this, a friend of Gita's was staying at Horsley House while Jim and I were away. Apparently they heard Elaine singing in the bathtub and, unbeknown to me, put her up for an audition for a record label who was looking for a black female singer. Was I jealous? Possibly. Resentful? No. I loved my sister and I knew that she loved me. I was aware how boring it was for her to be stuck out in the middle of the country miles away from London and I kept hoping things would get better. I really needed her support, but things just got worse. A long brewing tension came to a head and the argument finally spiralled out of control.

Elaine ran away and Jim and I went frantically searching for her. When she finally returned, she called my parents to tell them what had happened. Daddy insisted that I send her home immediately. As always, it was assumed I was the bad seed and everything was my fault.

This was the beginning of the end of our time at Horsley House. The outgoings of running such a sprawling home – to say nothing of the constant repairs to the Bentley! – were really putting a strain on our marriage, especially as mine was the only income financing everything. I knew that Jim loved me, but he wasn't doing a good job of managing me. We needed Robert and Barry to sort out recording dates, but Barry had his own problems, so I had to just be patient.

We couldn't afford to deal with the expense and responsibilities of living in the country, so, after a year, we decided to move back to London. Perry Press, our estate agent, found us a more sensible townhouse on Alderney Street in Pimlico, close to Eaton Square and Barry and I now started serious work on pre-production. I hated uprooting the children once again, but I had no choice. We had moved three times and they had always adjusted well. They were close to each other and adaptable and, while Debbie missed horse-riding, they were still very young at the time and seemed to not be fazed by anything. However, the fairy tale was over. And not for the last time.

31

1969 (London)

'Bury Me Down by the River'

Jim and I were happy to be back in London. Our new home in Pimlico made much more sense than a manor house in the country, but we were still struggling financially and working together was taking its toll on our relationship. Being on the road cost money and keeping a band together and shelling out for nannies was an added strain on our already precarious finances. When I came off the road to concentrate on finishing the album with Barry and on taking care of the children myself, Jim and I found ourselves arguing constantly. I was frustrated that he hadn't been able to move things along and Robert was offering no support in that regard. Barry was in no hurry, I realised – he was caught up in Bee Gee family politics – but I needed a follow-up to 'Angel of the Morning' and I needed it fast.

Barry's girlfriend Linda and I got along very well. She was a young woman with lots of leisure time who'd made a great catch and she spent much of her time making sure her man's huge sexual appetite was kept satisfied. I often went with her as she shopped for the sexy lingerie Barry liked her to wear, while Barry liked to buy gifts for Linda at Asprey's, the UK's finest jeweller. Sometimes we'd go to Soho to buy porn videos, which was illegal in those days, so you had to be very careful.

Sometimes I bought things for myself, but Jim and I had little money to spare. It wasn't always fun being an onlooker as another woman chose diamonds when I had none for myself, but I was happy for her and it's nice sometimes just to be a part of other people's happiness. We provided solid emotional support systems for each other and there was no hanky-panky. My ménage à trois with Mick and Marianne had been enough swinging for me. I had my children with me now and the Christian values my parents had taught me early on were deeply ingrained in my psyche.

When we weren't shopping, I was at Eaton Square rehearsing with Barry. I was really looking forward to finally going into the studio, but I was uncomfortable in the middle of all the politics. I wanted to create a better professional relationship with Robert, but I never succeeded. There were many problems between Barry and him and between Barry and his family and I was one of those problems. It was a delicate situation and he had such power over all my affairs.

I found a reliable babysitter that I could depend on, but felt guilty relying on nannies and tried to keep some normality going. The children's school was close by, so we could collect them, feed them and put them to bed before returning to Eaton Square and sometimes Jim would pick them up from school and bring them to the Square to play with Barry's little brother Andy, who was about four years older than Kevin. Kevin was mad about soccer and they played in the private square in front of the house while Debbie did her own thing. We always had toys and books in the car to keep them occupied. We spent our evenings making music, singing, drinking Asti Spumante and smoking the very good marijuana Jim was always able to find.

Barry rarely went out. When we hung out at Eaton Square, we did whatever he wanted to do. He had his own film projector and we watched many great movies in that house, which was very beautiful and full of antiques and paintings. There was a lot of complicated intrigue that I didn't really understand at the time – and the many joints we smoked did nothing to help with all the paranoia. Barry is a genius, but as communications were increasingly breaking down with Robert, he got it into his head that his life might be in danger. He collected guns and kept them in the house and whenever the doorbell rang unexpectedly, we'd have to get down on the floor and take cover. It was a bit frightening.

Really, we were all a little too caught up in one another's affairs and it affected our professional relationship at times. I don't think Robert or the family had anything against me personally, but I was still in the middle of their war. Robert had a lot of money tied up in the brothers, so it was a delicate situation.

It was a relief when we finally started recording. He had broken away from the family and was experimenting with his production skills.

In 1968, Maurice had fallen in love with the singer Lulu and she and the family desperately wanted Barry to produce her with

Maurice, but she was not Barry's cup of tea and he had no intention of doing so. She very much wished to be Britain's female soul favourite. I was this American outsider and she sometimes showed up at our sessions and put out very negative energy, showing me no love at all. By contrast, Dusty Springfield, who was Britain's actual female soul favourite, was always warm and friendly with me.

I loved most of the songs that Barry had written for me and in June and July 1968, we had laid down the following three power ballads: 'Bury Me Down by the River', 'Give a Hand, Take a Hand' and 'Let There Be Love'. Madeline Bell and Doris Troy sang backing vocals, Barry sang in the choir on 'Give a Hand, Take a Hand' and we were all stunned at how big the sound was. I could feel my confidence coming back.

The single was now slated for September release, for Polydor in Britain and Atco in the US. The B-side would be 'Give a Hand, Take a Hand' and the A-side 'Bury Me Down by the River', which had such a sad title. I loved my vocals on it, but it was also a bit depressing. I was worried that the lyric was a negative omen and sadly I was right: it wasn't a hit. Barry and I were both disappointed, but we were determined that we were on the right path.

There had also been talk of this being the first release on a new independent label to be launched by Barry and Maurice, named either Diamond or the Gee Bee. But this was not to be. I did some radio promotion in the US, but though the single got airplay, there was no follow-up and no completed album to inspire Atlantic to promote it properly.

We were back in the studio in November recording 'High and Windy Mountain' and 'Turning Tide', as well as a song I was definitely not happy with, called 'Picaninny'. I felt Barry meant no harm – I put it down to simple, foolish naivety as opposed to anything more insidious – and with all the uncertainty and problems surrounding the sessions, I didn't want to make any waves, so I recorded it. I shouldn't have done. I should have been stronger. I told myself that the lyric was being compassionate and empathetic about the civil rights revolution, but I still hated it. It had the racist slur that reminded me of a slave mammy singing to her child about the hard times ahead. As a black American woman, it was a bad time for me to be singing the song. Barry was depressed and under pressure and I seemed to be the recipient of this sad song, although I could hear Robin singing it. Perhaps Barry was missing Robin and was too stubborn to admit it? I wish that we'd had a conversation about it. We both should have opened up more.

Singing 'Picaninny' was good for one thing, however. It started me thinking about who I was. It helped me realise that so many of my white English friends had never really seen the real me. Every day since joining the Revue in 1965 – apart from a very brief period around the time of the *First Lady* album cover, when I wore my own hair in a bob – I had worn a wig. Even Jim rarely saw me without my wig on.

There was a lot of racism in the UK at that time, but it wasn't in your face as it was in the US – not for me anyway. In fact, I never really thought about it, because I had been accepted as a result of my talent. There weren't any real racist attitudes in the pop music industry, where everyone was a young revolutionary breaking down barriers and taboos and everyone loved black music and black artists. Again, I was being youthfully optimistic. There was plenty of racism – it was just a different, more insidious kind.

I had always put my communication problems down to my shyness. I wasn't particularly competitive, but even so, there were some that might have been intimidated by authenticity. This was certainly the vibe I got from Lulu. Perhaps not everybody around me was as liberal as I imagined. Being in the US promoting 'Bury Me Down by the River' opened my eyes to how things were changing there. Perhaps it was time for me to get back to my real self.

Whereas Andrew Oldham had had a definite vision for me, Robert seemed less focused. I liked Robert, but we were from very different worlds. He was all business and had no real interest in where I came from or whether I was authentic or not. He was a very successful, very clever, elegant man, but I sometimes felt that he was being needlessly cruel towards me. Mostly he just wanted Barry to get back to the business of the Bee Gees – his cash cow – and I was getting in the way. He certainly wasn't giving me the managerial support I needed to get my record finished and Jim didn't have what it took to keep the mercurial Barry Gibb on track.

He tried at least, until one day the situation came to a head. Jim began to press Barry to get back to work on the album, stressing, among other things, the economics of the situation as he saw them. Accusing Jim of hustling him, Barry snapped. And that was it. Without any thought as to how this might affect me as an artist, the productions were stopped. We'd spent nearly two years on the project and I had nothing to show for it. It was Immediate all over again. I'd been paid no advance and I had stopped touring in order to get the record finished. It's still a mystery to me what actually happened, but I was told that Robert didn't think that the tracks were commercial enough. I have no idea what the real reason was that caused Barry and Jim to fall out, but one thing was for sure: I was broke and I had no idea what was going to happen next.

32

1969 (On the Road)

Eric, Derek And Jim

To his credit, Robert didn't drop me when the sessions with Barry ended. He still had a large roster of acts, including Eric Clapton, who was about to set out on tour with husband-and-wife duo Delaney & Bonnie. The shows were also set to feature George Harrison and Billy Preston as special guests. It was an incredible line-up and Robert invited me onto the tour as opening act. It was a perfect fit for me.

As a player, I loved Eric Clapton, though I didn't know him personally. In fact, I hardly knew anyone that well any more. I hadn't really been on the scene since my kids had come over.

Delaney and Bonnie Bramlett were the white Ike and Tina, with a great blue-eyed soul, blues, country/gospel sound. 'Eric Clapton, Delaney & Bonnie and Friends' was their first tour in the UK.

Aged fourteen, Bonnie Lynn O'Farrell had backed blues acts like Albert King and Little Milton and was even the first white Ikette for a short while. The band itself was serious rock 'n' roll, with a funky, down-home backbeat: Delaney, Eric and George on guitar, Jim Gordon on drums and Carl Radle on bass, Bobby Keys and Jim Price on horns, Bobby Whitlock on keyboards and Billy Preston taking it to church on the Hammond. Bonnie was the lead singer, with Rita Coolidge and Bobby Whitlock on backing vocals.

Jim and I went to work putting together a great rhythm section of our own for the upcoming shows: Steve Howe on guitar, Tony Ashton on keyboards, Roy Dyke on drums and my good friend Kim Gardner on bass, with Lesley Duncan and Kay Gardner on backing vocals. Steve later went on to great fame with the band Yes, whereas Ashton, Gardner and Dyke are best known for the hit 'Resurrection Shuffle'.

It was a great tour and so much fun being around so many Americans. We all had a funky good time and being back on the road again after all the months of drama with Barry and Robert was just what I needed.

When the tour moved to Europe, we took a ferry across the Channel and I shared a cabin with Lesley, George and my old friend Billy. Of course, I had no reason to worry about him jumping my bones and, surreal as it was to be at such close quarters with George, he too was a perfect gentleman. These were good times and there was a lovely camaraderie on that tour.

After one particularly riotous night in Cologne, we were still in full-on party mood the next morning as the bus drove towards the airport, desperately trying to consume all the drugs that we had on board before we reached customs. Hash and marijuana were my thing and I had never before seen cocaine, believe it or not. Somebody on the bus gave me a big lump of coke and I thought it was white hash, so I crumbled it up and rolled it up in a joint I was making. The very first time I tried cocaine – and I smoked it. I could have flown home myself.

Kevin and Debbie had been in West Drayton with Jim's parents Doris and Jock while Jim and I regrouped. It was another move and another change of schools, but they loved Doris and called her 'Nan'. It had been hard for her to adjust to Jim and I being married. Mixed marriages weren't common in the UK and they brought their own baggage, but she accepted us into the family and was very fond of the children. She also thought our lifestyle was crazy – and she was right – and felt that Kevin and Debbie would be more settled living with her in West Drayton. Like my mother, she just wanted to help any way she could and it had been a while since she had children of her own to dote on.

Kevin joined the local soccer team and football would become a lifelong passion for him. All the changes affected him more than his sister and he wasn't really fitting in as the only black boy in his class. Debbie had a fun-loving, outgoing personality and made friends more easily than her brother. Nothing seemed to bother her and she especially loved Jim's dad, Jock.

By now it was clear that our marriage was failing, but Jim and I visited them often. Children need routine and security and Doris and Jock were such a blessing at this time. I wish I'd had the chance to see them again years later, to let them know just how much I appreciated them before they passed away.

Meanwhile, I needed some financial security. I had to find a way to move forward with my career. I had received no royalties from my two LPs for Immediate, the gig circuit put no money in the bank and I was learning that the artists paid for everything. Jim had some hustles I knew and asked little about, which now and then delivered a life-saving lump sum, but two years trapped in the middle of the Bee Gees feud had left us with nothing. Even Eric's tour hadn't left me with much once everyone was paid and the expenses had been covered.

Above all, what I needed was to make a new record, so Robert arranged for Eric to produce some tracks with me. Delaney & Bonnie were still in town and the line-up for the sessions was basically the same as the tour band less George Harrison and Billy Preston. Doris Troy joined Rita Coolidge and Bobby Whitlock on backing vocals. In fact, the band would soon be called Derek and the Dominoes. We decided to lay down some tracks to highlight my soulful R&B side as opposed to my pop side and chose three covers: Van Morrison's 'Brand New Day', the Stones' 'You Can't Always Get What You Want' and Traffic's 'Medicated Goo'. There was a lot of medicated goo being consumed in the studio and some of the jams went on for ever. I loved the soulful, churchy sound of the vocals we laid down; they were the real deal. Eric captured my essence and I had never heard my voice sound so good on a recording before. The good feeling didn't last, however. Robert heard the tracks and pulled the plug on the sessions. He thought they sounded uncommercial, so the master tapes wound up on the shelf for the next fifty years alongside the aborted Barry Gibb recordings. This was the start of my downward spiral.

Jim and I started just hanging around the house. Madeline Bell would come by with her then-partner Tony Garland and we'd play cards, smoke and try to stay positive, but we were running out of money and, to make matters worse, I found myself pregnant again. We knew there was no way we could have a child and decided to be pragmatic, but the subsequent termination just deepened my growing depression. We were forced to move out of the Pimlico house and were staying at our friend Adrian Hughes' flat in Chelsea. Thanks to Jim's mum, the kids were still settled with her in West Drayton.

Jim and I would argue frequently and with growing intensity, but we were both young and neither of us had the emotional tools to deal with our situation – professionally or personally. He had big ideas but no power to execute them and the war between Stiggy and Barry dominated everything. He was also undertaking in increasingly more destabilising underground dealings that were putting us both in jeopardy without my knowledge.

I was once again in a dire situation, waiting for the unexpected to show me the way.

33

1970 (London)

Catch My Soul

Jack Good had been manager of several of the big UK names in rock 'n' roll, including Tommy Steele and Cliff Richard. He had also made the first UK music shows aimed at teenagers in the 1950s and '60s – *Six-Five Special*, *Oh Boy!*, *Boy Meets Girls* and *Wham!!* – though I knew of him via *Shindig*, which ABC had broadcast in the US from 1964–66.

In 1970 he produced *Catch My Soul*, a rock musical loosely adapted from Shakespeare's *Othello*. He was close friends with Robert Stigwood, who secured a lead role for me alongside two other US artists: Jack's friends Lance LeGault (who played Iago) and P. J. Proby (Cassio). Welsh actress Angharad Rees played Desdemona and, in a role beefed up from the original Shakespeare character, I played Bianca, the harlot who is Cassio's love interest. Montano was played by Emil Dean Zoghby, a former South African pop star who arranged some of the music. Rodrigo was played by Jeffrey Wickham and Emilia by Dorothy Vernon, a brilliant actress who was very kind and encouraging to me. As for Othello, to the embarrassment of all the black musicians and actors and dancers involved in the production, Jack Good himself blacked up every night and played the role.

Angharad, Jeffrey and Dorothy were all trained, professional actors, but I knew nothing of theatre life. Lance was a guitarist-singer who'd also drummed for Elvis Presley. He was very professional, but Proby, who had pushed for his role, would show up every morning stinking drunk from drinking Apple Boone Farm wine. At one point he had to leave rehearsals to dry out. And while Jack was undoubtedly a great TV producer, his acting ability left a lot to be desired. He was also an awful singer. His big number, 'Put Out the Light', had to be sung by Bobby Tench.

My two songs were 'A Likely Piece of Work' and 'May the Winds Blow'. Considering I had no acting experience, I guess I wasn't too bad. It was a big production, with a very racially mixed group called the Tribe of Hell. Always at the front was Dana Gillespie, a statuesque actress with huge boobs. She was also a fine singer and we got on well. I was also good friends with Cassie Mahon, a Trinidadian girl who had been a *Ready, Steady, Go!* dancer. Marcia Miller also stood out.

The music was played by the brilliant British rock band Gass, with Emil as their band's musical director. Bobby Tench, later of the Jeff Beck Group, was their guitarist. I loved working with the Gass and I had a major crush on Bobby, but he had his eye on Cassie, who was in a serious relationship with her childhood sweetheart Junior Kerr. Junior would later become guitarist with Bob Marley's Wailers and change his name to Junior Marvin.

I was nervous and excited. I needed the routine and the professional discipline and the daily rehearsals, vocal and dance warm-ups were giving me back the confidence I'd lost. I was used to everything being structured around me, so being in the company with its rules and regulations offered a new challenge and I tried to stay low-key and just learn the ropes. Everyone called one another darling, but there was also a lot of bitchiness and competitiveness. Theatre is very different from rock 'n' roll and some of the more traditional actors were a little snobbish about my interloper status.

This version of *Othello* retained all the original characters but took several liberties with Shakespeare's original text. It's set in a remote commune run by Iago, for example, and Othello is not a general but a wandering evangelist. Iago loves Desdemona, but much to his chagrin she marries Othello. Iago then quietly manipulates Othello until he murders her. Even without the nightly blacking up, Jack's interpretation was straight out of a minstrel show. This was highly embarrassing to many of us, not to say insulting. In the early '70s, black actors just weren't being given the leading West End roles they deserved and would have loved.

P. J. Proby had sung demos for Elvis and portrayed him on stage in the US. He had arrived in the UK a little before me and had three or four hits before some trouser-splitting concert appearances scandalised everyone and he was banned by the ABC theatre chain. I may have played his love interest, but his good ol' boy Texan racism didn't sit well with me at all. He was a nightmare to work with.

One afternoon we had a big argument about him patting me on the ass. I complained to Jack and he also didn't like it. In another scene I had to come to Cassio during a fight scene with Iago and Proby turned around and intentionally knocked the shit out of me. I was shocked and livid, as was everyone else, especially the band. Like Jack, Proby was also blacked up. This had already caused tension, but now it was creating a racial divide within the cast, which became very uncomfortable for a few days. I kept as far away from him as possible during performances, which was hard as most of my scenes were with him. He gave me a phony apology and pretended that it was an accident, but the damage was done. I never really recovered from the incident and working with him became really stressful. I've never been an Uncle Tom and I knew exactly where he was coming from.

Lennox, the percussionist in the band, sensed my unhappiness and introduced me to yoga meditation, to help me deal with the situation. After all, just walking off the show wasn't a financially sound option.

Catch My Soul was at the end of its four-week run in the provinces. Before it opened in Manchester and toured on to Birmingham and Oxford, we all took a short break. I needed a rest. The racial politics of the show were bringing me down and I wasn't really happy doing musical theatre. I liked to sing freely and I wanted to stay connected to the recording industry. I was entering a depression that I couldn't seem to pull myself out of.

Returning to the show made me realise just how unhappy I was. I soldiered on, however, looking forward to its London debut at Camden Town's Roundhouse where my hard work would be realised and I would see the benefits of this entry into the world of theatre. The Roundhouse seemed the perfect venue and there was talk of it transferring to the Prince of Wales in the West End. On top of this, a live recording was being made. Alongside my two solo tunes, I also sang a duet with P. J. Proby and a trio with him and Bobby Tench. I desperately hoped these tracks would help me get another deal.

The longer we toured, however, the more depressed I seemed to get. Angharad left and there was talk of Marianne Faithfull taking over as Desdemona. The night she came to see the show, though, she got stoned and collapsed in director Braham Murray's hotel room. We had all hoped the show would get some exposure, but this wasn't the national news headline we'd been hoping for.

An actress named Sharon Gurney eventually replaced Angharad, but by then I had lost all interest. I was bored of my own two songs, I hated having to sing my numbers with Proby and our relationship was getting worse and worse. His racist personality was just wearing me down. Despite all this, when we finally arrived at the Roundhouse, we opened to rave reviews. The positivity was short-lived, however. One night, Proby and I had a big argument. His relentless bigotry was too much and I quit the show. No financial reward was worth this, but it felt like another door slamming shut in my face.

34

1966–70 (London)

Encounters and Farewells

In July 1969, Brian Jones was found dead.

I'd distanced myself from the hard drug scene around the Stones after I brought Kevin and Debbie to England, so I hadn't seen him in a very long time, but still, I was deeply saddened at his passing. The last time I saw him had been at the Speakeasy. He was stoned and really out of it and it was shocking to see him in that state. In his last words to me, he told me that I was a very special being and that I would play a very big part in changing the world in the future. He always made me feel like I mattered.

One Saturday morning in 1966 while I was still in Epsom, I'd received a phone call from Brian Jones inviting me to London. He sent his Rolls-Royce for me and I was driven to his beautiful flat in Courtfield Road, South Kensington.

When we rang the bell, Brian came to the door. He was soft-spoken and polite as always, greeting me warmly. I'd heard gossip from Mick about his drug habits but we'd never talked directly. Besides, all the Stones had shown us respect and love throughout the tour.

If Mick was an extrovert, Brian seemed just the opposite, but that was fine, as I too felt sensitive, vulnerable and wary. He rolled a hash joint and made me feel welcome as we talked about Epsom.

Compared with the modern space that was Mick's Harley House, Brian's flat was really just one huge room, a small kitchen and bathroom. It too was decorated with rich fabrics, rugs and embroideries from Morocco, but was fairly disorderly next to Mick's flat. A wooden staircase led up to a minstrel gallery and I loved its high-beamed ceilings, big windows and skylight. Magazines, papers and clothing were strewn everywhere. The antique chairs needed reupholstering and the bed was just a big mattress on the floor. There was a real hippy vibe, an intoxicating mix of past centuries with the psychedelic '60s, including Indian and Moroccan influences. The hash joint was also pretty powerful, but it helped me to relax.

Brian was annoyed about Mick's behaviour towards me, which was very sweet. I explained that Mick and I had not made personal commitments. Yes, I was hurt, but I was in no position to judge. I hadn't stayed in England to be Mick's girlfriend. I knew that Mick and Marianne had a thing going. Afterwards, I wondered if Brian's compassion for me reflected his own estrangement within the Stones camp.

He was very cute and sexy and looked aristocratic, eccentric and yet elegant in his flamboyant attire, his dandy scarves and beautiful smoking jacket. I thought he had a mystical charisma about him. I was never physically attracted to Brian and didn't want to send out the wrong signals, but he was a perfect gentleman and host. He played some blues and R&B and I felt at home right away. While we smoked, he introduced me to some mystical Indian sounds. I'd smoked marijuana with Gabriel and hashish with Mick, but this was my first time in an environment that let me experience its effects fully. There was a piano and a beautiful collection of guitars, mandolins and other exotic string instruments. I was in awe of his musicality. He was deep and very talented, but there also seemed to be a sadness about him.

We talked about my roots and family and he talked about music and art. I felt comfortable and safe, not intimidated at all. With so little experience dating, I still believed that if you were drinking and smoking alone with a guy, they wanted sex with you, but he made no advances and I appreciated this respect.

He had to go out for a while and after showing me how the rolling machine worked he left me on my own. I was very happy to be here. It was enchanting to be in among all this artistic bohemianism, listening to music and exploring my thoughts. I felt worlds away from LA.

After a while he returned with his close friend Tara Browne, the heir to the Guinness fortune. All the Stones were connected to the aristocracy, bad-boy favourites of the rebellious young debutantes, the lords and ladies, viscounts and viscountesses, dukes and duchesses, earls and countesses of the realm. The well-educated idle rich had thrown themselves into the new culture of hippies and happenings, which let them party mindlessly, experimenting with heroin, barbiturates and acid. If thesc walls could talk, would I even want to hear what they said?

Brian's vibe had drastically changed and the hash wasn't helping me join them. I suggested it was time for me to go. He urged me to stay over and said someone could drive me back to Epsom the following morning. I was apprehensive, but he assured me I had nothing to worry about. I decided to trust him and not get paranoid. I knew I had to learn to trust that I could handle myself in my new surroundings. As a black woman in a strange land, my reputation was very important to me, but I had to let go of a lifetime's fears about how I'd be treated in the company of white men.

It was a lovely evening in very interesting company, especially after the delicious Indian food they had brought back with them. Tara left in the early hours and I joined Brian in his one bed, feeling secure enough to enjoy a cuddle and warm, gentle kisses with him. He made no advances and was in no condition to have sex even if he'd wanted to, which was a relief, as I certainly didn't want to have to wrestle with him.

Brian was kind and had displayed genuine friendship. I felt true sensitivity towards him. It had been a magical day at a delicate time of transition and had helped me to put my decision to stay in England in perspective. He said I was welcome to visit whenever I got bored and I did so a couple more times, though I wish that I had been more open with him. I'll never forget his kindness. I was a long way from America's racism here and I had a lot to think about.

Not long after this, Tara Browne was killed in a horrific car accident driving with his girlfriend in his sports car in the early hours in South Kensington. The Beatles' 'A Day in the Life' later immortalised this tragic event.

The casualties were mounting in this blessed new world. In 1967, as Mick and Marianne communed with the Beatles and the Maharishi, their manager Brian Epstein overdosed, a sad shock for the whole scene.

In the aftermath of her relationship with Mick, Marianne was also addicted to heroin. Mick was seeing Marsha Hunt, flaunting her at the Hyde Park memorial concert the Stones played in honour of Brian. The news of Brian's death and Marsha's pregnancy by him sent Marianne over the edge. When she and Mick flew to Australia to film the Ned Kelly movie, she took an overdose of barbiturates and was in a coma for six days. When they returned to London, Marianne was moved out of the house in Chelsea and Marsha moved in.

I'd missed Jimi Hendrix playing the Isle of Wight Festival in June and was looking forward to connecting with him while he was in London. His death on 18 September 1970 was a huge shock and devastating to everyone.

My relationship with Jimi had been very private and I'd never had much respect for women who latched onto musicians just to be a public part of a scene. The horrible stories that his lover sold to the *News of the World* sickened me.

All of my rock star relationships were based on friendship before turning physical. For fear of rejection, I never got too emotionally involved. I was promiscuous like them and we were all experimenting. I knew I couldn't depend on them being faithful, so I pretended not to really care, but really I did.

One Sunday morning the phone rang and to my very pleasant surprise it was Cat Stevens. I hadn't seen him since long before

Immediate collapsed, so I invited him over for lunch. We were never lovers but we had been good friends. I would hang out in his flat above his father's Greek restaurant around the corner from Immediate, as he played the 45s and LPs released that week. It was so lovely to see him again.

He too was in an insecure and melancholy mood. He'd had major chart success since we last saw each other, but with success comes challenges. We had both loved Jimi and shared our sadness at his death. Sometimes the universe just brings souls together, to inspire or help one another and this felt like a day for two people to feel spiritually safe in one another's company.

I had posters of Angela Davis and Soledad Brothers up on the walls of the flat I was staying in, but they only emphasised what a stranger I was. Steve, who was English but had Greek heritage, understood my need to connect with my own roots and my moral upbringing. I had been going with the flow and digging the experience as Jimi advised me to do and I think Steve had been doing the same. He was incredibly gifted, as well as a kind and gentle spirit, but now we both felt at odds with this fast-paced, intoxicated culture and were looking to find alternative ways to express our faith. We shared our fears and anxieties about the future and many personal things. I missed my children, who were living with Jim's parents in West Drayton. The conversation was very emotional and open and it was a peaceful day. It was so good just to relax without sex getting in the way.

We ended our perfect day at his favourite Greek restaurant and I took a taxi back home. It was the last time I would see him for more than forty years.

35

1970 (London)

Searching for an Identity

Leaving IBC studios one evening, I shocked everyone by impulsively taking off my wig and throwing it into a rubbish bin. Underneath the wig, my own hair was a mess. Since my days as an Ikette, when Ike used to tug at our stage wigs, I always used hairpins to keep them on tightly. Since leaving the Ikettes this had remained my habit and now I literally had several bald spots and many damaged hair cuticles. Rather than feel embarrassed, it was as if a huge weight had been lifted. I was no longer a little black girl with straight fake hair. I was free to be me again. It was the last time I wore a wig for years.

The next day I had my hair cut into a short Afro. It definitely changed how people looked at me. I was no longer Penny Valentine's cute little 'chocolate button'. I no longer wanted straight long hair to make me feel acceptable. I was living in the UK, but I was re-emerging a proud black woman, increasingly drawn to Angela Davis and her revolutionary stand against the racist system in America. She seemed young, beautiful, intelligent and brave. Since my split with Jim, I had been staying at our friend Adrian Hughes's flat in Beaufort Mansions, Chelsea, still house-sitting while he worked on a film in Yugoslavia.

The cover image of *Kafunta* saw me looking like a beautiful African Warrior Queen. This was Andrew's idea, but it came to personify my own struggle as a single black American woman in the UK industry. And though I didn't know it at the time, *Kafunta* was a hit in South Africa, where the battle against apartheid ran parallel to the US civil rights movement.

As for my hair, well, today I see that putting my wig in the trash was needlessly extreme. All I had to do was to respect it, take care of it, style it for my chosen persona and not be ashamed of it. So much has changed since those days, including new hair products for black women, beautiful extensions – and hair has little to do with what's inside your heart, anyway. All women, black and white, wear wigs to change their looks and images when desired. I choose to wear my hair natural, but I know that hair doesn't have to be a statement any more. I change my hairstyle to suit my mood. I am an entertainer. We live and learn.

Other encounters were stirring my Afro roots in other ways. My friend Gita Renick now lived in a communal flat in Battersea and there I met a young Antiguan guitarist called Wendell Richardson, known as Dell.

Dell was a very lively young man who was also very flirtatious, even though he told me he was married. While I didn't fancy him, I warmed to him instantly. He was a great guitarist who knew so much about black American culture and wanted to know more. We exchanged numbers and he promised he'd play me some of his songs.

I hadn't met many black British musicians since coming to London and Wendell educated me on what was going on. He was the first to open up as a friend and communicate with me like a brother.

He was playing in a pioneering world music band Osibisa and in fact many Ghanian and Nigerian musicians were helping shape the rock 'n' roll sound in Britain at this time, including such great percussionists and drummers as Speedy Acquaye, Rebop Kwaku Baah, Rocky Dzidzornu, Remi Kabaka and Gasper Lawal, who worked at various times the with likes of Paul McCartney, the Rolling Stones, Steve Winwood, Traffic, the Animals, Ginger Baker and others.

Before Osibisa, Wendell had played in a black rock band called the Sundae Times with drummer Conrad Isidore from Dominica and Calvin 'Fuzz' Samuel on bass. Dell talked incessantly about Fuzz, who got his nickname from the fuzzbox pedal he played his bass through. (Americans called him 'Fuzzy'.) The Sundae Times were said to be the very first black rock band in the UK and they had been discovered by Eddy Grant, whose band the Equals were one of the first racially integrated pop groups in the country. Wendell, Fuzz and Conrad were the session rhythm section on the Equals number-one hit 'Baby Come Back' and in turn Eddy produced *Us Colored Kids*, their only album. But though the trio wrote all their own tunes, they never saw any royalties for these historic recordings.

Strangely enough, Jim had also been talking about Fuzz, who had recently secured himself a fantastic gig replacing bass player

Greg Reeves with US folk-rock supergroup Crosby, Stills, Nash & Young. Jim felt I should meet him. Wendell had some songs that I thought might be good for me and during the short break from the Catch My Soul tour we recorded some demos at De Lane Lea studio in Kingsway. Fuzz happened to be in London on a break from touring with CSNY and he turned up, too.

As Wendell was trying out ideas on a track, I chatted with Fuzz. He was good-looking and wore a great hat, like the one blues singer Robert Johnson wore on his album covers. He was quirky and nonsensical, which was very endearing. Anybody who can make me laugh is fine with me. I gave him my number and went back to work with Dell.

Fuzz wasted no time calling. I had a couple more days before I was needed back in Manchester, so he came round with some prime hashish and we spent a lovely afternoon and evening together. He had been homeless until a meeting with Stephen Stills had turned his life around and I was definitely impressed with him. But he had to be back in the US soon, for the CSNY tour. All of my peers seemed to be America-bound. The British invasion was in full force and I was feeling really left out.

We started having a fling and Fuzz flying back and forth from the States to see me helped lift my spirits in those torrid final days of *Catch My Soul* and I was so glad when he finally returned. We spent a lot of time together at Beaufort Mansions and it was nice to be with a black guy who wasn't macho and demanding. He was easy-going and covered up shyness with eccentricity.

Love and romance very much shaped my musical decisions on this next phase of my journey. I had a temporary roof over my head, but I had no idea where I was going.

36

1971 (London, Miami, Antigua, LA)

Trying to Find My Way

I started to get the word around that I was available for session work doing background vocals. Thanks to Madeline Bell, Lesley Duncan and Kay Garner, the first session that I booked for was *Jesus Christ Superstar* andrew Lloyd Webber's new project. He had wanted a soulful, gospel sound to accompany the backing tracks he had already overseen.

I had a very distinctive sound that wasn't right for a lot of sessions and I also didn't blend well with some English voices, so I mainly got calls from artists who wanted that special American gospel sound, which was fine with me.

Madeline had worked with Dusty Springfield and was the number-one background singer in London. She had sung on several of my sessions, released and unreleased and we often worked together. She had the clearest crystalline vibrato I've ever heard and her surname described it perfectly. Originally from New Jersey, Madeline had come to London in 1962 and Dusty had encouraged her to stay here. We first met when Ike and Tina were taping *Ready, Steady, Go!* and was a bold soul sister with an outgoing personality and a great sense of humour. Everyone loved her and she knew absolutely everybody. I love her dearly to this day.

I first met Doris Troy through Madeline, just before my sessions with Eric. Like Madeline, she was loved in the UK as a solo artist and was also in demand as a session singer. She and Madeline had known one another in New York and her 1963 hit 'Just One Look' (which the Hollies covered in the UK) had been one of my favourites. They were both East Coasters who'd grown up in the Pentecostal Church (Doris's father was a Barbadian Pentecostal minister), so the three of us all had similar backgrounds.

Doris was a larger-than-life character, with a big, confident personality and heart to match. She was so fun to be around. It was impossible to not like her. Upon her arrival in the UK, she had impressed George Harrison with her backing work on Billy Preston's 'That's the Way God Planned It', his debut for Apple Records. George signed her to Apple and co-produced her album *Doris Troy* with her.

Meeting her was a godsend. I still had no confidence taking care of my own business affairs, but Doris was a lot older and had a wealth of experience and expertise. She knew all about getting ripped off and she knew how to hustle and protect herself in the industry. The first and maybe most important thing she taught me was to always make sure I asked for the money!

With lots of time on my hands, the door to session work opened easily. My first session with Doris was with the late Nick Drake. She called me one evening and we went down to Sound Techniques Studio and sang on the track 'Poor Boy' that he was recording for his *Bryter Layter* album. Nick was extremely quiet and introverted, but he knew exactly how he wanted us to sound. The song was about a boy who felt sorry for himself and he wanted the sarcasm to come across. I didn't hear the end result until years later, but I love the sound that we got together that night. This was the only time that I met Nick.

Doris and I also sang together on 'Feel Too Good' from the Move's *Looking Back.* I sang on a lot of sessions at this time, including *The Worst of Ashton, Gardner and Dyke*, the Family Dog track 'I Wonder' and Mayfield's Mule's 'My Way of Living' and 'My One for Your Two'. I also sang on a few jingles that Manfred Mann caught on tape in his Old Kent Road studio around this time.

Fuzz had been calling me regularly from America. CSNY had split when the tour ended and he worked on five tracks on Stephen's first solo album, *Stephen Stills*, which also featured Jimi Hendrix and other well-known figures. Doris hung out with Stephen, who had his biggest hit with a saying she coined, 'Love the One You're With', off that album. Fuzz played on that track, but I hadn't met Steven yet. The house he was renting in Elstead, Surrey was down the road from Tilford, where Jim and I had lived for a time. Peter Sellers had lived there in the past and when Fuzz wasn't with me or in the States, he stayed there.

I was definitely attracted to Fuzz. We were both soulful young survivors integrated into the world of rock 'n' roll and it seemed we had a lot in common, though we were also very culturally different. Fuzz was a sideman with great ambitions that he wanted to realise and I had been catapulted into the limelight – a status I wanted to maintain. I didn't play an instrument but I felt that I could write songs if I found the right people to work with. Fuzz was a good songwriter, so I thought perhaps he could help me open up my creativity. We were both shy and looking for love and I was drawn to him.

Stephen was now putting together *Stephen Stills 2*. Some of it had been recorded at Criteria Studios in Miami and on one occasion I travelled with Fuzz to Miami where he was recording and stayed in a huge mansion house on Miami Beach that was rented for the entire band and their partners. There were two very cool, funky ladies there, Cindy and Gerri, who had formed a company called Home At Last. They cleaned and catered for rock 'n' roll artists, with healthy vegetarian home cooking and creature comforts. They were very smart and soon would become very rich young ladies when they later moved into real estate.

The Miami house had a big patio with a huge swimming pool. In England it's usually too cold, so this was my first rock 'n' roll sunshine experience. I bought a swimsuit and pretended I was used to such parties. I even embarrassed myself by jumping off into the pool like I knew how to swim before Fuzz had to save me from drowning.

Alongside the steady supply of marijuana, there was an increasing amount of cocaine. I wasn't really into coke and didn't understand Stephen's erratic behaviour. I knew that Fuzz smoked a lot, but I didn't realise how much coke he was doing.

From Miami, Fuzz booked a flight to Antigua. It was beautiful – and a bit of a culture shock. Everybody was black; in the banks, shops, restaurants, cafés and the marketplace. Even the policemen were black. I'd never been anywhere where black people controlled things. The capital, St John's, was not a modern city, but it was bustling. Its shabby-looking houses reminded me of wooden shacks in the deep south. This was where Fuzz was born and his family still lived.

Fuzz's mother was called Ruth and she looked me up and down distastefully when we arrived. Apparently she had plans for Fuzz to connect with some island girl, but his sister Junie welcomed me enthusiastically. Ruth stayed well away from me the whole time I was there, sitting in a rocking chair on the back porch smoking a pipe. I'm sure it had more than tobacco in it, which might have explained her red eyes. Her house was really strange, spooky, with handwritten prayers adorning the walls. Apparently she had a reputation of sorts in the town, but Fuzz didn't elaborate.

Junie was lovely though – a vibrant, happy young woman, very kind and hospitable, who cooked me delicious West Indian food. To be honest, given her attitude towards me, I'm not sure I would have been comfortable eating anything his mother had cooked.

We spent our days hanging out on the beautiful beaches and driving around in a rented car and Fuzz told me all about island life. It was clear he was glad to be back. One afternoon he took me to the parish where his grandmother lived, a place called Gray's Hill, in Liberta. She was ninety years old, a lovely little woman and Fuzz resembled her quite a bit. She lived alone and seemed healthy and strong. Her house was decorated very sparsely with nothing but a picture of General McArthur proudly displayed on the dresser, which I found both strange and funny.

Another afternoon he took me high up into the bush, to a place called Horsford Hill, to introduce me to his favourite Uncle David, who lived in a mud hut he had built himself. He was nowhere to be seen when we arrived, so we peeked inside. It was filled with books and everything was very neatly arranged, with just enough room for a bed and personal things.

Outside there was a very striking sculpture made from mud, iron, broken glass, seashells, tiles, pottery and junk, which reminded me of the Watts Towers, that iconic folk-art treasure built by an Italian immigrant in a backyard in Watts. It was evident that David was highly intelligent and artistic. He had been a pharmacist until he gave up on civilisation to become a recluse and a Rastafarian. The family shunned him and as a child only Fuzz had visited and brought him things. They definitely had an affinity.

When we finally saw Uncle David, he arrived dripping wet and carrying a fish. He was surprised and happy to see Fuzz and even happier to see me. He was a beautiful man and the first Rasta that I had ever seen. His eyes sparkled like diamonds and his finger was bleeding – where a fish had bit him, he said. It was obvious he caught his fish by hand while diving in the sea and as I wrapped his finger in the bandage material he gave me, he laughed at the fame Fuzz had found in the world. I could tell that he was happy his nephew was using his talents to survive.

Another highlight was a full moonlit swim in the sea at Fort James beach near St John's. I wasn't swimming to be honest, but the water was crystal clear and with Fuzz's help I could at least paddle around fearlessly. We parked the car nearby and slept on the beach.

It was idyllic.

On 8 February 1971, we travelled to LA and the atmosphere was strange as we arrived at the airport, the air acrid and smoggy.

A limo drove us to Hollywood and we checked in at the Chateau Marmont Hotel on Sunset Boulevard. We had dinner and a nice evening, determined to stay up and fight the jetlag. We went to bed late and when we woke, the room was shaking. We had flown in for the earthquake that killed sixty-four people and caused $2 billion worth of damage. I grew up with the occasional tremor, but this one literally shook me up.

Going home was very different this time. The California Department of Transportation was building a new freeway, the Interstate 105, as part of their master plan for the new freeway system. Most of the areas slated for demolition were African American and 117th Street had been included on the plan since at least 1947. Despite the strong feelings and opposition in the community, all the families were required to sell their properties to the city. They were being asked to move away from the places they'd migrated to and called home all those years.

This mass uprooting of our communities was devastating and coincided with a time of rising crime and gang-related activity. The drug and gun culture in South Central had grown so suddenly that many believed the government had a hand in it. All the support systems families had developed over the years, to protect their children who were so badly affected by the wave of crime, were suddenly gone.

It was the end of an era – and the beginning of a lot of unhappiness. My parents' lovely big sprawling house with its front and back yards would be destroyed. They sold their home and bought two lots with two buildings on each, one big, one small, as well as two small front lawns. The plan was to rent out the larger house and live in the smaller one. From one of the smaller buildings my father ran Cole's Upholstery, while the other was a little one-room house-garage they didn't really know what to do with. Investment in property to rent was smart and Daddy was happy having his independent business at last, but Mama hated its little kitchen and bathroom, its single very small bedroom and the cramped living room. She deserved better and I really felt for her. Daddy was definitely ensuring that none of us kids could come back home to live and I felt I had no roots left in LA.

Still, we were there for a week, so I introduced Fuzz to everyone. They threw the customary BBQ and neighbours and friends came to hear recent news of my life in England. They were surprised to see me with a West Indian rock 'n' roll bass player, but he was a hit, even though my family had been fond of Jim and didn't understand why we had split up. They had all taken Elaine's side after we'd argued at Horsley House, however and I think they were beyond trying to understand me. I couldn't really blame them. I didn't really understand what was going on with me either.

Thanks to CSNY, Fuzz had many contacts in LA. Stephen Stills was putting together a band called Manassas, with Chris

Hillman (of the Flying Burrito Brothers) and Al Perkins, which would include Fuzz. CSNY's managers had been David Geffen and Elliot Roberts and Geffen had recently formed Asylum Records. I had come to LA hoping that Asylum could help with our projects. Geffen and Elliott were very fond of Fuzz, but they weren't really interested in him as a solo artist and they definitely weren't interested in me. Also at the Chateau Marmont was Graham Nash, recording his solo album *Songs for Beginners*. He was involved with Rita Coolidge at the time and she and I had toured together with Eric Clapton and Delaney & Bonnie and Friends. We'd also sung backing vocals on the 'Military Madness' track.

Erma Kent and my brother Kenny visited us at the Chateau Marmont for some rock 'n' roll partying. I was shocked at all the cocaine, but I did drop a tab of acid – my first since Andrew had spiked my drink in Germany. It gave me the munchies and we went to Greenblatt's takeaway Deli and bought a watermelon. We took it back to the hotel and devoured it like it was the last one on earth.

All this was almost too much fun and I was glad to get back to London, where I had many decisions to make, about my children and about where we'd live. Back home, Doris was helping me capitalise on everything I'd done as a solo artist. 'It's all about the business,' she would say. 'They don't call it the music BUSINESS for nothing!' I always felt protected around her. At one point we had an idea for a project we were going to call Gospel Funk and we actually booked a rehearsal room. Our solicitor friend Tony Demetriades had a song that he thought might be good, but Doris didn't like it. Later it was a hit for another band he was helping out.

Doris called to say that Steve Marriott was looking for me. I hadn't seen him since the Immediate crash. The Small Faces had now disbanded and Steve had formed Humble Pie with guitarist and vocalist Peter Frampton (formerly with the Herd), Greg Ridley (ex-Spooky Tooth) on bass and a seventeen-year-old Jerry Shirley on drums.

With Claudia Lennear, Doris and I were booked to do a session with Humble Pie at Olympic Studio. We sang on 'A Song for Jenny' from the *Rock On* album (Jenny was Steve's wife and we're credited as the Soul Sisters). I was surprised when Marsha Hunt arrived with Doris. She wasn't booked to sing and no way did she have the confidence to sing with Claudia. I suspect she was checking Claudia out, but even showing up took nerve, so I give her that much credit. She was clearly uncomfortable and stayed in the control room, but the band were delighted to have all three of Mick's black exes in the room. Steve was as stoned and happy as ever and I was really happy to see him again.

Meanwhile, Fuzz was back and forth between London and the States and I was doing as many sessions as I could. One evening we went to the Marquee with Doris and her partner Chaka. To my surprise, Ian Stewart turned up. 'Pat,' he said, 'I've been looking everywhere for you! Mick's getting married tomorrow and he wants you and Doris to come to the wedding in St Tropez. Here's your tickets; you can both bring who you like with you. Make sure that you're at Gatwick Airport tomorrow morning.' He gave us the tickets and he was off. Mick had chartered a plane to fly seventy-five of his friends out there. How did Ian even know I'd be there that night? Talk about being at the right place at the right time!

At the airport the next morning, I was with Fuzz and Doris was with Chaka. Mick's parents Joe and Eva Jagger were there, as were Paul McCartney and Linda, Ringo Starr and his wife Maureen, the French film director Roger Vadim, the photographer Lord Patrick Litchfield, Marshall Chess of Chess Records, Eric Clapton and Alice Ormsby-Gore, Ronnies Wood and Lane, plus Ian McLagan, Stephen Stills, Nicky Hopkins, Jimmy Miller and Glyn Johns. Quite the guestlist.

The majority of us didn't actually see the ceremony. There were reporters everywhere and it was a chaotic day. Apparently Bianca hadn't expected to have to sign a prenuptial agreement and she was also taken aback by Mick's bank balance, which was far smaller than she'd expected after he'd had to deal with a huge tax bill. Eventually there was a wedding, however and everyone was styling at the reception. Mick took me out onto the dance floor with him to get the party going, at which point Fuzz got jealous and butted in. It was the first and last time I actually saw him dance. As we boarded the bus back to the airport, Mick gave me a big hug and a kiss. I wouldn't see him again until the Miss You tour in 1978.

By now Fuzz had a big following among the West Indian and African musicians in London. We should have installed a revolving door, so many people were turning up all the time. Still, soon it would be time to move on. Adrian was back from filming in Yugoslavia and needed his space, so Fuzz rented a flat around the corner on the King's Road and asked me to move in with him. I knew I was letting my heart rule my head, moving in with a musician. Fuzz was more used to communal living, so when we set up house together, I had to get used to his friends constantly dropping in unannounced and then outstaying their welcome.

One of them was Maureen Gray and it was clear she didn't get that Fuzz and I were now an item. She was very demanding, outspoken and confident, claiming to know about everything and everybody and she refused to identify with her black roots and culture. In fact, she pretended to be white and had an accent more British than the British, which is where we clashed. I wasn't a social butterfly; I was actually quite shy and boring. She'd come to London to find fame and had fallen in love with Stevie Winwood and since he'd dropped her she was always on the look-out for another British rock star. She definitely felt the need to compete with me, which just wasn't in my personality. Don't get me wrong – I actually liked her. She'd been a teenage pop idol in Philadelphia, with some great Philly sound teen hits. She was very talented and pretty, with dimples to die for. She sang and played guitar and wrote songs, which made me slightly envious, but I just felt she was wasting her time living off the success and fame of others. I put my foot down. She'd have to find somebody else to hustle.

I've always loved my privacy. I didn't know these people and some of them I didn't want to know. I was eager to get my own career back on track. I didn't play an instrument but Fuzz wrote songs all the time and we definitely had a nice vibe together. I wanted us to collaborate but we both had a lot of work to do if we were going to join forces. We needed to be alone to work out how.

Surrounded by my peers at Mick's wedding in St Tropez, I made a decision. I had to stop having doubts about my musical direction and commit totally to making a great record with Fuzz. With Mick, I'd hum melodies and lyrics and he would put chords to them and produce the music. Andrew presented me with songs from the various Immediate writers or else we recorded covers and he produced everything. Barry simply wrote and I sang. Like I said, he was a genius. He just pulled songs out of the air.

I simply assumed that Fuzz knew what he was doing. He knew who he wanted to work with, he was a great bass and guitar player and I liked all the songs he played me. We recorded some acoustic demos with just the two of us, including a Wendell Richardson song I also liked called 'Live and Love' and he played them to his songwriter-lawyer friend Tony Demetriades, who was now in artist management. Tony wanted to play them to some connections of his and I was encouraged by his interest.

But the hangers-on and groupie traffic at the flat was getting totally out of hand. If we were going to be together, a proper home for my children would have to be part of the plan. We decided to look for a house outside of London, somewhere in the country and we convinced ourselves that buying would be more economical than paying rent. We were a proper couple, so we needed a proper home. Our future looked bright, so surely it made sense to get a mortgage. Didn't it?

37

1971 (Cotswolds)

Hoplands

Fuzz and I were taking an enormous chance on one another. We were both excited about making music together and felt certain we could get support for our project, but we refused to consider the problems. He was making good money with two of the biggest bands in the US, but he knew nothing about being a part of a family and anybody in a serious relationship with me had to take on my children as well. I had three UK hits under my belt, but I needed further success to create some security. I had a lot more at stake than him and my dual needs to be a good mother and still maintain my career had become an obsession. I had convinced myself that I could make this record with Fuzz – but of course neither of us knew what the future held.

Tony Demetriades introduced Fuzz to an estate agent in Mayfair and they set up some appointments for us to view houses before Fuzz went back to the States on tour. One Saturday morning we set out to look at three houses, two of them in Berkshire. We thought that if we had the money for a mortgage we could live wherever we wanted to. This was our first mistake.

Of course, we knew that racism existed in major cities in the UK, even if it wasn't in your face. Popular culture might have embraced the music, food and fashions of black people, who were slowly beginning to be seen on TV and to hold prominent positions in society and mixed relationships were more common among young people, but beneath the surface racism was simmering. Police would stop and search young black men. There was fear of the National Front. Blacks and Asians were called 'wogs'. There was graffiti: 'Keep Britain White' and 'Niggers Go Home'. There were campaigns against immigration everywhere and most blacks lived in the poorest areas, segregated from the rest of society.

It was against this backdrop that we decided it was a good idea to find a nice village and move to the countryside. We didn't even consider that the colour of our skin would make us unwelcome. So, when we rang the doorbell of the first house we decided to view, the owners were visibly shocked to see this young black couple on their doorstep. Fuzz was decked out in his bowler hat and Hendrix hippie-style vest and I was dressed in my best funky look, with Afro hair. It was clear that I was no longer the cute little pop-soul singer that people might have known from TV.

The owner was very curt and rushed us through the viewing. It was obvious that they didn't want to sell their house to us and this jerked us back to reality. We might be accepted in the world of music, but here in the real world we were not welcome. Always in the past when looking for properties I had a white husband and white friends. Of course, there had been the politics of mixed couples, but mostly my children and I had been accepted.

The reception at the next house was even worse. The owner refused to show us the house and asked us to leave. Evidently, we were not welcome in Berkshire.

Our next viewing was in the Cotswolds near Oxford, in Milton-Under-Wychwood, a honey-coloured limestone house built close to the road, with 10 acres of land including grazing fields, a dilapidated tennis court and a huge back garden.

It had a warm family feeling to it and was a funky-looking house – not too flash, with a bit of history attached. Apparently two African missionaries had lived in it. An iron staircase at the far end had linked the upper and lower parts of the house and the two old ladies would go upstairs at night with candlelit lanterns and nightcaps on. Since then, a newish L-shaped extension had been added.

It was called Hoplands, because in the eighteenth century they grew hops there for beer (there was a 'Malt House' across the street). There were only some 100 households in the village and a population of maybe 750. It was about two hours' drive from London. We weren't put off by this, though we should have been.

Our bid of £18,000 was accepted and we were buying it fully furnished, which made moving less stressful. It seemed very welcoming, though it required a lot of upkeep. Apparently I'd learned nothing from Horsley House, though when you're young you think you're invincible.

Tony Demetriades sorted out the mortgage and I moved into Hoplands with Kevin and Debbie. My brother Kenny was flying over to help me settle in. He was a singer, as were all of my siblings – he had grown up singing in vocal groups with my brother Larry – and he was excited about being close to the English music scene. He would go to London with Fuzz and they always came back with good herbs. Kenny was four years younger than me, very hip and cool and full of the old-folk sayings from our Texas family.

Meanwhile, I registered Kevin and Debbie in the local primary. They were happy to be living with me again, but they were sad to leave West Drayton. Doris and Jock were worried about them adjusting but, contrary to our fears, they settled in quickly. Except for Marianne, I was the only woman my age with children, but I was uncomfortable in the wild and free communal atmosphere everyone seemed to enjoy and my kids grounded me.

I spent my days around this time cleaning, cooking, shopping and trying to be a normal mother. Milton was a small village and there wasn't much going on, that's for sure. There was a Gothic revival church, a pub, the Red Horse, the school and a little shop just down the road called Carpenters and very little else. I also loved shopping in Burford, with its medieval bridge, picturesque stone houses and lovely Tudor and Georgian fronts. 'Quaint' doesn't begin to cover it.

Our neighbours Mike and Monica were very helpful and we had a good relationship, but unlike the children I didn't connect with other grown-ups very easily and never really got to know anyone closely. We stuck out like a sore thumb and it made me very uncomfortable how people would stare rudely at us, especially in the grocery store. It was very optimistic to think that I could just fit in and adjust to living here. My utopian ideals would again become my downfall.

Fuzz was away a lot of the time with Manassas and he'd visit for a week or two at a time. I was always happy when he had time off and we went to local antique shops together. A black pop singer and a black rock musician living in the Cotswolds – I guess you could say we were something of a curiosity.

It bothered me that Fuzz never talked about his times on the road, which of course made me suspicious. I think if I'd simply been a regular wife or girlfriend I'd have dealt with this all better, but I was an artist myself and music was meant to be the thing that connected us. Yet he never talked with me about our work together, even though this was why I'd decided to be with him! Whenever he called from the road, he always cut our conversations short and that was frustrating. He hated confrontation and when he was home and we argued he'd drive off in the car and disappear, which just frustrated me more. The kids knew that I wasn't happy and I wasn't easy to live with. The arguments and tantrums would be awful. Like my mother before me, I would curse out my man. I'd throw and break things and make everybody miserable. The children would go to their rooms just to stay out of the line of fire. I was angry with Fuzz but I was also ashamed of myself.

Back in those days nobody in a serious relationship used condoms all the time, so I don't know why I was surprised when

I missed my period. The pill had never agreed with me and thanks to an infection I had recently had my coil taken out. I had become pregnant just before Jim and I broke up and had a termination. I had promised myself then that I wouldn't have another. However, Fuzz really wanted us to have a baby. I convinced myself that another child would bring more joy into my life and that we would be happy. We could get a proper nanny and then focus on making the album.

I had started to realise that we had a big problem, however. Fuzz was so used to being a loner. He felt he was doing his best, but he had never been in a proper committed relationship and I was a very strong character. Here he was touring to bring home the bacon and here I was being – in his eyes – overly demanding. Jim had loved doing things with the kids, but with Fuzz it was different. He didn't really connect with them.

Of course, having a baby was a stupid thing for us to be doing, but it was too late for that now. I wanted to collaborate with him and I thought being with him would help me open up and be more creative. I thought having his child might bring us closer, yet he still wasn't letting me in. He liked the idea of having P.P. Arnold as his woman, yet neither of us knew how to communicate with the other. Nevertheless, I would just have to deal with it. Given his success in the US, he wound up bankrolling the new house and our lifestyle, which I felt a bit guilty about. I was accustomed to being the sole earner and I didn't like giving up my own power, but I wasn't even doing sessions right now. Wasn't I just being jealous and selfish? I needed to stop thinking about myself and focus on my kids and the child in my belly. In any case, there was nothing I could do until after our baby was born.

Jim was moving on with his life after our split and I had done the same. He was a really nice guy and had been a real dad to my children and to be honest I often missed him. He might not have been a great manager, but with his friend Bill Kelsey he had started building the powerful PA systems that replaced the 200-watt PAs everyone used before this. Kelsey Morris Trans Atlantic Sounds were supplying the sound systems for the artists of the British invasion, including Eric Clapton, ELP and Pink Floyd and organising the equipment's transport. And they were doing very well. Jim was suddenly well on the way to becoming the young millionaire he always dreamed he would be.

However, Jim's illicit activities soon caught up with him and he was subject to a huge CIA drugs bust. The police came calling and questioned me as to his whereabouts. Apparently those container trucks touring the States full of speakers and amplifiers were also full of hashish, which was much more expensive in America. They'd fill the speakers in Europe and air-freight them across the Atlantic, putting bricks in them when they brought them back so the weight discrepancy didn't appear on the waybills. And they were raking it in!

Jim's partner-in-crime was a guy named Howard Marks, who already had quite a reputation as a drug smuggler. But it seemed Jim was the mastermind, with Swiss bank accounts and everything. Everybody was busted except for him and he became a fugitive and didn't return to the UK for many years. He never saw his parents again, either, which broke their hearts. I was as shocked as anyone, but he had always had a very secretive side. I often dreamed that I would see him again.

The baby was due in November and I decided I wanted to be in LA for the birth, where I'd have my entire family around me. Fuzz would be recording nearby with Manassas and if we arrived in time for the summer holiday, Kevin and Debbie could attend an American school for half a semester and return to Milton for the second half. There'd be disruption, but then we'd carry on as before. I put my career on hold and spent the next three months living life as a regular mother. I had myself checked out physically, drank a small daily bottle of Guinness, for the iron, and got into nutrition and reading. I was moving towards a more spiritual state of mind.

38

1972 (LA and Cotswolds)

Kodzo

The music scene in LA was on fire when we arrived. It was a thrill just to be able to turn on the radio and hear the latest from some of the greatest contemporary artists in the world: Bill Withers, Donny Hathaway, Elton John, Roberta Flack, Isaac Hayes – all incredible singer-songwriters. In addition, the early '70s FM rock scene was hitting its apogee: the Eagles had a crossover hit with 'Take It Easy', while CSNY were all enjoying solo chart success – Neil Young with 'Old Man', Graham Nash and David Crosby with 'Immigration Man' and Manassas with 'It Doesn't Matter'. I was happy for Fuzz. And happy too that my pregnancy was coming to an end.

Fuzz had rented an apartment at the Chateau Marmont and paid $7,000 cash for a brand-new BMW Bavaria. A Mexican woman named Ana Maria was offering a short rental in Studio City, which suited us perfectly. It was on Irvine Avenue, on the other side of Laurel Canyon and close to the Hollywood Freeway, which was good for Inglewood, where my parents now lived. The kids would be attending Colfax Elementary, practically around the corner. The house had a swimming pool and a puppy named Pinchita, or Pinchy – a very anxious little spaniel kept chained up by the garage. The first thing that we did was unchain her. She was frightened of everybody and Debbie was the only person she let get close.

Not many black families lived in the San Fernando Valley then, so once again we were integrating neighbourhoods. The children made new friends without problems and they all spent a lot of time in our pool, scaring the life out of me by diving in from the roof of the garage. They were both very athletic and had no fear, but I did and I insisted they only jump in from the side of the pool.

Shortly after we arrived, my grandfather Theodra Cole passed away. It was the end of an era and I was so glad that I was able to say goodbye. Poppa Thea was born at the beginning of the century and his life marked the progress that my family had made together, moving away from the racist south. He had been a wild, whiskey-loving, womanising blues lover with no time for Christianity. He'd had very little education and nor had my grandmother, who'd stood by him all those years despite his curious ways. She was the love of his life and he respected and trusted her even when he strayed. They had worked hard and saved and acquired LA real estate, but her life would never be the same.

I had loved him and though I didn't understand many things about him, I felt that he had loved me, too. I knew he didn't understand my choice to move so far away. Had he been insulted when I returned with a white English husband, after all he'd endured in the Jim Crow south? My determination to make my family proud never left me, but every time I came home and saw my friends and family face to face with racist America, I knew I didn't want to live like this.

And, of course, when I look back, I realise I was probably also running away from all those beatings, from the abuse my mother suffered, from David's abuse and from the shame I'd put everyone through. I had come back to be closer to my family while I had my baby, but I had chosen to stay in the Valley, where very few black families then lived. Patricia Ann Cole was now P.P. Arnold, living in England in an integrated, cosmopolitan society. Would I be accepted in my new persona?

It was always an occasion when family and friends came out to visit us in Studio City. The older generation couldn't understand why I didn't just live where black folks lived and I tried to explain that with Fuzz recording we had to be close to Hollywood and the music scene. They shook their heads and didn't visit very often. Hollywood was too far for them to travel, they said. This was also the reason they gave for not visiting me in England, although to be honest I could understand them not caring to fly for ten hours.

It was nine years since I'd last given birth and all I could remember was the pain. This time I wanted a natural birth, so Fuzz and I would take Lamaze classes together and Elaine came with me when Fuzz wasn't able to. By the time school started, I was heavily pregnant and I spent most of my days shopping for clothes and furniture and preparing for the birth. This time, I was excited about the forthcoming delivery.

Lunch with Andre and Maxayn Lewis and her delicious, powerful chocolate mousse started my labour the evening of 5 November. I was hoping that Kodzo wouldn't be born on the Ike Turner birthday date.

By the time I was wheeled into Culver's Brotman Memorial Hospital on 6 November 1972, Calvin 'Kodzo' Samuel was well on his way. And after just four hours in labour and a totally natural birth, our beautiful baby boy came into the world.

Fuzz was totally unprepared for my labour. We'd learned all the rhythm and panting at the Lamaze classes, but he nearly passed out when my boy slid out without help of clamps. The colours of the umbilical cord attaching him to my womb were amazing. It was truly a wonderful thing and I thanked God for his delivery. Fuzz's mind was blown and he disappeared for a while after the birth. He needed to finish that joint – something of an irony, as his pregnant partner had brought his son into the world drug-free.

Fuzz had asked our Ghanaian percussionist friend Rocky Dzidzornu about African names and Rocky had sent us a list for girls and a list for boys. In Ghana, your name depends on the day of the week you were born and a Monday boy-child is called Kodzo, so there it was.

Paulette Parker was an ex of my friend Jimmy Thomas and I first met her in 1968 when she was an Ikette, performing with Ike and Tina for their second Stones tour. Now she was in a soul/funk group called Maxayn with her husband, keyboard player

Andre Lewis, guitarist Marlo Henderson and drummer Emry Thomas. Paulette herself was a decent pianist and – rumour had it – a first-class French horn player. Marlo I first met in London when he was there with the Buddy Miles band. He had played with Stevie Wonder in the first incarnation of Wonderlove. Andre specialised in electronic sounds and he had played with Buddy too, as well as Frank Zappa. I liked their progressive funk/soul approach and the idea of a line-up with a female leader was similar to what Fuzz and I wanted to do.

Now that I was no longer pregnant, they were interested in recording a couple of tracks with Fuzz and me. In retrospect, the concept was black ABBA, with Paulette and I fronting a band of great musicians and songwriters. I wasn't so sure. They were all very talented musicians for sure, but only Marlo had written any songs of note – including two for Minnie Riperton. Even so, I was excited about going in the studio and I thought that there was no harm in checking out the possibility. At this stage, I had nothing to lose.

I should have trusted my gut. It was a classic case of 'Hot-Lick Syndrome'. Instead of simply laying down some good commercial tracks, everyone was hell-bent on proving how hip they were. It became an ego jam session. Neither Fuzz nor I were accustomed to this and we didn't get along well with hard, egotistical characters. Andre didn't think much of Fuzz's bass playing and Paulette was riffing all over me.

Most of the R&B female singers in America at that time were into a new funk style of singing. I'd spent the last eight years developing my natural old-school gospel/soul style in the UK, so

I already had a unique sound of my own and I was closer to the European pop sound that they saw in ABBA.

In the music business, sometimes you have to be able to fight your way into the limelight and once again, it became clear that my shyness was proving to be an unhelpful character trait. This did not bode well for our forthcoming project together.

Meanwhile, Tony Demetriades had played our acoustic demos to his friend Mickey Shapiro, a top Hollywood lawyer. Mickey was impressed and so were EMI. They wanted to sign us through Back-A-Yard, the production company that Tony had advised Fuzz to form and to give us an advance to start recording.

The timing was perfect. We were about to return to England. Again!

Kodzo had certainly brought Fuzz and I closer. When Manassas were recording their *Down the Road* album at the Record Plant in Hollywood, Stephen had liked a blues piece that Fuzz had written and it had turned into 'Rolling My Stone'. I sang backing vocals on it as well as on the album's title track. Soon Fuzz would be touring the album with Manassas and he would follow us to England once the tour was over.

It was strange to be back in the middle of the English countryside again and I would have to introduce the three-month-old Kodzo to his new surroundings. I remember the woman who ran the little local shop exclaimed, 'He's such a cute little picaninny!' when she saw him. My blood boiled. That word again! So much for progress. Integrating into white society still wasn't going to be easy. I told the woman that they don't call us that any more and she apologised. I was probably the first black person that she'd known. (Ironically, her daughter later married an African and I became the only person in the village that she could open up and talk to about it.)

I settled in with my young family once again and waited for Fuzz to return, praying everything would come together with EMI and we could start recording. Aside from a few sessions and the odd jingle, my solo career had become landlocked.

One band making a lot of noise in 1973 were Rufus. Their original singer Paulette McWilliams was replaced by her friend Chaka Khan and by the time of their second album, *Rags to Rufus*, they had scored their first Grammy win. Chaka Khan became the new Queen of Funk. Alongside Maxayn, Mother's Finest, Earth, Wind & Fire and Stevie Wonder, Rufus were the driving inspiration for the music that we wanted to create. It was a tall order for two people who'd never done anything together before.

I would wake early and fix breakfast for the kids, then do my chores as the stereo blasted out the latest progressive sounds from these amazing artists. They were spiritual, socially aware, tight funk rock. I would sit in my living room nursing my baby, looking out on my garden and the fields full of horses and cows, listening to all of these young, gifted black artists, scorching the grey English earth with their revolutionary messages. To keep me peaceful and thoughtful on the long rainy afternoons, I'd put on Miles Davis's *Sketches of Spain* or *In a Silent Way*. My education had been cut short by motherhood at fifteen, but I still had a thirsty, academic mind. And when I put Kodzo down for his nap, I would turn to my books for comfort and enlightenment. It was a peaceful time for me – but it wouldn't last long.

39

1974 (London)

The EMI Recordings

In 1973, the Manassas tour ended and Fuzz came home. At the EMI offices in London, we met Roy Featherstone, then head of A&R and quickly signed. Our advance was £10,000; it sounded like a lot of money at the time considering we'd only played them a couple of demos, but it was relatively small in comparison to some of the deals being done at the time. However, it was my first ever advance. I felt happy and validated. I like to think that Fuzz playing with CSNY as well any 'P.P. Arnold' brand credibility had helped to secure the deal, but in the end, it's down to who you know. You're in luck if you have a manager or lawyer or who's already in with the label. And we were in luck. Now we just had to deliver.

We called our band Axis in tribute to Jimi Hendrix. I was putting all my faith in Fuzz's production ideas – though, truth be told, I really had no proof of his abilities yet. For the musicians, we assembled our friend Wendell on guitar, plus Robert Bailey from Osibisa on keyboards, drummer Alan White (who was managed by Tony) and percussionist Gaspar Lawal. Fuzz would play bass and I would sing. The record was going to be built around songs Fuzz and I had written and then we'd put a touring band together. Tony had booked us in at Advision Studios and Eddie Offord would engineer.

It soon became clear, however, that life was in danger of unravelling ass backwards. In reality, Fuzz and I had spent little time getting to know one another or creating any emotional attachment before moving to the country. Alongside this, Fuzz had mostly been on the road and was yet to form any sort of serious bond with my kids. And, of course, we'd been too blind to notice we'd established a professional relationship before any sort of artistic or creative one.

Fuzz was a wild, untamed young man with no strong ties and I knew nothing about the hippie communal culture that he'd grown up in. Sure, I smoked marijuana, but I was still more inhibited than many of my peers and I hadn't thought about any of this before jumping into a life with him. Having Kodzo in LA was such a beautiful experience that I'd simply forgotten about the isolation that I'd felt before. Newfound contentment has a way of shielding you from the past.

Nevertheless, we were moving forward, so I had to get my shit together. Fuzz had a nervous disposition and, as I was just discovering, a passive-aggressive streak. He was even more introverted than me but he hid it by being comical, nonsensical and eccentric. Sometimes he'd just leave without saying anything and would drive around for hours visiting friends such as Stevie Winwood who lived not far away. This made me jealous: I'd have loved to sing or record with Stevie. On other occasions, Fuzz wouldn't even say where he'd been.

As a musician, he was self-taught and very talented, but communicating with him musically was a nightmare. Like me, he didn't read music, although this was true of most musicians I knew. I often have good musical ideas but as I didn't play an instrument I had little confidence in my writing. I hadn't written any songs since my *First Lady* album and I was hoping that working with him would help me to open up. I was good at getting my ideas across verbally, but he would then incorporate them in a different way without crediting me. Rather than argue, I decided just to focus on the songs accepted by EMI. They were good ideas; they just needed to be developed. Another difference was that there was always an arranger on hand at Immediate or when I worked with Barry. Fuzz had no experience as an arranger and it became clear that we should have bought one in. All the recordings I had done in the past had been built around me, whereas now I was just letting him get on with it. I had to trust him; I had no other choice. Maybe once we got the first few tracks down, things would fall into place, I thought.

When we began recording, the musicians we'd assembled didn't get any musical direction from Fuzz. There were no rehearsals and the songs were all being worked out in the studio. All the experimental ideas seemed horribly underdeveloped. Sometimes songs were recorded in the wrong key for me and I sounded terrible. Too often, the direction certain ideas were being taken was a surprise to me and I never had enough time to find the right style to sing them in. Time was of the essence, too; we had a limited production budget and were on the clock. I tried to reason with Fuzz but he wouldn't listen.

A lot of marijuana was being smoked and everybody thought – surprise, surprise! – that everything sounded great. It didn't. We recorded five tracks at Advision, but they were all just long self-indulgent jams. The vocals were a mess. The band overpowered the melodies and the hooks were boring and repetitive. I thought that Fuzz was more concerned with how the backing sounded than the vocals, but I didn't want to make a scene. I was the only woman in the studio and I had no production skills. Had I been the bitch they all believed I was, I might have been able to salvage something. The intimacy of the original demos was long lost and Fuzz was stubbornly, irresponsibly taking us down the wrong road.

The legendary blues producer Mike Vernon owned a studio near us, in Chipping Norton and I had sung backing vocals for him on the brilliant title track of Freddie King's album *The Burglar*, alongside another American singer, Misty Browning. Mike's studio was great and Fuzz decided to do the next sessions there, as it was less expensive and much closer to home. Any savings we may have made, however, were soon swallowed up by a litany of supporting musicians that Fuzz flew in from all around the world.

Kevin and Debbie and some other Milton children sang on one nice track, 'Hello Sunshine'. They all enjoyed their day in the studio but sadly these sessions were no better organised than before and the other songs just weren't working. The words I was singing might have meant something to Fuzz, but I just couldn't find my way in. They had no real melodic structure and there was no beauty in the arrangements. The wrong keys forced strained vocals and the painful ad libs sounded excruciating. I complained, but it made no difference. I sounded like shit. A song called 'Soulful' wasn't even in the same postal district as soul. We were totally lost in his own one-man Hot-Lick Syndrome. I couldn't recognise the P.P. Arnold who had sung on those beautiful '60s productions.

Everyone else was having a good time, but all the marijuana was having the opposite effect on my brain. I was smiling and laughing on the outside, but I was dying inside. I had given up my power and had no idea how to turn things around.

Things got worse when Fuzz spent a lot of time at the Manor, the huge house in Shipton-on-Cherwell owned by Richard Branson, which he used as a residential recording studio for Virgin artists. The guys often went there to hang out, but I only went on a couple of occasions. It was an all-male club house vibe and I desperately wanted Fuzz working on material with me at home. I hated being left behind all the time.

The mixed tracks were handed in to EMI and we were called in for a meeting with Roy Featherstone. Tony Demetriades should have been with us; I needed someone to speak on my behalf. Fuzz was a great musician, but he wasn't a producer and he definitely wasn't a suitable advocate. I was nervous as hell and it turns out I was right to be. Featherstone was blunt and to the point. He said they sounded nothing like the original demos, which was true and that he had no idea how they could market them. I was not at all prepared for what came next. EMI wanted to market me as a punk artist and record a Rolling Stones song called 'Star Fucker' – in my mind one of the lowest points of the Stones' illustrious recording career. I was totally insulted. I told Roy what he could do with 'Star Fucker' and Fuzz and I walked out. I couldn't quite get my head around it. Was that his sarcastic way of dropping us? What made him think that a young black woman would sing such vulgar, insulting lyrics? Was he insinuating that I was a groupie? I was mad as hell!

We now had no management, no agent and now no record company. After paying costs and with no money coming in, we were now in a perilous position.

It was a stressful time. I realised I'd made a mistake in placing Fuzz on this pedestal. In simple terms, his work on the tracks wasn't fit for purpose and in music one of the hardest things to admit is when your absolute best wasn't good enough. You can't turn mutton into lamb. You have to be honest. I'd fallen in love with a talented musician, but I didn't yet have the faculty to make good professional decisions for myself. I had allowed my P.P. Arnold persona to become lost in the Axis band concept.

If the music we'd made had been on fire, it would have been accepted. Sometimes people just don't get it, I understand that, but on this occasion the honest reason was that the music was just not good enough. I was trying to do something outside the box but nobody wanted to hear that. I was a pop singer and I should have recorded material that reflected that fact. It turned out that Fuzz had been mixing tracks at the Manor with his club house pals all along. Far from being a liberated woman, I was trapped in a professional and personal relationship that would end up being my downfall. Subsumed, I had lost all sight of who I was.

It felt like a real low point, but if nothing else, I'd become used to expecting the unexpected. When you think there's nowhere else to go but up, there's always another level down. Fuzz had been meeting in Portobello Road with the deputy managing director of Virgin Records, Steve Lewis, who was delighted to find out that Fuzz's partner was his favourite female soul singer. Steve's friend Brad Misell worked in a shop where one of his customers was Stephen Fishman, a producer who also made radio commercials for Virgin, including one for an album by Tangerine Dream.

Fishman wanted to make a radio ad – 'something soulful' – for his sales recruitment company, Sales Associates and asked the Virgin boss if he could recommend anyone. Turns out he could.

The ad had a great response and Fishman formed a company called Eclectic to sign me and Fuzz. As Steve Lewis remembers it: 'He then offered to sign you to all kinds of deals, including, I think, records and publishing. He threw a lot of money around and was a bit of a groupie, frankly. I remained very wary of him, but you and Fuzz both dived in!'

It certainly seemed like the answer to my prayers, but it was the beginning of yet another downward spiral. Today, a 'how-to' manual on how to break into and sustain a career in the music business is just a click or two away, but in the '60s and '70s, artists held to the belief that raw talent alone was enough for them to be successful. Without any driving ambition, I had been lucky enough to be in the right place at the right time, landing in the hands of some of the most successful movers and shakers in the British music industry. What I really should have realised by then was that it was always about who you knew and who they knew. Fishman had money, but he was no mover and shaker. He wasn't going to open any doors for me. If anything, he was using me to open doors for himself.

Fuzz jumped in like white on rice, but my loyalty to him was still holding me back. I was a mother with lots of responsibilities, so I let Fuzz be the one to hang out with Stephen. Fishman had financial credentials and that's what we needed. He would be our manager and the executive producer for the new Axis session. We felt we'd learned from the earlier sessions and that we could turn things around with the right support system. We knew we needed better recordings and optimistically imagined he could steer the project to a more successful conclusion. Perhaps if Steve Lewis had been involved, things might have been different.

We were planning to record in LA and Fuzz and I now flew back over. His quirky and wild island-man personality was starting to wear thin on me, but it humoured people that didn't know him quite so well. From his commune days, Fuzz knew Malcolm Cecil of electronic duo Tonto's Expanding Head Band. 'Tonto' itself was a pioneering multi-timbral analog synthesiser, the first of its kind and Malcolm had worked with Stevie Wonder on several albums, winning awards as producer-engineers and programmers.

Visiting Malcolm at Malibu, where Tonto was set up, Fuzz discovered that Bob Dylan was moving out of a ranch house just down the street, high on the hill on Birdview Drive in Point Dume, with views of the ocean. It was a sprawling four-bedroomed place, painted yellow, modern and funky. It was available for rent and was just right for us.

I thought it was a magical place and not only was it completely furnished in a durable, child-friendly way, it was only a 75-minute drive from Hollywood. We'd become used to a two-hour commute by now, so in that regard, Point Dume fit the bill. The rental price was $750 a month. We didn't know how long we'd be in LA, so we agreed a short-term lease, figuring we could always extend it.

The first indication things were about to go badly wrong was when Fishman showed up in a BMW sports car with a sixteen-year-old girlfriend. The second sign came soon after, when the visitor's visa we'd put in for my nanny, Beverley Mollyneaux, was declined. Stupidly, Fishman had told them she would be working for me, so it was turned down. Beverley's visa not coming through was the warning sign I ignored. She had become an integral part of my family and without her I knew it was going to be difficult for me.

I was torn, but the lure of the Hollywood dream and my family being close for much-needed support tipped the balance. Kevin and Debbie had only just settled back into the UK and Kevin was becoming a valued and excellent player on the local soccer team. I knew we could always return to Milton, though and I wanted to give us one more chance to get it right. Fuzz left the final decision to me. I try not to live with regret in my life, but this one still haunts me.

Here's the thing. Everybody believes they can make it in Hollywood. Wrong. Hollywood is where you go once you already have things happening. Everybody and their mother is already in Hollywood trying to make things happen. This move was the hardest thing I've ever done and the most selfish: I packed up Hoplands and broke the children's hearts. But I was still young and stupid and scared and my pride wouldn't let me admit I needed professional and spiritual help and advice. It wouldn't let me learn from my mistakes and it wouldn't let me talk honestly with my parents or my grandmother. Deep down, I secretly knew that the Axis dream was over, but I had sacrificed so much for it already.

If only I'd been able to see the writing on the wall.

PART 3
The Way Gets Harder

'You may hinder me here, but you can't up dere.'

– 'Go Down, Moses'

40

1975 (Malibu)

Nightmare in Paradise

We arrived at Birdview Drive after a long, exhausting flight and everybody's spirits lifted immediately. It was a lovely house in a stunning location and the kids warmed to it straight away. They were just excited to be so close to the sea.

In the past, Point Dume had been known as the Malibu Ghetto, though it was beginning to gentrify, with wealthy residents from the entertainment world moving in. Surrounded by exotic shrubbery and trees, the house was modest and reasonable compared with some of the mansions being built nearby.

I breathed a sigh of relief. There were stables just down the road, so Debbie was happy and she lost no time befriending the owners. She was a skilled rider by then and they let her take the ponies out for short rides.

The local elementary school was two streets away. As was often the case, we were the only black family in the neighbourhood – I hadn't even realised this would be so – and they also stood out with their English accents. But, as always, they made friends quickly, even though they were so different. They were both very beautiful-looking, so confident, smart, athletic and fun to be around and of course their parents were musicians. Bonus points!

Fuzz instantly transformed the big garage into a rehearsal space and we hired a white Mustang. People knew we were looking for players and before long we were rehearsing the nucleus of the new Axis band daily: Leon Rubenhold and Cedric Jackson on guitar; Gregory 'Slim' Lewis on keyboards; 'Bags' Costello on Hammond organ; Steve Lacy on drums. Fuzz was on bass of course – and my brother Kenny was on vocals! Others who came around would include keyboard player Michael Stanton, who'd played with Marvin Gaye, bass player Greg Brown and Michael Moore, who would later replace Steve on drums. As word got around, musicians would just turn up. There was a lot of jamming, but the sound was starting to sound tight.

Those early days in Malibu were good and it was just nice to be close to my family again. I remember everyone driving out for Mother's Day dinner, including Mama, Grandma Stel, my aunt Catherine Cole and Elaine. This was truly a wonderful thing, as some of them rarely strayed far from home. Even my father was there. To me it was just a pleasure to be able to honour them all together. Elaine remembers telling one of the musicians in no uncertain terms that he wouldn't be eating anything until the mothers were all taken care of.

Fuzz met a really cool guy named Jimmy Mayweather, who was the engineer at Clover Studios and could get us some recording time on spec. He was brought into the Axis project to engineer and co-produce with Fuzz. I was just glad there was someone else on the production side.

Jimmy also introduced us to his guitarist friend Leon Rubenhold. I liked him because he was down-to-earth, solid and drug-free. He was naturally spaced-out and astral. As Leon remembers it, the reason Fuzz was holding the band together was that people knew about his high-profile background. 'I felt like, *Okay, this guy has some connections, he'll be able to hopefully send this through the channels and get it listened to* . . .' Meanwhile, I was cooking and looking after the kids. I was a house girl, occasionally coming out and throwing on some vocals when I had a break.

After a few weeks, we noticed that Stephen Fishman was never on hand when you needed him. I naively assumed that he had amassed record-industry contacts before leaving the UK and he was checking in with them one by one. We would see him from time to time and he would give us positive feedback regarding how he was getting on. We were busy settling in and putting a band together and Stephen was busy making connections for the band. Or so we thought. Our beautiful Bechstein upright piano that Fuzz had stupidly shipped from Milton was waiting to be collected from the docks, but, for all the money Stephen had flashed back in England, he was steadfastly refusing to pay for it to be moved. Eventually we arranged for delivery ourselves. As it turned out, the container had been busted during the shipping and the piano was ruined. It was a bad omen.

We hadn't realised that Stephen had never been to Hollywood before and that he knew nothing about the inner workings of the music industry there. He might have been able to make moves in London, but Hollywood was a whole different ball game. But here he was in Hollywood flashing his money around under the impression that Fuzzy Samuel and P.P. Arnold were his red-hot meal tickets. Fuzzy might have been a part of the crowd, but, let's be brutally honest here, he was a sideman to the main event, and P.P. Arnold was not box office on the West Coast.

Everyone with any influence soon tired of his pushy salesman persona, while the more opportunistic Hollywood vultures sensed an easy prey. One morning, he showed up in a terrible condition and unable to sit down. An all-night session with the liggers he was hanging out with had ended with him being subjected to painful and abusive acts. Hollywood had proven too much for him. It had humiliated him and beaten him into submission. Defeated, he made a quick exit back to London and we were left in the shit.

I was determined not to panic. I spent a lot of time walking down to the beach with Kodzo on my shoulders and on rare occasions Fuzz would join us. We saw the grey whales on their annual migration from Alaska to Baja and I would also run, two miles south-east to Paradise Cove or north to Zuma Beach. This was exercise for my sanity and my physical wellbeing.

So many people came to the house every day that I was starting to freak out. I was constantly cleaning up after everyone. Musicians brought their girlfriends and it seemed everybody except me was having a great time. What were they all doing here? I didn't like them being around the kids.

One day, a tall, slim, good-looking white guy appeared. His name was Jack Vos and Fuzz had met him on tour, I think in

Baltimore and approached him for investment to keep us afloat. As usual I had no idea who he was or what the actual agreement was, but we were running out of money. As Leon Rubenhold said to me recently: 'It was kind of like this mysterious arcane thing going on all the time, that you really didn't know what was happening. You thought, *Is this guy the manager? What's that all about?* Those kinds of things: you never knew what was happening. There was always some kind of rumour that Jack Vos was going to put some Carnegie Mellon money into the band.' The Mellons and the Carnegies were real old money types from back East, with interests in banking and the steel industry and Andrew Carnegie had been Booker T. Washington's benefactor, helping create the National Negro Business League in the 1900s. If Jack was the heir to all these fortunes, I sure wished he would just show his hand!

One afternoon my dear friend Gered Mankowitz came to visit with his wife Julia. He remembers an aggressively unfriendly atmosphere: 'The music was incredibly funky, but Fuzz and the band were not remotely interested in being pleasant, polite or nice. Fuzz was certainly not welcoming. I remember the whole vibe being uncomfortable. Julia and I felt extremely unwelcome and very conscious of your discomfort at what was going down. You hadn't bought into all that heavy macho energy and you were not happy.'

A solicitor friend of Fuzz's named Joel Turtle got us some dates up north in Berkeley, two at the Long Branch and another two at the Keystone. Both played to full houses and great reviews, but they were the only gigs the band ever performed.

We also started laying down tracks at Clover Studios. This was why we'd made sacrifices and uprooted our family, to record material and – finally – land that elusive deal. But our home was fast becoming one big party spot and that wasn't part of the plan.

As I felt that I had been totally disregarded in the EMI recordings, this project was hugely important to me. The EMI tracks had turned into laborious long jams and I'd been so unhappy about how I sounded. Having a great co-producer like Jimmy made a big difference and even the legendary Steve Cropper – who was one of the partners in Clover Studios – gifted us with some contributions. We cut nine tracks over a period of about six months in Hollywood and I felt that we were finally on point with what we were doing. We had better songs, proper arrangements and amazing musicians. For all my other worries, it was starting to happen.

I'm amazed when I hear those tracks back. Sadly the masters were burned up in a fire at Clover Studios, or so I've been told, so I only have rough mixes.

After the highs of the recording, I was brought back down to earth again. Fuzz had thought that CSNY's co-manager Elliot Roberts, given his close links with that group, might be interested – but we had no such luck. As for me, I had no contacts in the industry in LA. The tracks were shopped around, but we were unable to get a bite. Not one single crumb of interest. Personally, I thought the problem was that we were presenting the project as a band, with all the economic demands that implied. The band concept suggested a heavy load and anyone interested in just Fuzz and I together would be put off. Coupled with that, our lack of organisation erred on the shambolic. It was obvious to everyone.

We had also not prioritised our family responsibilities. There were too many pressures to cope with and I started having panic attacks. Things were going downhill. We kept rehearsing, but neither of us had the business connections we needed.

Once again, we had overstretched ourselves. There was no collateral in hopes and dreams and we could no longer afford to pay the rent. It was yet another upheaval, another home, another heartbreak for my children.

When would I learn?

41

1976 (Malibu and the Valley) From Moorpark to Bluebell

My children were crushed. They were not happy about leaving another school and Debbie especially was having difficulties. They knew that we didn't have the money to stay, but we also didn't have the money to return to England. And, anyway, we were behind on our mortgage payments there. We were running out of options as to where to turn next. To make matters worse, Fuzz and I were arguing constantly and the atmosphere was horrible.

After a couple of weeks at Elaine's, friends and cheap motels, Fuzz found us a two-bedroomed apartment in Studio City on Moorpark Avenue, not far from Irvine Avenue. It was far from ideal, but we took it. Colfax Elementary was close by, so the kids already had friends in the neighbourhood. Kevin was now too old for Colfax, though, and I had to register him at Walter Reed junior high.

It was a stressful time and, subconsciously, I think I've chosen to suppress a lot of those memories. Marlo and Michael from the band lived close by, so Fuzz was hanging out with them. I preferred this to lots of guys smoking weed around the kids, though as usual I wasn't sure what else he was up to. He always had good smoke and grass certainly helped calm my nerves in those difficult months. This wasn't a big house, so when the kids were home we smoked on the balcony or in our bedroom. It's not something I'm proud of.

By summer 1976, we had found a house a bit further into the Valley, in Bluebell Avenue – a very modest suburban white middle-class neighbourhood, tree-lined with manicured front lawns. The house was a sprawling bungalow, with front and back yards. It didn't look so big, but it opened up inside, with a spacious living room, a nice-sized kitchen/dining area and a door into an L-shaped garage which was perfect for a music room that wouldn't infringe on family space. Off the living room was a hallway with three smallish bedrooms and a bathroom, then a master bedroom with en-suite bathroom at the end of the hall. Everybody was happy to have some space after living in the apartment on Moorpark, but three big moves in fifteen months was crazy. The worries and stresses had taken their toll and our musical hopes seemed dashed. Fuzz and I were sleeping in the same bed, but that was it.

Like everybody else, my friend Doris Troy had arrived in Hollywood looking for fame and fortune. I was overjoyed to get a call from her. None of us realised you only did well here if you had a strong support system and already had something going on. Unlike me, however, Doris knew how to hustle and network. She also rented a house in the Valley and would pass by and pick me up. When she realised what a state I was in, the first thing she said was, 'Baby, you've got to fluff up. Being depressed is not going to get you anywhere.' She made it sound so easy.

She took me to the studio where she'd recorded her biggest hit, 'Just One Look', for which she was still chasing royalties nearly fifteen years later. Another time we went to see her good friend Nina Simone. Just being in the room with these two legends and listening to their tales of rip-offs going back to the '50s made my obstacles sound petty.

Hanging out with Doris from time to time did lift my spirits, even though she had her own problems as she tried to break into the in-crowd. Singers here were a dime a dozen and you didn't get into the session scene without serious connections. An artist from the UK might request you, but otherwise it was all sewn up.

At this time, Fuzz professed not to believe in anything except music. But, as we were no longer creating any music together, that didn't really give us much of a shared spiritual platform and we argued a lot about his non-belief in God. I had been disillusioned by religious institutions after all the hypocrisy when I became pregnant, but I never lost my faith in prayer. We might have made it over the hump if we'd been able to come together on some level: praying together, planning together, laughing together, making love together. I even asked Doris if she could help. She was a good mediator, but Fuzz was better at being stubborn, so things just continued to get worse. Whatever common ground we once shared was crumbling beneath our feet.

Around this time I heard that Stevie Wonder was looking for a singer and through Hank Redd, his saxophone player, I got an audition. It did not go well. My confidence had been shot to pieces. There were always young female singers in Hollywood who hadn't been through everything I'd been through – innocent, excited, enthusiastic and eager to learn. My ten-year fairy tale had turned into a nightmare and I didn't have the energy to battle for a backing vocalist gig, even with Stevie. I had lost the connection with my roots and my fears about being accepted were turning people off. I felt washed up and scared. I was only thirty.

If the '60s had been a decade of peace, love and revolutionary change, the '70s were the comedown: corrupt political leadership, terrible economic problems, disenchantment and asinine fads. Every woman I knew in a relationship was having problems. Women were no longer prepared to stay in unhappy relationships or abusive marriages, not even for the children. Although I had escaped my abuse in the '60s, for many of us, women's liberation actually took place in the '70s. Fuzz and I had spent the past five years trying to make something happen, but we were going nowhere. I was determined to take back my power.

All seemed well with the kids on the outside. Debbie had lots of girlfriends and they liked to come to the house and would sing in a group together. She was starting to sound really good and she'd always been a good dancer. Kevin also had a natural singing voice. They were both serious Jackson 5 fans, but also very much into British pop and rock. Kevin's true passion was soccer, though. He played it wherever he could and had reconnected with his friends René and Hugo Elizondo, who played in tournaments all over the San Fernando Valley. René went on to direct videos and Janet Jackson.

Since we moved from Malibu, Debbie hadn't found a passion to truly replace horse-riding, but she loved swimming and ice-skating. Her friends all enjoyed sleepovers, but I felt they were a little wild. She could be naughty and adventurous, but was also sweet and lovable. She had a wicked sense of humour and an infectious laugh. Everybody loved her. She was like a magnet.

Bluebell Avenue was not a harmonious home, however, and she hated all the tensions in the house. Like all brothers and sisters, she and Kevin fought. Kevin would deliberately tease her, which would drive her nuts. One time we had a big BBQ and somebody called the police. I remember Debbie ran to me saying, 'Mommy, the pigs are coming, the pigs are coming!' She had grown up in a rock 'n' roll household and was warning anybody who was smoking marijuana. She knew all about it. What I did not know was that both Kevin and Debbie were now smoking themselves.

The first signs that I had of any delinquency was when I discovered that some of the girls supposedly at our house had actually run away from home. They were only twelve, thirteen, fourteen years old! Once I realised that these were girls with teenage problems, I found myself taking them home nearly every weekend. I would check in with their parents to make sure Debbie was where she was supposed to be and in turn they would check in with me. I felt most secure when everyone was at our house singing and dancing. In England, my kids had been naughty, like all children going through puberty, but it was innocent naughtiness. Down in the San Fernando Valley, I was encountering something very different.

Naively, I also hadn't realised just how much the situation with Fuzz and me was affecting my kids. I'd also imagined that Kevin and Debbie would spend time with David, but although he and Lan did take them to the beach a few times, I had no real support from him. He was a father only when it suited him. All the good reasons for returning to the States had disappeared.

The happiest time for Fuzz and me had been the birth of Kodzo. Otherwise, our relationship never got past the honey-moon stage. Looking back, I believe I'd have been better off dealing with my three kids on my own and pulling my own career together. But we were just too young to make mature decisions like that. Hindsight is a bitch, as we all know.

Fuzz and I were just about able to make Christmas happen that year, but we also knew we'd come to the end of the road.

All the mental, emotional and sexual frustration had gotten to be too much. First we decided to sell Hoplands before we lost it. We would split the money and break up amicably. He couldn't travel in and out of the US as his work permit was no longer valid and he still only had a passport for Antigua, so I would be going to England. In six years, the house had more than doubled in value. In fact, we'd been stupid not to rent it out while we were away, but it had taken us this long to realise that we wouldn't be returning together. We couldn't make plans until the house was sold and we needed the money to let go and move on. Breaking up is hard.

Kevin had a tournament coming up, so I left him and Kodzo with Fuzz. In early February I flew to England with Debbie to put Hoplands on the market. It was so nice having those couple of weeks with her. Time had stood still in Milton-Under-Wychwood. Memories came flooding back and it was very sad, especially for her. As we walked through the fields and visited the wild garden with its swans and ducks, our mood was downbeat. I think she suffered more than all of us.

She was happy to see everyone riding their ponies and going about their normal life, but I think that trip back and knowing we weren't returning contributed to her state of mind in the months to come. She didn't like her teachers at junior high in North Hollywood and the home environment didn't help. I was determined to change all of this and we talked about the future before we flew back to LA together.

I wanted to create a more solid home base for my kids in their adolescent years. The last two years had not been good for any of us. Fuzz and I were not married and, to be fair, Kevin and Debbie were not his responsibility. So many bad situations had just taken their toll – not all of them out of my hands.

It didn't take long to get an offer for Hoplands. It was a choice piece of land. We could have kept it if we hadn't been so desperate for money, but we had no one we could ask for a loan. No one was getting royalties out of the Immediate money and we'd barely been surviving on royalties from CSNY and

Manassas. This was the only way for us to get our shit together. I left Debbie in school this time and returned to London alone.

I had come back to the winter of discontent. The scene in London had changed so much and I could understand this revolutionary distrust of the government, all the outspoken protests about oppression and racism and the rebellious art and philosophy. I got where the musical influences were coming from, too, but I found the aggressive fashion alienating.

It was a welcome relief, therefore, when I ran into my old soul brother Stevie Marriott one afternoon. I hadn't seen him since that early Humble Pie session and it really was a magical reunion. He had re-formed the Small Faces with Ian McLagan, Kenny Jones and Rick Wills and they were finishing up some tracks and then going on the road. He wanted me to tour with them. 'It would be like old times,' he promised.

I needed to get back to LA, though. Debbie was missing me and she wasn't happy living with Fuzz and Kevin. She and her brother were arguing constantly and Fuzz couldn't control the situation. I had had no opportunities in LA, however, and this short tour might be what I needed to open things up for me back here. I could even make some money. Maybe, just maybe . . .

The Small Faces sessions were taking place at Grange Sounds Studio in Chigwell, Joe and Vickie Brown's home studio and they were so much fun. Vickie and I did backing vocals on three tracks – 'Never Too Late', 'Find It' and 'Looking for a Love' – but it was just great to be there with them. Steve was on top form. He was married now with a toddler called Toby.

For the tour, we travelled in dark blue Range Rovers. Except for Ronnie not being there, it was like old times. A few technical problems aside on the first night, the band were always on fire and Rick slipped easily into Ronnie's shoes. He was a great bass player, even if he wasn't as Small as the rest of us.

Off stage, it was another story. The scene had gone from dope, acid and uppers to cocaine, heroin and heavy drinking. Steve was into everything. All those US tours with Humble Pie had changed him. A couple of times he scared the life out of me mixing coke and heroin, speed balling together. He almost OD'd at least twice on that tour. And that was just the times I was there.

I'd enjoyed reconnecting with everybody, but I had to get back to LA. Debbie was in tears every time I spoke to her. Things were clearly not right.

42

1977 (Hollywood)

Debbie

I had been anxious as I flew back to LAX. Really I had wanted to stay in London and put the pieces of my career back together. LA was not the place for us, but first, I needed to get my kids out of that Valley neighbourhood. We'd sold the house, so Fuzz wouldn't have to support us any longer. He would fare better than me financially, but that was fine with me. I was sure we could find a way to share our responsibility for Kodzo.

My babies were at the airport to meet me and I was shocked at the energy surrounding them. They ran to me and hugged me so tight, but there was such a sadness there. Fuzz was unresponsive and I asked him what the hell was going on. The airport was not the place to get any answers, however, so we rode home in the car making small talk.

By the time we got home, Debbie was crying uncontrollably. She told me she and Kevin argued like crazy, while Kevin told me that Debbie was out of control, not showing up to school and sneaking the car out at night to joy-ride with her friends. He sometimes ditched classes too, but he at least attended school on a daily basis. Fuzz knew nothing about any of this. In my absence, it seems his duties as a guardian had pretty much been limited to making sure they had some food before taking Kodzo into the garage where he played music and hung out with his mates smoking.

I was angry. We'd agreed I had to go to England and I thought the two-week tour wouldn't make a difference. I knew the Valley was far from South Central, but couldn't somebody have helped out? Why didn't Fuzz call my family? Why hadn't he told me? I might as well have taken her with me if she wasn't going to school.

Kevin also told me that he and Debbie both stole from both Fuzz's stash as well as mine. I had no idea how things had escalated so fast. Most kids do things their parents aren't aware of, but the neighbourhood kids in North Hollywood were wild and delinquent and Kevin and Debbie had become very influenced by it all. I needed to get them out of there.

First of all, I grounded them both. They were allowed no visitors and no sleepovers. They weren't allowed to do anything except go to school. I knew they would smoke regardless of what I said, but I talked to them about the dangers of choosing to do so at such a young age. It could affect their concentration and I told them about the heightened physical sensations I didn't feel they were ready to experience. They knew I smoked so I could hardly condemn them, but I wanted them to know what they were getting into. I asked if they were doing any other type of drugs and they assured me that they weren't. I begged them to start communicating with me.

Everybody on the rock 'n' roll scene smoked pot or drank heavily. Marijuana was the lesser of the two evils for me. I didn't need uppers unless I was totally exhausted and had to work and I didn't do barbiturates. I never understood why people took Quaaludes, Mandrax and other downers, especially mixing them with alcohol and I avoided all that party drug culture. When I was working in clubs, I had to keep my shit together as a singer-performer. This and my responsibilities towards my children had saved me from many things.

I was embarrassed about what a mess my life was in. About what a mess my children's life had become. I wanted to talk to my parents, but I didn't feel that I'd get the support I needed and I couldn't discuss the dope with them, as Daddy didn't like the fact that I smoked. This was my mess and it was down to me to clean it up.

A couple of days before Mother's Day, Debbie ran away with some of her friends. I waited to see if she would call, but when she did she wouldn't tell me where she was. I could hear laughter in the background. I didn't want to call the police, so Kevin and I went around the neighbourhood to ask her friends if anyone knew anything. She kept on calling to let me know that she was okay. Only Debbie would run away but keep in touch with me so I wouldn't worry!

We continued to search for her, however and I remembered she had a crush on a cute little guy named Chris. Chris told us where she was: with her friend Meg in Culver City near Santa Monica. I never beat my kids, but this time I gave her an old-fashioned whipping with a belt. It wasn't as bad as the ones I'd taken for almost nothing when I was a child, but it was effective. I finally understood what my father had meant when he said, 'This is going to hurt me as much as it's going to hurt you.'

I found a house on 8th and Spaulding near Wilshire Boulevard, close to my brother Kenny. The move went as smooth as moves go, but then I guess I'd had enough practice by now. We'd been living in furnished accommodation, so it was merely a matter of packing clothes and private bits and pieces. It would mean a two-hour drive for me each morning and afternoon driving them from LA to school in North Hollywood, then picking them up at 3 p.m. every afternoon before the rush hour. After driving them to school every morning, Kodzo and I would spend the day shopping, unpacking and organising our new home. He was four years old now and would soon be starting school himself. I was rebuilding my family and my career – now if only I could make some money.

Debbie would be fourteen soon and had recently started her period. Soon she'd be going to high school, then college and hopefully university. She had to start concentrating on her schoolwork and leave drugs alone. She told me that she definitely wanted to dance. She also wanted to sing. As soon as we moved house, we would get her started in dance classes, starting with tap.

Initially, because they didn't kick up a fuss, I thought she and Kevin liked the house on Spaulding. It had a huge split-level living room with a large fake fireplace, a cosy warm look that reminded me of Hoplands. French doors on the left side of the room made it light and airy. Debbie had a very funky, classical style of dancing and she would dance on the split-level platform like a ballerina as if she was dancing on a stage. She loved all the new disco music and seemed so happy and sweet, like her normal self again.

One day, Debbie and I went to shop for tap shoes. I was going to take classes with her and we decided on some Red beginners. They didn't have Debbie's size in stock, but I could pick them up in a couple of days. Back home as I fixed dinner, Debbie gave Kodzo his bath. They loved each other so much and when she and her friends were at the house, he was always eager to tag along. It was a peaceful evening and we went to bed a little later than usual. I was just dozing off when I saw Debbie coming towards me sleepwalking. She'd always been a sleepwalker and when she got in bed with me, I gave her a strong cuddle and we turned on our sides, our booties touching. I fell asleep that night with my daughter lying beside me feeling safe, thankful and grateful.

Getting dressed the next morning, I couldn't help but notice how beautiful she was. She was just glowing that day, with the most gorgeous peachy-coloured skin. She was very petite, with the cutest little figure and a smile and energy that lit up any room. I couldn't keep my eyes off her. Kevin's skin was darker, but he also had those peachy tones and he was very handsome, self-assured and clever. Kodzo was just the cutest, sweetest toddler ever – definitely an old soul who had been here before, for sure. I knew he'd miss hanging out with his daddy in the garage beating on drums and shaking tambourines and I hoped Fuzz would continue to spend quality time with him. I loved my children very much. I was so proud of all of them.

It was a sunny morning as we drove over Laurel Canyon and for the first time in a long time, I was filled with real optimism. They were running late for school when we arrived and I kissed them all goodbye.

At 2 p.m. as normal, Kodzo and I drove to the Valley to collect Kevin and Debbie. Kevin was there as normal, but there was no sign of Debbie. Kevin had no choice but to tell me that she had not gone to school that day. I immediately drove to Bluebell Avenue, but there was no sign of any of Debbie's girlfriends.

Then a neighbour told me there had been an accident.

Apparently everyone had been taken to a hospital, but no one seemed to know where. I drove to LA as fast as I could and called around frantically. Finally tracking down the hospital, I asked about Debbie Arnold. How was she? Was she okay?

I was told that my daughter had been killed in a car accident that morning.

I dropped the receiver and ran screaming toward the bay window. Someone caught me just before I crashed through it and I continued to scream as Kevin and a friend tried to calm me.

And then I had to tell my son that his sister was dead.

Everything happened in surreal slow motion after that. David and Lan suddenly appeared. They were just dropping by to take the kids to see the new Star Wars movie. I called the hospital again who told me I should come immediately and the rest of the day is a blur.

One of Debbie's best friends, Fran Berman, was also in the car that day. She too was fourteen years old. Here is her diary record:

> 26 June 1977
>
> Dear Diary,
>
> Well here I go. I'm writing on this cause it's gonna be long and sad. I haven't written since June 1st cause I wasn't home to write in it. I was in a hospital bed. Me, N, D, C, J and Debbie were in a car accident. Deb, my best friend, was killed. D, a broken arm, C, a crushed pelvis, crushed bladder, crushed legs, glass stitches, J, glass and stitches, hurt legs, N, bruises, me 3 fractures on my shoulder. A brace for 3 weeks. C is still in the hospital. When I think of Debbie I cry. I loved her a lot.
>
> Well to start, Deb called me the night before to ask me if I wanted to cut and go to the beach. I never said yes or no. I wanted to though, I asked N and she wasn't sure.
>
> We left for school and met at the wall. We waited for Deb and finally she came. Then D and C wanted to come. So, we were finally ready.
>
> We started thumbing from there. This guy picked us up, me and J sat in front. We thought he was a cop cause he had a CB. He wasn't. Then we got picked up again. Me and J sat in the front again. The next ride we got picked up by a truck. We sat in the back going over Topanga Canyon.
>
> (I told my mom we took the bus part of the way, dad I think knows, mom doesn't) (I don't think)

It was fun until we got over. I remember wanting to go to the beach right there. But Deb and J said Zuma was gonna be good. We thumbed again and got picked up by a little car. I forgot what kind. I remember it had red puffy stuff on the ceiling and on the back seat it was carpet. The guy was driving and J sat next to him and I forgot if Deb was sitting on J or C. But then J wanted to drive. (N, D, me in back) So he pulled over and J got in the driver's seat. In the front it was J, the guy and D on C's lap. Then left to right in back, N, D and me. J was driving good on the freeway. She was going fast. At first I was gonna get out when J was gonna drive, but as dumb as I am, I stayed. We drove on the freeway for a while. Then Deb said I know the best hill, which Deb and J had been to when they ditched at other times. She made a left turn at a light, at a Mayfair market. The brakes had to be pumped a little. So we drove a minute or two and we were on top of the hill, we started driving down and we were going fast, it didn't seem fast and then I think it swerved 2 times and we crashed sideways into a pole. Where I was sitting that was where we hit the pole. So, I'm not sure if I was knocked out or not, but when I got up, I thought the car was going to blow up. So N was up, we both hopped out. D wasn't in the middle of us any more. No one is sure how she flew out; when I got out she was on the floor face down. I'm not sure where she flew out from. I guess the back. Me and N hopped out fast and we crossed the street and laid down, cause the wind was knocked out of me. We walked up the block cause the kids were running and coming from the school across the street. (Deb graduated from that school)

We had blood on us. We were walking and I felt like passing out. But we stopped in some bushes cause N had to pee. Then we sat on some side of a ladies porch. Then I started getting pain. We knocked on a door and no one answered. We ran across the street. We heard the sirens. We knocked on this door and this girl answered and we asked if I could lie down. We told her we fell off a bike coming down the hill. We both had blood on us. She got a sheet, which I laid down on. I was in a bit of pain, so we told her the truth. N called the ambulance I think. Then N called her mom who called my mom. Then someone said to N's mom it was probably the ambulance guys when they came, that there was a fatality, but N's mom knew it wasn't N cause she talked to her. N I think told her I was ok. The ambulance guys asked my name and age about 20 times. They put sandbags around my head so it wouldn't move and put a sling on and put me on a stretcher. It hurt. I had a bump on my head, too. They took me and N to Westlake Hospital. They asked us a lot of questions. They asked who was driving we the said the guy. They soon found out it was J. We were so scared. We got to the Westlake hospital and everyone else was already there. Deb and I think C went back by helicopter. And the rest by another ambulance, I think.

I know that everyone thought Deb flew out the window. The impact was so strong that C was under the dashboard with Deb under the dashboard on top of her. Deb snapped her neck. They said she died instantly.

My parents were hysterical. Just like everyone else's. No one knew Deb was dead. Pat didn't until the afternoon either. I was the only [one] who knew Deb's phone number. But no one asked me cause I had a big bump on my head. And I guess they thought I wouldn't remember.

I waited around two hours until they took X-rays . . . Everyone was getting glass taken out. They soon transferred me to Kaiser. N went home. At Kaiser I got a little figure 8 brace. It hurt a little. Not as much as x-rays, that hurt the most. I stayed at Kaiser that night. They took out my phone. I didn't know why. They woke me up every hour to take my blood pressure, temp and check my eyes. That night hurt, the next morning my mom took me in another room and told me Deb was dead. I was the last one to know. My best friend was dead. I cried for a long while and I felt so ashamed. I kept asking myself why I did it and why I was so dumb and felt so ashamed. Everyone in the neighborhood knew.

C is still in Westlake Hospital. Everyone else is home. Me and N got grounded. I went to Pat's and she asked me everything. I told the truth. She almost blew it. She said, 'everything is open now right?' (in front of my dad) 'Were you guys high?' I don't think my dad heard. I said no. (we weren't) No one was high. Just J and D were smoking. Kevin was really upset. The guy in the accident, Manuel Gamboa, 26 I think, broke his leg and hurt his ribs. An investigator came to my house, said the car skidded 210 feet on an angle before we hit the pole and he said in the trunk in his suitcase there were 3 pairs of girls panties. He had no insurance and he just came from Santa Cruz, where some girls were raped. (I'm pretty sure Santa Cruz)

He was looking for a good time. He got off and they are pressing charges. It was in the papers. The funeral was a week after. There were hundreds of people. I cried through the whole thing. The casket was open. I had already seen her at the wake, she was beautiful. She was in her Indian stuff, her nails were done. She was gorgeous. We didn't go to the graveyard. We were all hysterical. It's all over and I'll never forget this. It was a terrible thing and I'll always remember Deb. She was my best friend and I love her.

I guess I'll just stop here. I might continue a diary next year. I'm not sure.

P.S. I'm still grounded. It's June 27th.

Denice Molina was also in the car. She was thirteen years old. As she remembers it:

That day, I remember us all meeting at the wall to go to the beach. I remember us catching a ride straight away in two different cars, because there were six of us and I remember we made it a game to say who could beat the other group to the beach. We'll meet you on Topanga and PCH. Somehow we managed to get there around the same time. We wanted to stay there but Debbie and Joy wanted to go to Point Dume, I guess they'd been there before. Debbie was saying she wanted to go by her old school and that's how we ended up hitching again and we got in the car with that guy. He was driving a Corvair, for sure I remember it totally and so does Fran. I was in love with a guy and his father had a Corvair, which is how I always remember it was a Corvair. We got in the car, I was in the back in the middle, Nori was on the right of me and Fran was on my left. Debbie was sitting on Charlottes lap, Joy was in the middle and the guy was driving.

I don't remember at what point Joy started driving, but I remember that happening. I don't think that Joy drove a long way; I don't think it was that far, but it was far enough. I remember Joy saying, I know how to drive, like I can drive and I don't know that I was scared, I don't know that I trusted Joy, I just don't know what I was thinking at the time. At that time in my life I was in such a place that I probably just didn't care.

I remember when we got to Point Dume and started going down the hill and it was really fast. I remember us kinda like shouting weee rollercoaster for a second and then I don't remember anything, except that I woke up on the ground, I was lying there I must've flown out of the car and I blacked out, but in my blackout I had this incredible dream, and the dream was that the hill goes down (it goes flat in reality), but in my dream the hill goes down and then it goes back up and I dreamt that there was an ambulance, a beautiful white ambulance and it takes off and it just goes up the hill and into the sky, and this was the dream I had. This white beautiful ambulance going up into the sky – I always remember that. It's always been to me some kind of spiritual thing. I can see it in my mind now as vivid as I did then, but that's what I dreamt. I was knocked out. I woke up and Debbie was next to me and they were trying to resuscitate her. I don't know if she was

> gone already or not, I just know that they were doing CPR on her. I was laying there, I opened my eyes and I turned my head and she was right there next to me nobody else was there, it was just me and Debbie. I don't know where anyone else was. I just started crying. Then they took me off and put me in the helicopter.

I cannot describe the shock and devastation as we digested the news. We were all crying in disbelief. The fact that David just happened to pass by was so surreal. My parents took me to Westlake Community Hospital to identify her body. I remember being taken to a room and seeing Debbie's body on a gurney. I felt so guilty for not being around to protect her all those weeks I was away in England. I knew we were in a bad place and I tried so hard to get away, but I was too late. She was only thirteen years old.

The guy who had picked them up had been taken to the police station, but the police had let him go, which none of us understood. Apparently he was on his way to Mexico and obviously up to no good picking those girls up as they hitchhiked on Pacific Coast Highway. Had the accident not taken place, the girls might've been in a different kind of danger. Debbie was the only black girl in that car. Would they have let him go if one of the white girls had been killed? We should've had lawyers investigating why they just deported him. But the devastation of seeing her body on that gurney had blown my mind completely and suing the police didn't occur to me. The other parents were more focused on suing the parents of Joy, the girl who was driving the car. I just wanted to be able to take my daughter home. She wanted to be a dancer, but her foot had been damaged in the accident. I felt if she'd had a choice, she wouldn't have wanted to live. It would take years for me to process Debbie's death. That night I had to focus on getting her body moved to a funeral home.

The accident had taken place around the corner from Birdview Drive and across the street from the elementary school Debbie had graduated from. Debbie was taking the girls to the place she'd been happiest since leaving Milton-Under-Wychwood.

Was there anything I could have done to save my daughter from this tragic end? I felt it was my fault. I had taken my children from a safe environment to follow an impossible dream and ended up sacrificing my daughter. The ramifications of the choices I had made would torment me for years to come.

The next few days are just a rush of moments, glimpses of painful memory: funeral details, people coming and going, confusion and disbelief. I had no insurance, so I paid for the funeral in cash with my part of the money from selling the house. Debbie had grown up in England and liked to dress in a hippie way. I didn't want to put her in an ordinary dress, so I just followed my intuition. I bought a beautiful sky-blue sari, her favourite colour and a purple sari for me to wear. I asked a friend of mine, Mom de Leo, a Rasta Sister, to come to the mortuary with me to help me prepare and wrap Debbie's body. I somehow felt this would help me to let go of her physical body. My family thought I was mad, but that's what I did. I painted her nails and made up her face. She was so beautiful. Her skin was still glowing the day of the funeral. She looked like the princess that she was. I placed a beautiful Egyptian necklace over the sari and buried her with it.

The third day after she passed, I sat down in a chair and closed my eyes, as I'd had hardly any sleep. I had a vision of her standing on the seashore looking straight ahead as the tide came in. The sun was shining brightly and she was wearing dark glasses, looking very brave. She was never afraid of anything. I woke with a start, unable to stop my tears.

On another evening, my house was full of friends and family. One of my brothers-in-law was in my bedroom going through my things and he ran out in a fright saying that he'd seen Debbie in my room. I knew she was around. I could feel her, protecting and watching over us. Kodzo kept telling me that Debbie lived in the top of our house and I believed him.

Her funeral was held at the Harrison-Ross Chapel on Adams Boulevard. After the processional I sang 'Never Grow Old', with my cousin Frank and my fellow Ikette Gloria Scott. Brother Al MaKay spoke, as did Reverend J. Hitchens. My friend Renita Lorden gave a reading and my dear friend Jody read the obituary. My cousin Reverend Jerrell Harvey did the eulogy. It was a very beautiful, peaceful service and the chapel was filled with family and friends, including all of the girls in the accident and their families.

I buried Debbie at the Rose Hills Memorial Park in Whittier, an open and hilly location that I thought she would love. Whenever I'm in Los Angeles I go there to pray and meditate, though I know that her soul or her spirit does not reside there.

Joy Snipes was fourteen years old at the time. She was driving the car that tragic day so long ago:

'Back Then n When'

Tribute to Debbie by Joy Snipes

There are no words for what an amazing friend you were to me back then and when. I never did actually get to say these words to you, so 'thank you' from the bottom of my heart. We lived n loved a lifetime back then. It was as if we knew each other from another place n time on another star perhaps back when. Once we met, we stuck together like glue n there wasn't anything we couldn't do. We were a force to be reckoned with, you and me. You were such a free spirit. We were young n full of life with no fear. We shared a love for imprinting with so many people and different places. Going to the beach n how the waves would draw us in to go for a swim. Looking at the stars at night, they were so beautiful n bright. They helped guide us home after sneaking out at night, to simply talk as if we forgot to say something to one another that day. I can still hear your beautiful English accent as I write about you, which I'm sure if you could, you would have something to say about this back then . . . It still makes me laugh when I think about making up words no one would understand back then – and it worked, nobody knew or maybe they did, we just wanted to believe no one knew our very own special code. I miss listening to your stories. I especially liked the story about when you were out riding horses English-style when you lived in England; riding English-style meant riding bareback. But you were not riding bareback the normal way that day; you were riding bareback 'backwards' and ended up getting in trouble, but said they'd have to catch you first as you laughed and rode away, only to do it again one day. I miss hearing you sing with such passion, your voice was bigger than you were! I especially liked when you sang those songs you liked by Barbara Streisand, 'I Won't Last a Day Without You' or 'The Way We Were' and of course 'Memories'. I remember listening to you when you sang your accent disappeared but your voice was so pretty. I was always amazed at the way you could hit those really high notes and hold them for so long and so effortlessly. You sounded like an angel, your voice was so light but huge at the same time. I'd know your voice anywhere. Just like the day you laid next to me on the ground. The last thing I heard your voice say that day was 'everything would be okay'. Until you reappeared in my window telling stories, jokes n pokes, just like you my friend from back when. I will always cherish our friendship n how you were such a beautiful friend to me. You taught me what it was like to be free from any n everything I knew. We were on the run laughing n having so much fun, imprinting everywhere we went. Most importantly, thank you for the imprint on my heart, because I would not have lasted this long without you. With that, my friend, it gives me great sorrow to say and do this, but I kept my promise. I never let go, but I may have held on too tight. Now is the time to release you and let go. Like you said to me, I'll say to you: 'Everything will be okay.' Until we meet again, my friend, in another place n time back then n when. Love always, your friend Joy <3 <3

Up to the evening of the funeral, my house had been full for a week. That evening when everyone went home and Kevin and Kodzo had gone to sleep, I was alone at last. Debbie had wanted me to listen to her latest favourite album, Supertramp's *Crime of the Century*, but I'd been busy and hadn't taken the time. The image on its sleeve now shocked me, with its astral resignation before fate. I put it on and I cried and cried and cried. It seemed to describe how she felt about school and everything she had been going through. The doorbell rang. A friend had come by to see if I was alright. He offered me some cocaine and I said yes.

It was the beginning of months of self-medication when I almost lost my mind.

43

1977 (Hollywood)

Kevin and After

When I lost Debbie, I lost Kevin, too.

Both my children had grown up during the P.P. Arnold heyday – a 'heydey' that felt like it belonged to somebody else. They were accustomed to living well; we had nice houses and materially speaking they always had everything they wanted. Kevin was very self-sufficient and intelligent, polite, charming and extremely good-looking, but he was also extremely self-centred. If ever he didn't get his way, he would give me a hard time.

At first, my mother had looked after them on 117th Street and they played with the McDade children next door. After my first hit record, I had brought them to live with me in England, so, just like me, they had gone from a South Central LA neighbourhood to living in London penthouse apartments and townhouses. They had nannies and toys, but no other kids to play with, so they were extremely close. When I married Jim Morris, we had a good family life together. He was great with them, always planning family outings and his family embraced us all.

After Immediate went bankrupt, Kevin and Debbie were doing okay in school. While they were young, the constant moving around didn't affect them so much, but as they got older it became problematic. When Jim and I split, they lived with his parents, which was a nice, stable environment.

The children weren't happy when I decided to be with Fuzz. I thought Milton would offer a healthy and secure family environment, but the problem was all the rock 'n' roll craziness that surrounded us. Around then, I think my children began questioning my choices and judgement. They were right to. They knew I wasn't happy being with Fuzz and my career had gone the wrong way. And after that it all just got worse and worse.

When I lost Debbie, I felt so guilty for everything. It was eating me alive. Kevin and I were in so much pain and I was upset with him not letting me know earlier just how out of control his sister had become. We blamed ourselves and we blamed each other. It was a mess. We both should have been in therapy.

David wasn't helping matters either. He knew he could and should have been there for his kids and he tried to make it up by giving Kevin money behind my back. Having a dad who was suddenly being so cool was creating friction between us. I resented this and meanwhile Kevin was a fourteen-year-old boy out of control and smoking grass.

One evening we got into a big argument. I called David and told him to come and get Kevin. I was fed up with David not taking responsibility, financially and in general, and Kevin was constantly making excuses for him while giving me a hard time. I felt that it was time they got to know each other. Fuzz loved Kodzo and was trying to get to grips with fatherhood. Perhaps if David had given him some kind of support, Fuzz might have managed things better with Kevin and Debbie. Being both Mama and Daddy to all of them had taken its toll on me.

But David was the worst person to help us mend our relationship. Kevin took his pain out on me and refused to visit me all the rest of the time I lived in LA. Even when he moved to Miami to live with me, it took us thirty-five years to mend those broken fences.

So, as I say, I lost them both when I lost Debbie.

Kodzo alone gave me a reason to get up in the morning. He was my rock and we clung to each other for dear life.

Meanwhile, the cocaine was turning me into someone I didn't recognise. Kodzo was the only one I did not feel judged by. I woke up in the morning to look after my baby, clean my house, shop for groceries, cook and do the laundry – just the mundane chores. I couldn't deal with Hollywood.

For money, I became a disciple of the devil. I knew nothing about coke or dealing, but Kenny gave me the connections and I had no problem finding customers in Hollywood for pure Peruvian flake. Which meant my profit margin wasn't as generous as it could have been. My customers were mainly musicians and I won't name names, but let's just say that they were regulars.

I only went out of my house to go to the store. My family's lives had gone on without me and I felt we weren't connected any more. I had always been the black sheep and after losing

Debbie I felt more isolated than ever. I was now a stranger in my own hometown. The neighbourhood I had grown up in had been torn down, drugs and gang culture had taken over and many people were dealing with tragedy and displacement.

I tried to focus on music and for a while Gloria and my cousin Frank came by and we'd work on ideas. I have cassettes of some of those afternoons and it doesn't sound like me at all. I sound possessed; you can hear my demons.

I was really pleased when Madeline Bell showed up unexpectedly. She'd had a lot of success with a band called Blue Mink while I'd been away from England. We cried together and she left me with some of her strength. She knew my children well and she also knew how fragile I was.

I also called Steve Marriott, to let him know what had happened. He was grieving over the loss of his dog and I was a bit put out. It seemed to me like no comparison to the loss of my daughter, but I guess he really loved that dog.

The Rastafarian sister Mom de Leo had helped me wrap my daughter. Pregnant and about to deliver, she was also homeless and needed my help. It was my pleasure to come to her aid. Our time together was supportive and educational. Her son Hamisi was born prematurely and I became his godmother.

When we were still in junior high, Mom de Leo was plain Delores Johnson. Now she dressed and behaved like an African Queen and she declaimed all the Rastafarian expressions with an amazing Jamaican patois. I did not follow the Rastafarian way of life, whereas Delores was wholehearted about it, which caused a bit of friction.

She followed all the Jamaican reggae groups and went to their LA concerts religiously. She also smoked ganja from sunup to sundown, which suited me fine at the time. Besides Hamisi, she had another son, Dar, a gorgeous, sensitive child who was company for Kodzo, so for a while we were able to live together and our religious and philosophical differences paled beside the love she had bestowed upon Debbie and me.

I think my family liked my music, but I sensed it just wasn't black enough for black folks and I hadn't had the exposure I needed to appeal to crossover audiences in America. Since I'd been in LA, I'd let myself become overshadowed by Fuzz and the others – even though most of them, great as they all were, were sidemen. People knew that my professional name was P.P. Arnold, but everybody just related to me as Fuzz's old lady Pat. My confidence was at rock bottom.

Today, people can just Google your name and everything about you will magically appear, but not in 1977. People didn't know that the British artists that they worshipped had all been my peers. They didn't know I had been 'The First Lady of Immediate Records'. Even I didn't know that *Kafunta*, with its futuristic African Queen photo, had been such a massive hit in South Africa. I had been foolish to think I could be a successful female artist here in Hollywood, but this all seemed irrelevant to me now in the light of losing my beautiful daughter.

I went to see my father and discussed my idea for a 'Third World Habitat'. I would make cushions and pillows with my brother Ronnie, who was very talented and build the frames for them in my father's upholstery workshop. I told him about a friend in London, Sue, who sold East African Kangas and could send me fabrics and we could add other durable and artistic fabrics from South America, Asia and American Indian designs. It would be a low pillow furniture designed for young couples and students, similar to futons but before they became popular. The frames would have large pillow backs and comfortable pillow seats and they could also be slept on. I needed to get my head into a creative sideline before I lost my mind and I was looking forward to spending time with Ronnie. Daddy had always wanted his children to be a part of his business and I thought my project was a good idea. I'm sure that he could also see that I was falling apart and so he was willing to help me do something.

I had met Linda Alhadeff through Jimmy Mayweather and she would visit me if ever she was in LA. She was very knowledgeable when it came to cosmic, metaphysical things and introduced me to the Urantia Book. It helped a lot. I was totally out of control and I needed to get mind, body and spirit together. The drug abuse was taking its toll. Linda lived near San Francisco, where she knew lots of healers and alternative therapists and she invited me there to go cold turkey. And that's what I did. Cocaine is a horrible drug and those two weeks at the beginning of December were hell. But with Linda's help I got through it. I succeeded in cleaning up. For my family, my career, myself, I vowed to stay away from coke.

I was back home in time to celebrate Christmas. Kodzo had the measles and he was so sad. I had ordered my first Kangas from Sue in London and we started making our first 'Third World Habitat' creations, with my father's help. 1978 was a new year and Ronnie and I both had to move forward. This project had given me direction.

I found a new place to live just off Olympic and La Brea, a couple of blocks from where Kenny lived. It was a spacious apartment with a strange set-up: four bedrooms plus a really large living room which I used as a showcase room for people to see the pillow-furniture samples. I would then take orders. It was a nice, relaxing space and working with Ronnie was great. I'm so glad we had that time together.

I rented two of the rooms out to two young, creative women: Terry Hart, who was studying fashion design at the Fashion Institute; and Renita Lorden, who worked in the film industry in the prop department. They would both become lasting friends and really helped Kodzo and me make it through the next phase of our lives.

I remember this as a time of strong emotional and physical transition. Kenny practised Shotokan karate and suggested that I practise with him to help deal with my grief. My parents had never really encouraged me or Elaine in anything sporty. Then I'd had my kids so young and never fully developed my physical potential.

Shotokan karate was my first adult sporting challenge and Kenny and I trained outside at a local park, with a sensei named Santee. My body responded to these exercises well and I really enjoyed working out in such a natural environment.

Practising karate helped me to heal more and grieve less. I also found I had a talent for long-distance running. I never ran for competition; I just ran for my life.

To this day, I am still running, still healing.

44

1978 (Hollywood)

Sgt Pepper Comes to Town

It always startled me that I was so easy for people to find, especially when I was so far off the Hollywood radar. This time it was Jim's old friend Dick Ashby, who was also now Barry Gibb's personal manager. Even after all this time, no one knew where Jim was.

The Bee Gees had produced a film version of *Sgt Pepper's Lonely Hearts Club Band*, which was both ambitious and ill-fated as it turned out. I was so out of touch with the industry that I'd heard nothing about it, but the movie was set to receive its premier on Sunset Boulevard. Dick was sending a limo for me and a guest of my choosing and wanted my address. I was touched to hear from him out of the blue like this and I accepted of course and immediately called Kenny to see if he would escort me.

I hadn't seen Barry or Linda since 1970. We'd been such close friends and it meant so much that they'd thought of me.

I hadn't been invited to an event for years. Debbie would've loved *Saturday Night Fever*. Funny to think that Debbie and Kevin had played in the garden at Eaton Square as Barry and I worked on songs.

But Hollywood is a long way from Eaton Square. Had they heard I'd lost Debbie? As their star had risen, mine had dramatically tumbled. Everything was different now; *I* was very different now. Nevertheless, I was looking forward to seeing my friends.

As the limo turned up in front of the theatre, we stopped directly in front of the Bee Gees' own limo. Kenny and I were stepping onto the red carpet just as the brothers stepped out of their limo. There were so many people there and I could hear everyone whispering, 'Who's that? Who is she?' But Barry and Linda spotted me and gave me the biggest hugs. So did Maurice and Robin. Even Stigwood acknowledged me! It was overwhelming and I fought back my tears. We all went in to watch the movie and while I tried to concentrate, it was all I could do not to cry throughout. Grief is a powerful emotion.

After the premier, Kenny and I were driven to the Beverly Hills Hotel and escorted into the lounge for a proper reunion. My old friends seemed genuinely pleased to see me again after such a long time and offered their condolences over Debbie while embracing me warmly. Barry told me that if I ever came to Miami we could finish the recordings we'd started all those years ago. He didn't say when, but it didn't really matter, because what he gave me that night was hope. And hope was something that was in short supply in my life.

With my grief overwhelming me, I left them to the party at the Beverly Hills Hotel. It was neither the time nor the place for me to break down. Once again, the unexpected had come into my life. Magic, serendipity, destiny: my life had been full of these moments. One minute I'd be in hell, the next minute I was lifted up to heaven. The return of Sgt Pepper took me on another strange dream of a journey.

I'd heard the Rolling Stones were coming to town. They were touring *Some Girls* and would be playing at the Anaheim Stadium, but when nobody remembers your name, trying to get in touch with a Rolling Stone in Hollywood! Good luck! However, Peter Tosh, one of the original Wailers, was a support act on the tour and I knew Sandra Isidore, who happened to be Peter's friend. She arranged for me to travel on Peter's band bus to the Anaheim show. Bob Marley had just performed at the Hollywood Bowl and she was going to hang out with him in Santa Barbara.

My friend Junior Marvin had called me when Bob arrived in LA. He had heard about Debbie's accident and I'd visited him at the La Hermitage Hotel. Bob and the band had all given me their condolences and watching him performing the music from *Exodus* had been a very spiritual and magical life experience.

The first person I saw as I got off the bus was my dear friend Ian Stewart, who'd helped me escape from Ike Turner a lifetime ago. 'Pat!' he screamed excitedly. Then he saw my dreadlocks and said, 'Hate the hair!' – which made us both break into laughter. He gave me the biggest hug and was genuinely saddened when I told him about my daughter. 'Come with me,' he said. 'Mick is really going to be surprised to see you.'

I adored Stew. He'd been so kind to me when I first landed in the UK. He knew Mick was a bit of a scoundrel and had genuinely been worried for me. Soon I was backstage and everyone was hugging me – Keith, Bill, Charlie, Shirley. Ronnie Wood was now a Rolling Stone and Ian McLagan was on keyboards on this tour. It was like a big old family get-together. It's funny what comes around.

Mick seemed genuinely excited when he saw me. He was a little awkward and uneasy expressing his sympathy, but many people are like that. Death is a difficult thing to face up to. I don't know if Mick even knew until then that I'd lost my daughter, but I still felt his sincerity. He introduced me to Jerry Hall, his latest beau and I almost laughed when I saw her; she was so tall, skinny and country in manner. I remembered Mick trying to talk like a black man, but I knew back then he'd never marry a black woman. Country was as close to black as he was gonna get. But I would always be grateful to him. He had helped open me up beyond the ideals I had grown up with and I had been a whole lot more innocent and sweeter than the black sisters who arrived after me, that's for sure!

Anyway, as usual, it was all about Mick. Marsha Hunt had just slapped him with a paternity suit for child support for her daughter Karis and Mick was almost in tears about this. He understood that I knew exactly what had gone down and he was eager to talk to me about it. He gave Stew instructions that I was to be put into a limo after the show, to take me back to (as usual) the Beverly Hills Hotel.

Stew took me to a VIP seat. I loved Etta James, but I'd missed her performance while I was backstage as well as half of Peter

Tosh's. I hadn't seen the Stones live since 1966, which was long before these huge stadium tours. 1966. It seemed like another lifetime.

As they started 'Jumping Jack Flash', I was taken out to where the limos were waiting. I was stood there listening when someone touched me on the shoulder. I turned around. It was Jim! I shouted his name in delight but he put his finger to his lips to shush me: 'Don't call me that. My name is Richard now.' I didn't care what his name was; I was just glad to see him. He gave me a big hug and kiss and slipped a piece of paper in my hand with his new name and phone number. And then he disappeared.

I had always felt I'd see him again. We were actually still legally married, but I'd had no idea of his whereabouts. He had been a fugitive for some seven years now – the only one that got away in the Howard Marks bust of the early '70s. Rumour had it that he was off in Asia living a life of luxury.

I was ushered into the limo with the other VIP guests and taken to the suite at the Beverly Hills Hotel. This was very different from hanging out with the Bee Gees. Don't get me wrong, the Bee Gees also knew how to rock and roll, but they had a respectable front. Their parents and family travelled with them. With the Rolling Stones, though, the party was *on*.

I was nervous as soon as I saw all the cocaine being passed around. I was there on my own and I was still battling my own Class-A demons. A musician I knew really well called for me to follow him into the toilet. He was trying to shovel coke up my nose, but when he dropped his pants and pulled his dick out, which was bigger than he was, I totally freaked and ran out of the toilet. I burst into tears, ran for the elevator down to the lobby sobbing and asked the concierge to get a taxi. I didn't wait to see Mick; I just made my way home. When I got there, I felt so stupid and prudish, but I just couldn't believe that an old friend could have been quite so insensitive. I had never been a groupie and I didn't appreciate being treated like one. Is that what people thought of me now? Is that all the respect my intermittent career in music had afforded me?

I phoned Jim, remembering to call him Richard, as silly as that seemed to me. He was very brief on the phone, but wondered why I had left the hotel so suddenly. I told him I'd had a panic attack. I gave him my number and address and he said he'd call later. He seemed so secretive, so furtive. Everything about being on the run, it seems, required such caution and discretion! I really looked forward to seeing him, but I knew that he'd be distraught about Debbie.

True to his word, he came to see me that evening. It was a very emotional reunion. We both wept and he comforted me as no one had been able to. He was very concerned about Kevin and wanted to see him. We talked about Barry saying he'd produce some tracks with me if I came to Miami. But I'd have to relocate there and my financial situation was not good. The 'Third World Habitat' was still a drain on money and energy, although to be perfectly honest my heart just wasn't in it. It was great working with my brother, but marketing and promotion weren't for me. I just wanted to sing.

Jim thought that I should definitely go. I told him that I didn't have much money left and he told me he would sort that out for me. I figured it was best not to ask him how! We met again on a couple of occasions in LA and each time we did, he gave me a bundle of cash. Jim reasoned that if I was serious about getting my career back on track, Miami was my last resort. Barry and Jim were the only people throwing me a life raft – and there were certainly more unreliable life rafts than one belonging to Barry Gibb. I had to grab on and see where it took me before I drowned in despair.

I hated to see Jim go and hugged him tight. I knew he had moved on and now lived in a clandestine world of intrigue and danger, but I really missed him. I'd been such a fool.

The previous year I'd bought a sturdy Volvo, so if I drove to Miami, at least I'd have transportation when I arrived. The money Jim gave me was generous, but it wouldn't last for ever. And I could hardly bear to leave Debbie in the Rose Hills Cemetery as well as Kevin with David. I couldn't guarantee this move was the answer, but it did seem like my best hope. I stored the majority of my belongings in the basement of the Full Gospel Church, which my Grandma Stel owned and moved the pillow furniture into my parents' garage. Ronnie could sell what he could and I'd review the project at a later date. Daddy was disappointed at me giving up so soon, but I had to get out of LA.

I packed our suitcases and said goodbye to my family. Kodzo and I drove onto the Santa Monica Freeway I10 East, which would take us all the way to Florida.

Oh, and because I couldn't help but hitch myself to trouble at any opportunity, Fuzz came, too.

45

1979 (Miami)

Lost In Miami

The drive was long and tedious. The last time I had taken such a road trip, I was on that big old raggedy bus with Ike and Tina. And I'd forgotten how big and sprawling Texas was. Fourteen years and the civil rights movement had brought some changes. There were still rednecks and the Ku Klux Klan, but now there was legislation to counter the absence of respect African Americans had to face back then.

And this time we could stop wherever we liked. I gained 10 lbs on that journey eating Mexican and soul food as we passed through Arizona, New Mexico and Texas – and another ten along the Gulf Coast! We stayed overnight in the French quarter in New Orleans, the birthplace of jazz, where slave traders from Holland, Portugal, France and England had once exchanged Africans for rum, sugar and tobacco at the largest slave mart in the US.

As we drove, Fuzz and I laughed and talked together for the first time in for ever. It was a relief. Kodzo seemed happy to be with us both and I prayed that this time, everything would be alright. When we finally made it to the East Coast, we turned off Highway 10 onto the I95 and stopped at Cape Canaveral and the Kennedy Space Center so that Kodzo could see where all the spaceships were launched.

Just outside Tallahassee, I heard a siren and saw a red light flashing behind me. I looked down at the speedometer: 65 mph. Generally, you get 5 mph grace, but this was five more than that. I pulled over and put on my best English accent: 'So sorry, officer!' But with Fuzz's thick Antiguan accent and my LA licence, we didn't stand a chance. This ticket would have serious repercussions.

Finally, we pulled into the Coconut Grove. It was a shabby-looking apartment complex that Fuzz had rented and would act as cheap accommodation for me and Kodzo while I was finding my feet. The situation was far from ideal, but I heard Jim's voice reminding me that I was here to work with Barry again. There were two bedrooms, a living room, kitchen and bath. It had a tiny air conditioner and it was hot. There was no swimming pool. It was decorated in true laid-back hippy-musician style, but at least it was clean and I endeavoured to keep it that way.

I had only been in Miami two weeks when Kevin called. He hadn't wanted to speak to me when I left LA, but now he'd fallen out with David's partner Lan. Lan was the one who paid the bills and she was laying down the law for everybody living in her house. Kevin was realising that living with Daddy Cool wasn't as cool as he thought it would be. He and David were so similar. He wanted to come to Miami and live with me and it wasn't long before we were all in a tacky two-bedroom apartment – me, Fuzz, a fourteen-year-old, a five-year-old and the increasingly motley crew of hungry musicians that Fuzz had collected along the way.

This set-up was not going to work and I realised that if I was going to stay in Miami, I would need a job. The last regular job I'd had was working as a file clerk back in 1964. Singing had been my life since then and while it was all I really wanted to do, I had two sons to think about.

Phyllis Shenker was a hip young New York Jewish woman who'd moved to the Coconut Grove with her daughters Kim and Nicole to open a lovely little clothing boutique called the Chelsea Morning. It was a mixture of vintage and London hippie chic, with exotic styles from Bali, Thailand and India: beautiful colourful cottons, perfect for Miami's tropical humidity. The clothes reminded me of my King's Road days. She and I hit it off straight away and very soon she hired me as a part-time manager. I could pay rent and utilities and feed my boys. If I was careful, the money Jim had given me could go a long way.

Martha Gonzales was another good friend, as mad as a hatter, but she helped me find a bungalow, on 33rd Avenue near Coral Gables and the Coconut Grove. It was full of light, had a good feel and I was thankful to have found it.

Martha's son Terry was the same age as Kodzo and while he was wild and out of hand, he and Kodzo got on well. I enrolled Kodzo into the local elementary school and Kevin into Coral

Gables High, where he would eventually graduate. Kevin and I were still rebuilding our relationship and we were both still grieving, but we were also moving forward. Things were finally settling down and so I rang Dick Ashby to make an appointment to see Barry.

The entire Gibb family had bought mansions on or near Bay Shore Drive, the most exclusive neighbourhood in Miami Beach. I was a little nervous when I arrived. Barry and Linda's waterfront estate was magnificent, with a crystal chandelier in the luxurious reception foyer and the garden backed onto the bay, where a number of boats were moored. There was a large swimming pool and the view of Miami Beach was breathtaking.

Miami was perfect for them. They looked radiantly healthy and suntanned, Barry as handsome and sexy as ever and Linda with her dark, elegant Scottish beauty. They had always been so warm and kind to me and I loved them both.

Over a cup of tea and a spliff, we talked about life and the family and the tough time I'd been through. I explained how much I'd love to be able to work with him again, but I could tell from his nervous energy that I wasn't going to hear what I'd hoped to hear. The good news was that he was putting the finishing touches on a Greatest Hits album and also producing tracks for his younger brother Andy. He asked me if I would like to do a duet with Andy, on the Carole King classic 'Will You Still Love Me Tomorrow'. Andy was now an artist in his own right, riding high on his own wave of celebrity. He was as handsome as Barry and with a very similar voice. I loved this song and felt it would be an honour to sing with him. The last time I'd seen him he'd been maybe twelve years old. This was a golden opportunity for me and it wasn't hard to say yes.

The bad news was that he didn't have time to do more than one song. The Bee Gees were currently recording their *Spirits Having Flown* album and then they'd be touring. He would soon be producing Barbara Streisand, Olivia Newton-John and Dionne Warwick, artists he'd always wanted to work with. I was just one in a long line of artists all seeking that Gibb magic. Plus the brothers were back with RSO and I knew that Robert Stigwood would never support him making a record with me. I was quietly crushed but I had to try to make the best of this situation. It seemed like Jim had rather oversold the Miami dream, but I had a job, both of my boys were with me and I was alive.

As well as being a musical genius, Barry is a kind and loving human being with a big heart. He reached out and touched my sensitive soul many times, but sadly the politics of the industry combined with family commitments impeded our ability to work together more fruitfully. Who knows, with better management or a label behind me things might have worked out very differently – another one of my life's great 'what ifs'. But I will always be grateful for the friendship that Barry and I shared.

They say you can't always get what you want, but sometimes you get what you need and I needed some spiritual support around me. It came in the person of my dear friend Naima, a beautiful model and actress I had met during our last days at Hoplands. Both American ex-pats living in a strange country, we had bonded over distance running. When I left England for LA, Naima had followed me and when I moved to Miami, she came too and lived with us while she was sorting herself out. She had become a flight attendant for Eastern Airlines and travelled quite a bit. She, Martha and I would smoke a bit of herb together, although I learned to tread carefully around their tastes for something stronger.

The day before my thirty-third birthday on 2 October 1979, I received a shocking phone call. My eldest brother Ronnie had passed away suddenly at just thirty-six from cirrhosis of the liver. We hadn't been able to develop the 'Third World Habitat' before I left for Miami, but it had given us precious time together. Ronnie was an inspiration for how to deal with a handicap. He had perfected the wearing of an artificial limb and worked at UCLA teaching people how to walk with the prosthetics of the day.

He could draw anything and planned to become an architectural draughtsman. He left school with great grades and much optimism, but then ran into prejudice against his disability – and of course it didn't help that he was a young black man. It was all bullshit, as his disability didn't affect his skill at composing drawings or communicating ideas visually, but there was very little sensitivity in the workplace in those days and this left him angry and depressed.

He started drinking heavily and taking barbiturates, which led to his liver disease. His many operations had given him a high tolerance towards pain and he hadn't realised how bad his condition was until it was too late.

To be honest, my mother never really recovered from his death. I remember her once saying that losing Ronnie was harder for her than losing Debbie had been for me, which hurt me deeply at the time. But I understood how much they had been through together and for so many years and I knew how much she loved Ronnie, so forgave her the remark, but you can't measure pain that way.

I wanted to go home for the funeral to celebrate Ronnie's life, but the flight would be expensive. It was only thanks to the gracious generosity of my dear Barry Gibb that I was able to attend.

Around this time there was a celebration at Andy's house in Malibu for the release of his Greatest Hits album, which featured our duet. I remember coming out of the bathroom to find Andy waiting for me in a mischievous mood. It seems that he wanted to show me his personal appreciation for our musical collaboration and it was very hard to refuse. In fact, it was impossible. He was so sweet and naughty. I should have been flattered, as he was only about twenty-one and I was twelve years older, but instead I was a bit embarrassed and flustered. I wasn't sure if our absence had been clocked, but I hoped Andy would keep it to himself. Nevertheless, it certainly gave our duet an even more special meaning.

I was eager to make some music. Buddy Zoloth, who had been road manager for Stephen Still, was also tight with Martha and he called to say that a happening Miami disco group, Niteflyte, were looking for backing vocalists. The other singer was a young girl named Jaqueline Demeritte. She was about seventeen, the age I'd been when I hooked up with Ike and Tina. And she was so cool. I was thirty-three and had already been to hell and back. Jacqui was young, fresh and innocent. Everything was in front of her. I was green with envy.

We sang together with Niteflyte for a little over a year. It was the lifeline I needed, but it was a strange gig. Frontmen Sandy and Howard were both on huge ego trips. They both had the Jeri-curl soul image, but Sandy was a Barry Gibb lookalike and made it quite clear that he was the star and Niteflyte was his project. None of this impressed me. It was just a gig for me, but the money was good. I was on a rehearsal retainer of $350 a week and they paid $1,500 per gig.

They broke up at the end of 1980 and I was uncertain what to do next.

I heard John Cougar Mellencamp was looking for a backing vocalist and I did a session with him at Criteria Studios and then an appearance on *American Bandstand.* He was from Seymour, Indiana, which is not the deep south, but even in 1981 only 1 per cent of its population was African American and he had a somewhat crude attitude towards black women. For starters, he thought that it was cute to introduce me on *American Bandstand* as an 'old floozy' and Dick Clark had to pull him up on it. He liked my sound and wanted me to tour with him, but I found his attitude intolerable. When I told him that I was thinking of going back to England to get my solo career back on track, he told me I was a fool to turn him down because my career was over. It was rude and unnecessary, but boy did it strike a chord.

46

1981 (Miami)

After the Love Is Gone

Once again, I was struggling financially. I'd now had to give up the bungalow and I'd sold my car to send money to Kodzo, who was back in LA with my parents. My friend was out of town for a while so I was house-sitting for her. I'd just done a ten-day fast: maple syrup, lemon, cayenne pepper and distilled water, running a couple of miles each day. I was cleansed, recharged and this extreme diet hadn't been a problem in the past. But my state of mind wasn't strong.

All I needed right now was some distilled water and food to break my fast.

The friend I was house-sitting for had left the keys to a truck parked outside. If I could make it to the grocery store, I would be able to fill up my bottles at the distilled water dispenser outside. I ran out of the house barefoot, jumped into the truck and drove to the store. I filled up my bottles and had a good drink. Driving back home down 163rd Street, I saw a red light flashing behind me. It was the police and I was being pulled over. My friend hadn't told me the registration was out of date and I had run out of the house with my last $20 and no ID.

I explained I had been in a hurry and I was on my way home, just a couple of blocks away, but they started firing questions at me. Who did the truck belong to? I had no idea. Could they see my driver's licence? I didn't have it on me. Name? Social security number? They ordered me out of the truck and laughed at how small I was driving a truck that big – and also for having no shoes on.

They told me to get back in and ran a make on me. As I waited, I ate as much fruit as I could and drank some more water. This turned out to be a good idea. They had found the old warrant for the Tallahassee speeding ticket from three years previously and, without fanfare, I was handcuffed, put in the police car and driven to the station. I couldn't even call anyone to come and help as I didn't have my handbag and address book with me.

It was early on a Friday evening and the station was already busy. They put me in a holding tank with lots of young prostitutes and I was scared to death. I had never been arrested and the experience was terrifying. One girl boldly lit up a spliff and when the policewoman asked who was smoking marijuana, this girl laughed and pointed at me. I denied it, but there I was, barefoot in shorts and the only woman present with dreadlocks. So, of course, I was strip-searched. In the cell, in front of everyone. I had never felt as humiliated and low as I did in that room. I'd heard it wasn't a good idea to cry in jail, though, so I fought back the tears and kept my mouth shut.

After a while my name was called. I was fingerprinted and allowed to make a phone call. The only number I knew by heart was, weirdly, Bruce Hensall at Criteria Studios. I was told I'd be held overnight in the cells and taken to court the next morning. With all the noise, this section reminded me of the lower levels of Dante's Inferno. I wasn't even sure if I'd make it through the night.

They showed me to an empty cell and I instantly assumed a lotus position and started praying. Before long I had cellmates, some of whom I recognised from the holding tank. I had made up my mind not to sleep that night. Most of them were no older than Debbie would have been and most were scared like me. They were interested in my lotus position and after a while started talking to me. I explained that prayer and meditation helped me stay calm. We introduced ourselves and explained why we were there. They laughed at how breaking my fast had led to me getting arrested. It made me laugh, too. It was so stupid.

They were intrigued by fasting and I listened to their stories in turn, horrified that they were choosing prostitution as a profession at such a young age. For some it was for drug money, some were supporting children, some were being pimped and some were just plain lost.

Several of women I knew dated men they didn't really like but they bought them clothes and took them out for good times. Some married rich businessmen who made good Sugar Daddies. I had never gone down the road some of these poor young women were now travelling. I had only slept with idiots to satisfy my sexual needs, never for money, but was there any difference? Probably not. As a successful artist who survived via the talents that God had given me, I put myself on a pedestal. But, in reality, it was me who was the idiot. I would have been better off with a sugar daddy.

I learned a lot about myself that night and I even managed to doze off a couple of times.

At around 6 a.m., an officer ushered us to a canteen area. We were offered breakfast in what looked like dog bowls. I passed. Then we were brought before a judge. The judge must have taken pity on me because I was released on my own recognisance without bail. I collected my keys and my change and got out of there as quickly as I could.

I was thankful and grateful for all that I had achieved in Miami, but this really was a sign that it was time to say goodbye.

47

1982 (LA)

Dancing with the Devil

Broke and broken, I was back in LA. I hadn't lived with Mama and Daddy since my Ike and Tina days. I was glad to be alive and living with Kodzo again, but everyone was traumatised since losing Debbie and Ronnie.

The personal items I'd left in the church basement next door to Grandma Stel's house were gone. Nobody seemed to know what had happened to them. I was glad to see her though. She had always been my guiding light.

Kodzo was happy and loved and Daddy was teaching him how to make upholstery buttons. I was happy they'd bonded.

One Sunday morning, Marsha Hunt phoned my parents' house. I didn't really know her that well, but our paths did seem to keep crossing. I had been a fully paid-up soul sister from the university of hard knocks, while she'd attended Berkeley, dropped acid, dropped out and protested against the Vietnam War. This time she was working on a musical theatre project, called *Clair de Lune*. As I was getting dressed, she came by and entertained Mama and Daddy with stories of how she'd never slept with a black man. They wondered why she was telling them this but by now they were used to my more exotic friends. We laughed about the encounter for some time afterwards.

Marsha was planning to make a demo for her new project and wanted me to sing on it. I wondered why she wasn't singing herself, but anything musical was okay with me. She introduced me to Linda Lewis, who was also asked to sing on the demo. I hadn't been in England at the time of Linda's success, but she was a sensitive, sweet woman. She was also a bit lost since her husband Jim Cregan had decided, brutally, that he no longer wanted to be married to her.

She lived in a beautiful house in Laurel Canyon. In the grounds was a log cabin, which Marsha thought could work out perfectly for me. She thought I could befriend Linda and keep an eye out for her, which would be good for everyone. Linda agreed to let me live in the cabin. I had no independent financial means so I was grateful for her generosity.

Linda warned me that Jim Cregan visited from time to time. He knew I was staying, but it might be best if I stayed out of his way. I didn't have a clue who he was. I really felt for her when he walked down to the patio to hang out at the pool, laughing and having fun with his Hollywood friends and groupies. I was also still quite fragile, but I was stronger than her. I could feel her loneliness. My job was to water the roses and the garden and clean the swimming pool. It was the least I could do to repay her for her kindness.

When one of Linda's friends arrived from England to look after her, it was time for me to move on. Wendy seemed to think I was just some hustling American, but I was in this predicament because I *wasn't* a hustler. Had I been one, I'd have been a lot more successful.

My friend Renita had a suggestion. Her mother Delores was an ex-girlfriend of Johnny 'Guitar' Watson. She felt Johnny might be able to help me and she invited me along to his birthday celebration. He had a beautiful spread in Encino, a very well-to-do part of the San Fernando Valley. The driveway had a gate decorated with a guitar and a huge patio and swimming pool for entertaining. I helped myself to refreshments and stayed in the background. After all, I was a guest that no one really knew. But I was glad I had come. Johnny was dressed '60s pimp style, very flashy, stylish albeit a bit garish with a great big smile full of gold teeth and plenty of ostentatious jewellery. He was, it was clear to see, something of a character. He was a very cordial host.

I knew of Johnny from his days with *The Johnny Otis Show*. My Uncle Book was a big fan and so was I. He was an astonishing performer, an exponent of that Texas Blues sound and he influenced everyone from Jimi Hendrix to Stevie Ray Vaughan. Etta James once said, 'They call Elvis the King but the sure-enough King was Johnny "Guitar" Watson.'

Renita had played him a cassette of some of my recent recordings. At this point I was desperate to work with an American producer. Johnny had an old-school blues and R&B pedigree, but he was also known for commercial rock. Perhaps he had some advice or, even better, he could introduce me to someone who might be able to help.

As people started to leave, Johnny asked me and a few others to stick around. Renita was there with me so I felt comfortable staying. It was a big house with many rooms and he led us to his bedroom, where he had his studio set up. This was his inner sanctum: a sitting room with a bed in it, decorated very comfortably. As a friend rolled some joints, Johnny began to play the tracks he was working on. Then he told Renita she had to leave, but he hoped I would stay. Did he want the party to get more grown up? I tried not to panic and certainly didn't want to appear spooked, so I told Renita that I could hold my own and would call her when I got home.

When the coke came out I explained to Johnny that I was happy just smoking a joint. He laughed, cracked his knuckles and by the end of the evening I had the nickname 'church girl', which suited me fine. But, despite everything, I still found Johnny charming and funny with an extremely cool, old-school air. It helped that he was respectful and seemed genuinely interested in me.

He had an apartment in LA that was empty and said I could stay there if I liked. I told him I couldn't afford to pay rent and that what I really needed was some work. His friend Paul – who up to this point appeared to be on hand solely to roll the joints – said he might be able to help out. He told me that he had connections in casting at Universal City. His friend there hired extras and might be able to get me some bit parts.

I started to relax a bit more and found I was actually enjoying myself. Johnny was a genial, entertaining host. He also had some serious big cosmic energy.

As the night wore on, however, the drugs became more intense and when the pipe came out, I knew that it was time for me to go. As I left he gave me a very sensual kiss, even though his old lady was in the room. As I said, a very cordial host.

True to his word, Paul drove me to the Universal Studios casting office to meet his friend Ruth. She was intrigued by my English CV – a rare commodity in LA in the early '80s – despite my limited experience. It had been a few years since my brush with musical theatre. She explained that she booked for various sitcoms and movies before reeling off a list of shows that were currently casting for extras with my profile: *St. Elsewhere*, *Quincy*, *Knots Landing* and *Fame*. And as strange as it sounds, it really was that simple. I was now P.P. Arnold, Hollywood extra. The money was great and I would now be able to rent Johnny's apartment.

My parents were pleased I was earning and able to rent an apartment, though Daddy was dubious about Johnny, whose street reputation was not dissimilar to Ike's and he warned me to look after myself.

Ruth took a liking to me and carried on hiring me as an extra. As well as being at the studio from 6 a.m., I was sometimes working late in the evening for overtime. My dreadlocks were unusual at the time in the media. I was not a Rastafarian; I just wanted to be a natural black woman, which meant rejecting all the perming and weaving that had once been the rage. All you do to grow your hair long is stop combing it and train it into ringlets. I kept my locks well-groomed and they looked good.

Johnny's apartment was working out well. Our hours and routines were very different and as I was working all the time I didn't see him much, but he took to visiting unannounced. He would also drop by if I had a day off. I wanted to stay on his good side and to have a relationship based on friendship and music, but he was the 'Gangster of Love' and I didn't want to be a part of that. As time went by, my 'church girl' ways began to piss him off. He wanted more control over me.

The vibe on the Burbank lot was pretty intense. This was Hollywood in the '80s and cocaine was high on the menu. It was all about staying up all night and sleeping all day. Sometimes when I was tired, I would toot a little coke to stay alert, but I didn't like the way it affected my voice – and there was no way that Johnny was getting me to hit the pipe. I was always waiting around to sing and then leaving because I had to get up early to work. This annoyed Johnny. I think he was regretting letting Paul introduce me to Ruth. All the groupies, prostitutes and musicians might have been having fun, but I'd grown up in the church. I was a church girl meeting a real blues man and totally out of my depth.

Paul was with him a lot of the time and sometimes Sly Stone would come over, too. On those occasions, they would not be in good shape. Sly's glory days were long behind him and now he was mainly known around town as a drug addict. He was a mess, with awful matted dreadlocks under his wig. I couldn't connect with him at all. I told him I knew a hairdresser who could sort his locks out, but when he took the wig off he was totally bald on top. The dreads were only at the sides and back. I gave him my friend's number regardless, but I doubt he ever went to see her.

Fuzz had moved back to England and was living in Fulmer, Buckinghamshire, so I sent Kodzo to be with him and start school there in autumn. I was planning to return to England for Christmas 1982 and Fuzz had offered to let me stay in Fulmer while I sorted myself out in London.

I still hadn't done any recording with Johnny. Increasingly, he wasn't in a good place. His good friend and musical collaborator, the great Larry Williams, had been shot the previous year and then the English record company he was with folded. He had problems with his new label, A&M and this had escalated his drug-taking. I knew that he liked me and I liked him too – we definitely had an affinity – but I found it hard to relate to the hard drugs and all his women. He was a lovable, warm guy, but my life was already complicated enough.

One of his women was a cute little Mexican girl and he started bringing her round to the apartment from time to time, especially on the weekends, when I didn't work. She always wore a red Fedora. If I was sleeping, he'd just come up to my room and wake me up and they would start smoking the pipe with no regards to my dislike of it. I'd end up rolling a joint almost out of politeness. I might've been paying rent, but it was Johnny's apartment. He had keys and he was still helping me out. I knew what he wanted of me, but I was not going to be drawn into his game. He soon began to lose his patience with me and his attitude started to change.

One evening after a long day at Burbank, I went to the studio as I normally did. Johnny was working on a song he wanted us to do together, but he and his entourage were also partying hard that night. I felt that he was testing me. I'd been up since 4 a.m. the previous morning and I was tired. I was waiting to sing and starting to nod out in the control room. As I fell asleep, he woke me up saying, 'Okay, Pat, are you ready? This is called "Can You Hang"?' He sang me my parts and phrases. His part was already recorded. I knew it was a set-up because he was laughing and acting crazy, but I made some coffee and went out into the studio and laid down a vocal. He started giving me a hard time, wanting me to do it over and over, until I finally snapped: 'You know what, Johnny? I can't hang.' I got my things and left.

By now I had realised that the LA inner circle just wasn't a healthy option for me and I was getting Johnny's message loud and clear. Johnny was basically an artist who produced himself. He was having problems with his own career and understandably that was his priority. It was time to leave LA.

Before I left, I tried to explain to Johnny how cruel I felt he'd been that last night in the studio. I'd been up nearly twenty-four hours. He started talking about my plans to return to England and I admitted that I was ready to make that move. I had only been waiting to see whether or not he wanted to do any serious recording together, but it was evidently up to me to find my own way again. He was furious and I saw a side of him I'd never seen before. He looked me dead in the eyes and said, 'If you go back to England, you're going back to the grave.' And he turned and walked away.

That was the last time I saw Johnny 'Guitar' Watson.

I was glad to be on my way out of LA.

48

1982 (London)

'The Light at the End of the Tunnel'

It was a cold December morning when I flew into Heathrow, but this was still the best present I could've given myself. Fuzz met me at the airport with Kodzo. They had moved back to England earlier in the year. I was grateful Fuzz had stepped up like this and I was just ecstatic to see Kodzo.

We drove out to Fulmer. They were staying in a property not far from the manor house where his friend Wink Lorch and her family lived – a lovely location, complete with stables and horses. Kodzo had been a baby at Hoplands and didn't really remember England at all. He'd been at Fulmer Infant School since the autumn, which he hadn't minded aside from being the only black child.

Kodzo had been my rock since losing Debbie and it was a joy to be with him again. He was just four years old when she passed, with only scattered memories of bus rides with her to

Malibu or the mountains, but he'd loved being with his big sister, following her around and tagging along when she was singing and doing dance routines with her friends. I have a cassette of one of those afternoons and you can hear his little voice calling her name.

We had been invited to join the family for a traditional Christmas lunch. Mr and Mrs Lorch were very kind, as was Wink's sister Janet. The food was delicious but my jetlag was kicking in, so Fuzz, Kodzo and I made our way back across the fields to the house. I couldn't help thinking how much Debbie would have loved it there.

Wink was a really nice young woman who sold and bought wines. She was also Fuzz's current partner, which he had failed to tell me. We were actually staying in her house, but he had asked her to stay with her parents when I arrived. It wasn't until Boxing Day when I opened a closet to find all of Wink's clothes hanging there that I realised not everything was as it seemed. As for Wink, she had been under the impression that I was only there for Christmas. As usual, Fuzz was not being completely honest. I knew that I had to leave. I was not about to disrespect this girl who had been kind enough to let my son stay at her house. It was a new year in a couple of days and I wasn't going to start it off dealing with Fuzz's chaos.

I found accommodation in a shared flat in Plumstead. It wasn't ideal, but Kodzo could live with me as I sorted myself out. It's not easy to reconnect when you haven't lived somewhere for more than ten years. London had changed and everybody had moved on. Friends seemed thinner on the ground.

Finally, though, I got in touch with someone who did seem genuinely happy to hear from me; David Charkham, an old friend of Jim's. He was a charming, witty, elegant hippie and I'd always liked him. He'd been a child actor in several '60s TV shows and he'd also been in the original cast of *Jesus Christ Superstar*.

We met at a restaurant near his studio flat in Pimlico, where he told me about the Pineapple Dance Studio in Covent Garden owned by a woman called Debbie Moore. He would make an introduction and arrange a meeting.

I turned up to the meeting with no professional biography. I explained I was returning after eight years and was basically starting all over again. I told Debbie about being a principal performer in the *Othello* musical and singing on the original *Jesus Christ Superstar* album. This got an instant positive reaction, as she was casting for Andrew Lloyd Webber's new musical, *Starlight Express*. I was asked if I could roller-skate. Of course, I said yes. They were looking for skilled skaters and I hadn't skated since I was a kid, over twenty years ago, but, come on, how hard could it be? An audition was set up for the following day.

I was terrified. I'd never done a proper audition before and Andrew Lloyd Webber was there alongside choreographer Arlene Phillips and director Trevor Nunn. When the pianist asked what I'd like to sing, I asked him if he knew 'Everything Must Change'. They didn't have the music so I asked if I could just sing acapella. First hurdle cleared.

Andrew asked me if I could roller-skate. I said that I could and they asked for my shoe size and gave me a pair of skates to try on. In fact, I'd only skated in shoe-skates a few times. My father hadn't let me go to the rink much, so I did the bulk of my skating in the street, in the metal skates with a key to adjust for all sizes.

It was explained that *Starlight Express* would be a unique and groundbreaking musical. All the actors would play trains and all performances would be on roller-skates. The script was built around races and they were looking for skilled skaters to tackle all the necessary choreography.

'How hard could it be?' This was clearly a whole different ball game.

It was very quickly apparent that my kind of skating was not what they were looking for. I apologised for my lie and asked if they could give me time to work on my skating. They said that the part they had in mind for me would have to be decided within three weeks. I pleaded with them to give me that time. I probably sounded pretty desperate, but I was not proud. The part I was auditioning for was Belle the Sleeping Car. Belle had once been famous, had lived the high life but had fallen on hard times.

Sound familiar?

I was given the address of a skating rink in Old Street. A man named Sammy came in daily to help anyone who needed it and I needed a lot of help. Sammy was seventy years old and had been British World Champion in his day.

Learning to roller-skate again was fun. After a couple of intense days, the muscle memory and the moves came flooding back. The Savoy Skating Rink had been the place to go back when I was a teenager, even if Daddy didn't often let me. It was very hip and cool but it was well out of our neighbourhood on 78th and Central. We teens had circled the wooden rink, doing our own versions of the cha-cha and the Slauson shuffle. Our arms moved, our feet glided and our bodies swayed to the Motown greats.

Sammy was getting me working on my speed, which I loved. Once I was confident, the harder work began, including perfecting how to spin. That, I can tell you, was not so easy.

But as my spins were getting better I still found the three-point turn a challenge. This is one of the basic turns in figure-skating, the most common way beginners learn to change direction. And it was tough. One day I took a particularly bad tumble and landed squarely on my coccyx bone. I was in agony. That was it. No more for the day! The pain was excruciating and I cried all the way home to Plumstead.

When I got home to an empty flat, however, the tears turned to anger. I was angry at everything I'd been through since losing Debbie. All the disappointments, all the cruelties, all the suffering and all of the stupid, misguided decisions I had taken in pursuit of . . . what? Happiness? My career? Companionship? I needed this show to get me back on my feet again. I was doing it for me, for both my sons and I was doing it for Debbie. My inner spirit told me to go back to the rink and that's what I did. I let go of my self-pity. I was determined to learn, determined to succeed. I pushed myself. Hard. And everything changed.

From then on my skating improved every day and I looked forward to my next audition with skates. This time it was held at the Covent Garden roller rink. I think everybody was surprised by my progress. Arlene was particularly impressed. I discovered later that she could barely skate herself.

When they formally offered me the part a few days later, I was thrilled. I still had a lot of work to do – I was still going to have to learn to dance on skates – but it was great to know that my efforts weren't in vain. I hadn't performed in the UK since 1971 and it had been a long time coming.

Ray Shell, who was playing the lead role of Rusty the Steam Engine, was a very talented singer and actor, an African American from New York who'd arrived in the UK in 1978 with the gospel musical *Little Willie Jr's Resurrection*. We became instant friends after we met in the Covent Garden practice hall and he invited Kodzo and I to a gathering at his flat in Chiswick where I met his family.

Word seemed to be getting around that I had landed the role of Belle. Keyboard player Pete Wingfield, who had worked with Fuzz and me long ago, had since done well for himself as a producer. It was through Pete that I featured on the Kane Gang's 1983 hit 'Respect Yourself', leading to a live appearance on *Top of the Pops* with them. Things were starting to happen.

Rehearsals for *Starlight Express* were held for two months at the youth centre in Kensal Rise, before we transferred to the Apollo Victoria theatre. I already knew some of the team, but I was excited to meet everyone properly. It was comforting to be part of a big ensemble piece. Professionally, I had often felt so isolated in the US.

The rehearsals were intense. This was an innovative but high-stakes production and learning the moves and the songs was a lot harder than anyone imagined: frightening, dangerous and exciting, often all at the same time. We poured all our energy into that show and I'd never worked so physically hard in my life.

On opening night, as I got ready in my dressing room, surrounded by flowers and cards, nervously putting on my make-up, costume and skates, I thought of my beautiful daughter Debbie. I had no doubt that her spirit had helped carry me throughout rehearsals and that helped me overcome all the pain of the past and rise to these many new challenges.

Starlight Express was the perfect show for me at a time when I needed it most. It helped me regain my confidence and was a life-changing experience. After years of searching, upheaval and instability, its message of willpower and determination was more real to me than fantasy. I don't think Andrew could have realised quite how pertinent it was.

I had become strong again.

I had survived.

Epilogue

It's hard to believe that it's been nearly forty years since Bell reinvented herself on the *Starlight Express*. I've found the light at the end of that dark tunnel I got lost in. It set me back on track once again. Fast-forward to 2022 and I'm happy to say that I am still going strong. I was unaware of the many twists and turns that would lie ahead, but, as Daddy used to say, 'You've got to go through it to get to it,' and I would learn from even more experiences exactly what he meant. I still had many tests to pass and challenges to rise to that would show me what a true soul survivor must endure.

They would start with my own tragic accident – being crushed between two vehicles and told that I would never run or dance again.

I thought 1986 was the beginning of my next chapter. *Starlight Express* had been a big success and I was excited to regenerate my solo music career off the back of it. Both of my boys, Kevin and Kodzo, were doing so well and I was so proud of them. I had just returned from Kevin's graduation from the prestigious Howard

University in Washington, DC, and was starting rehearsals for my first global tour supporting Billy Ocean. When the going gets tough, the tough get going – this turned out to be a literal truth for me.

Rushing to get to rehearsal, I had negligently left the lights on in my car the night before and needed a jumpstart to get me on my way. I approached a workman who was working next door for help. We pushed my Saab out of my drive and he moved his vehicle to assist me. While positioning the jump leads, my spirit warned me to turn around. I did, but it was too late.

It was a rainy morning and the driver's wet boot had slipped off the brake and onto the accelerator of his automatic car. I saw it lunge at me, but was unable to get out of the way in time. I was trapped between the bumpers of the two cars. All I remember was seemingly invisible beings lifting me up and placing me in the front of my car. I looked down to see that the muscles in both my legs had collapsed. 'No, no,' I cried to God, 'not my legs,' but then a voice in my head answered, 'Your legs are going to be alright.' When the ambulance men arrived, I was repeating this reassurance over and over again. The two men looked at one another sceptically, so I said to them, 'I don't care if you don't believe; I believe my legs are going to be alright.' The three weeks that followed were intense and too much to describe here.

Although the accident would put my solo career on hold for some years, the work I had done with Nick Drake on his *Bryter Layter* album would re-emerge, bringing me acclaim for the backing vocals I had provided with Doris Troy. I also recorded with Peter Gabriel in 1986 on his *So* album, which was released later that year. I was proud of the contribution I had made to the recording: my vocal sound shone through clearly on 'Sledgehammer' and 'Big Time'. It had been a lovely afternoon working with Peter and his producer Daniel Lanois at his Ashcombe House studio in Somerset, with Dee Lewis and Coral Gordon also on backing vocals. I was surprised to see that Peter had a pair of anti-gravity boots in his fitness room. I also had a pair and he was the only other person I knew who used them! We had a lovely dinner after recording the tracks and I remember the wine was very nice. We also sang on the track 'Don't Give Up', but this became a duet with Kate Bush on the album, so our vocals were not used. I'd still love to have a copy of that original version.

Unable to do any 'live' work at the time, my dear friend Linda Hayes – another American singer who, along with Madeline Bell, was one of the top session vocalists of the time – was kind enough to introduce me to David Mindel of Mingles Music, who produced jingles and commercials. I would also work with him years later on the *Issues* project with Band of Sisters. Linda's introductions to other advertising companies would thankfully provide me with a way to survive financially in the later years of the 1980s. I also met jingle producers Manda Glanfield, Paul Carter and Richard Walmsley, who would become house-music DJs under the name the Beatmasters. I recorded a number of jingles with them and then ended up collaborating on their top-twenty hit 'Burn It Up', which led to an interesting few years recording on the London house-music scene. I was back on my feet again, but I still had dues to pay.

The '90s would test me further. I struggled with finding the balance between working as a backing vocalist to survive while holding onto my credibility as a solo artist. It was difficult. Without having the protection of a management, I negotiated various projects for myself, always fighting for the respect that I felt I deserved for the contributions I made to the projects at hand. I was aware that my unique sound and energy meant a lot more than just a session fee at times.

In 1992, I got the opportunity to work with Roger Waters on his *Amused to Death* album, duetting with him on the legendary 'Perfect Sense', which would open the door to later tour with him for many years.

Collaborating with my friend Chas Jankel of Ian Drury and the Blockheads fame on an independent project was also a creative highlight for me. Although the music was turned down by record labels at the time for not being commercial, times have changed and tracks from those sessions will now feature on a soon-to-be-released box set, which will include unreleased tracks from several projects I've been involved in. It is a joy that this music that will finally be heard and appreciated by my fans.

On the last night of the 1994 Birmingham Rep production of *Once on This Island* (the Olivier Award-winning musical in which I played Erzulie, the goddess of love), I was called to the stage door and presented with flowers by a local band, Ocean Colour Scene. This introduction, coupled with the revival of Steve Marriott and Small Faces, would lead to renewed respect for my work.

This started with an album that was produced to raise money to help Ronnie Lane, who was ill with MS. I collaborated on a cover of the Small Faces track 'Understanding' with Primal Scream, which we recorded at the legendary Regent Sounds Studios on Denmark Street. What a fun night that was! After they'd had a few drinks, I couldn't understand their Scottish accent at all, but the track turned out amazing.

Ocean Colour Scene were also on that album and it was the catalyst to me connecting with Steve Cradock and recording then later touring with the band. It's a beautiful thing that they gave me a little more recognition. Though my relationship with the band became a little rocky due to management problems, my relationship with Steve Cradock grew stronger over time and we have continued to collaborate. My most recent album, *The New Adventures of . . . P.P. Arnold*, is a masterpiece that he produced as a monument to our twentysomething-year friendship.

Fifty years after recording some of my most important music, produced by Barry Gibb and Eric Clapton, I finally acquired the licence to release it. In 2017, with the help of Steve Cradock, Paul Weller and my supportive solicitor Simon Long, these recordings were made public. Both albums have been enthusiastically embraced and I'm humbled by the love and respect I'm receiving at this point in my life.

Mama and Daddy, Grandma Stel and Big Mama, dear friends like Jim Morris, Steve Marriott, Doris Troy, Kim Gardner, my beautiful Naima, the one and only Jimmy Thomas and the special Jimmy Mayweather – all have passed on. I miss them so much, but their memories continue to inspire me and help me reach higher every day. Relationships are karmic. I believe that we choose the families we're born into; the extraordinary people who pass through our lives are souls that we've known before in another time and space and souls we will meet again. The universe is so vast and there is a whole lot going on that we don't understand. This thought is a comfort to me.

Moving to Spain twenty years ago has also been extremely challenging but stimulating. I've been able to continue my alternative healing journey and learn to be tranquil. It has helped me to grow into a better version of myself. With the help of my daily meditations, yoga and fitness regime, I now live in gratitude.

The music industry is constantly changing, as is the world we're living in. Surviving in the industry as an independent female artist throughout the years has been interesting, to say the least. The music industry isn't called the music *business* for nothing. Living in a man's world can be hard for an independent female like myself who refuses to give up.

Let's just say that I've got a lot more stories to tell. I'm a thriving soul survivor still going strong.

Acknowledgements

To my sons, Kevin Lamont Arnold and Calvin Kodzo Samuel, I thank you for your patience, understanding and love that have always kept me rooted through the ups and downs of my turbulent life.

Thank you, Renita Lorden, for the constant encouragement and advice you've given me from the very beginning of these writings. You gave me the confidence to believe in my voice, in my natural way of writing and expressing myself, and in the importance of sharing my unique story with the world. Thank you, Erma Kent, for being such a beautiful loyal friend throughout my life, too.

Tina Turner, you turned my life around and are 'simply the best' example of what being a thriving soul survivor truly is. I have always loved you dearly and I feel so blessed knowing God made you the answer to my prayer that Sunday morning so long ago. Your longevity, courage and strength have always been my soul inspiration.

The loving friendship and opportunity that Mick Jagger gave me to dream the impossible and to take that giant leap out of an uncertain future was another blessing for both me and my children. He opened the door for me to embrace unknown cultures; he was the catalyst for me to break down the barriers, attitudes and ways of being that growing up in a racist society had created; and he helped me believe in myself as a solo artist. The love you showed me in those heady days of my youth was such a great gift and I will always love you for that in return.

Andrew Loog Oldham, your vision and creative guidance encouraged me to take the steps that created me as 'The First Lady of Immediate'. Thank you for believing in me when I didn't even know who I was. I was so young, shy and inexperienced. I am so grateful to you for those magical, exciting times of my life. I was truly happy to be a part of the Immediate industry of human happiness. The legacy has lived on and I'm glad that we're still friends, in spite of the dues we've had to pay.

Gered Mankowitz, not only are you the culprit that named me P.P. Arnold, but you've also been a supportive friend throughout my career. Thank you for creating the wonderful creative images that document the majority of my professional life and for all the memories, advice and wisdom that you've shared with me during the writing of this book.

Barry Gibb, I thank you for all the love, friendship and help that you gave me during those lost turnaround years of the '60s and the kindness that you bestowed upon me after the devastating loss of my daughter. I'm so glad that I managed to let the world hear the work that we did together so many years ago.

You are all the template and inspiration for my story.

When you're down and out in this business, you're lucky to have any professional support systems behind you, but my solicitor, Simon Long, has come to my rescue many times, helping me to connect and find a way to stay in the game. Thank you, Simon, for being a patient, understanding friend. I'd also like to thank Heather Taylor for helping me to finally get this work published and released. These may be old memories, but they will also be a great part of my new adventures.

Leon Rubenhold and Steve Lewis, thank you for sharing your memories. Thanks also to Fran Berman, Denice Molina and Joy Snipes for sharing the tragic memories of the day that we all lost

Debbie and for giving me permission to use their words in this memoir. I'm sure Debbie had a hand in bringing us together after all these years so that we could get the closure we needed.

I don't believe in coincidences, so, when I received a phone call from Pete Selby with an interest in reading my book, I had a really good feeling about him. It turned out that my instinct was right and I'd like to thank Pete Selby, Mark Sinker, Melissa Bond and all at Nine Eight Books for the enthusiasm, guidance and support that you've given me to help edit this work without losing the heart, soul and essence of my story. Editing down 400,000 words has been quite a challenge for us all! There's certainly a lot more of my journey to share one day. . .

Rest in power and peace to all my musical peers who have moved on to that great gig in the sky. I'll always remember you: Jim Morris; Jimi Hendrix; Steve Marriott; Doris Troy; Kim Gardner; Tony Ashton; Naima 'Jody' Sherwood; Jimmy Mayweather; Jimmy Thomas; Leslie Duncan; Kay Garner; Keith Emerson.

Credits

Page numbers refer to plate section. All images courtesy of the author unless otherwise stated below.

p. 2 (top): Courtesy Everett Collection/Alamy
p. 2 (middle): Ron Howard/Redferns/Getty Images
p. 2 (bottom): Giles Petard/Redferns/Getty Images
p. 3 (top): Evening Standard/Stringer/Hulton Archive/Getty Images
p. 3 (bottom): Daily Mirror/Mirrorpix/Getty Images
p. 4: Giles Petard/Redferns/Getty Images
p. 5 (top): Keystone/Stringer/Hulton Archive/Getty Images
p. 5 (bottom): Michael Putland/Hulton Archive/Getty Images
p. 8 (top) Fox Photos/Stringer/Hulton Archive/Getty Images